NEEDY MEDIA

NEEDY MEDIA

HOW TECH GETS PERSONAL

STEPHEN MONTEIRO

McGill-Queen's University Press
Montreal & Kingston | London | Chicago

ISBN 978-0-2280-2598-6 (cloth)
ISBN 978-0-2280-2599-3 (ePDF)
ISBN 978-0-2280-2600-6 (ePUB)

Legal deposit third quarter 2025
Bibliothèque et Archives nationales du Québec

Printed in Canada on acid-free paper that is 100% ancient-forest-free, containing 100% sustainable, recycled fibre, and processed chlorine-free.

This book has been published with the help of a grant from the Federation for the Humanities and Social Sciences, through the Awards to Scholarly Publications Program, using funds provided by the Social Sciences and Humanities Research Council of Canada.

Funded by the Government of Canada | Financé par le gouvernement du Canada | Canada | Canada Council for the Arts | Conseil des arts du Canada

We acknowledge the support of the Canada Council for the Arts.
Nous remercions le Conseil des arts du Canada de son soutien.

McGill-Queen's University Press in Montreal is on land which long served as a site of meeting and exchange amongst Indigenous Peoples, including the Haudenosaunee and Anishinabeg nations. In Kingston it is situated on the territory of the Haudenosaunee and Anishinaabek. We acknowledge and thank the diverse Indigenous Peoples whose footsteps have marked these territories on which peoples of the world now gather.

Library and Archives Canada Cataloguing in Publication

Title: Needy media : how tech gets personal / Stephen Monteiro.
Names: Monteiro, Stephen, author
Description: Includes bibliographical references and index.
Identifiers: Canadiana (print) 20250180243 | Canadiana (ebook) 20250180286 | ISBN 9780228025986 (cloth) | ISBN 9780228025993 (ePDF) | ISBN 9780228026006 (ePUB)
Subjects: LCSH: Human-computer interaction—Psychological aspects. | LCSH: Digital media—Psychological aspects.
Classification: LCC QA76.9.H85 M66 2025 | DDC 004.01/9—dc23

This book was designed and typeset by studio oneonone in Minion 12/15.
Copyediting by Lesley Trites.

McGill-Queen's University Press
Suite 1720, 1010 Sherbrooke St West, Montreal, QC, H3A 2R7

Authorized safety representative in the EU: Mare Nostrum Group BV, Mauritskade 21D, 1091 GC Amsterdam, the Netherlands, gpsr@mare-nostrum.co.uk

For Manisha and Dhruv

Contents

Contents

Figures

Acknowledgments

On the journey of researching and writing this book, I have had the encouragement and support of many people and institutions. Aspects of this research were presented at conferences held by the Canadian Communication Association, the Society for Cinema and Media Studies, and the Canadian Science and Technology Historical Association. I would like to thank the organizers, audiences, and co-panellists at these events for their attention and feedback at critical moments in the development of my hypothesis and argument. Elements of the research on facial recognition and photographic practices found in chapters 4 and 5 have been published in *Information, Communication & Society* and *Media, Culture & Society*. I am grateful to the editors and anonymous reviewers at these journals for the opportunity they offered, as well as their suggestions, which helped shape my presentation of these topics. I am deeply indebted to my colleagues in the Department of Communication Studies at Concordia University. They offer a welcoming environment of intellectual and creative exploration that always amazes and motivates me. In particular, the Media History Research Centre has been a source of stimulating discussion and exchange, feeding my work in untold ways. I also must extend my gratitude to my students, who have sometimes been the unwitting first audience for ideas or examples that made their way into these pages. Their reactions and responses often impacted my subsequent steps. The editors and staff of McGill-Queen's University Press have been helpful throughout the publishing process. I especially thank Khadija Coxon for enthusiastically agreeing to take on this project and Kathleen Fraser for deftly overseeing production. I am grateful to two anonymous readers for the press for their many helpful suggestions and to Lesley Trites for expert and sensitive copy-editing. I have immense gratitude for my family in Canada, India, and the US. They have always had my back and offered extraordinary encouragement and patience as I took on research that was not always evident. In closing, I would like to acknowledge those who do the thankless work of building and maintaining the devices and networks at the centre of this book. We may take these devices and networks for granted, but they require the untiring efforts of many, who often work long hours, under hazardous conditions, for a small fraction of the profits reaped by the technology corporations behind them.

NEEDY MEDIA

Introduction

Our encounters with portable networked media unfold in all manner of circumstances throughout the day, often from shortly after we wake to the final moments before sleep. Sleep may suspend interactions for a time, although a chime, vibration, or flash of light from our device can disrupt our slumber, and wearable devices – like a smartwatch or fitness tracker – may continue to interact with our unconscious self. These exchanges between us and our devices are so frequent in part because our smartphone, smartwatch, or smart display need do little to get our attention. Responding also requires little of us: glancing at an object from our pocket or on our wrist, touching a screen, or saying a name. Through the simple gestures, decisions, and habits that unfold in these moments we frame, engage, and shape our world, orienting ourselves in relation to shifts in data that we both produce and receive within the networks we access.

However, even as we use these networks, we also orient ourselves toward these lively objects themselves, taken by the small but satisfying ways they appeal to our senses. They may serve as our closest companions and confidantes, appearing to know more about us – and how to gain and keep our attention – than our closest friends and family. They are privy to our cultural preferences and behavioural idiosyncrasies, and they adapt accordingly. Sometimes they seem to know us better than we know ourselves.

At the very least, they can imply as much through the diverse ways they produce appealing sensations and individually tailored information. If we had to identify the object most necessary to making our way through the world from day to day, it would very likely be one of these compact, connected devices. Sharif Mowlabocus describes this dependency as making "an investment of power in our devices; a power to 'hold us,' to 'know us,' and to be there for us … Arguably this is the reason why we become so upset and agitated when our smartphones stop working, run out of battery, get stolen, or otherwise 'abandon' us."[1]

This book traces the roots and implications of the transformation of networked interactive devices from supplementary communication tools into essential components of our sense of self by exploring how the idea of "personal" media has coalesced around the physical design and interactive functions of digital objects in recent years. User interfaces (UI) and user experiences (UX) have implicated people in increasingly subtle, complex, and frequent exchanges with their portable, personal devices. Often these exchanges are initiated by the user, but at other times they are initiated by the device, sometimes based in part on the user's previous behaviour. Simply put, we need these devices, in part because these devices seem to "need" us. They are not only tools but also animated companions. Accordingly, this book contends that the intimate and nuanced relationships that exist between users and their portable smart devices often have as much to do with the affective value of the multi-sensory, rudimentary exchanges that take place between user and device as they do with the exchanges with other people and systems typically carried out by texting, calling, posting to social media, scrolling, and related actions.

In arguing that contemporary consumer technology blurs the line between intimacy and solitude, sociologist Sherry Turkle has provocatively called technology "the architect of our intimacies." She asserts, "Technology is seductive when what it offers meets our human vulnerabilities. And as it turns out, we are very vulnerable indeed."[2] Accustomed to the intimate, material relationships that develop between us and our small, smart objects we perhaps have become more interested in personal media feeling personal to us than we have in maintaining control over the personal information and behavioural data shared with tech companies and service providers through these devices. The physical and psychological intimacy we develop with these objects, this book argues, belies the non-intimate nature of networked living, where personal data is extracted and converted into assets that can be exploited across products, platforms, companies, and governmental agencies.[3] The fight against this data capitalization and surveillance may not stop at privacy policies and platform algorithms. In the economy of the social the battle may also unfold in the minefield of device features and technologies that build both dependency and trust between user and object, whether that be a screen that responds to the faintest touch or a lens that can detect a face and a smile. Attempting to understand the historical and technical origins of this intimacy with smart devices, then, is a step toward gaining greater control over our relationships with devices and networks in what is a critical juncture in twenty-first-century communications and social conditioning. On the one hand, computing and the Internet of Things (IoT) threaten to further erode individual control of data in the guise of the convenience of ubiquitous connectivity and synching across platforms, devices, interfaces, infrastructures, and wider data-based systems. On the other hand, the rollout of powerful artificial intelligence (AI) and machine learning models across devices and networks can help build even more seductive and individualized interactions with devices as our networked objects may start to appear empathetic and sociable (as well as all-knowing).

Of course, our relationship to these devices has already become both personal and interpersonal as we may speak of them both as an extension of our being and as another subject with whom we interact. In 1960 personal computing pioneer J.C.R. Licklider expressed a hope that "human brains and computing machines will be coupled together very tightly, and that the resulting partnership will think as no human brain has ever thought."[4] It would appear that this goal has been achieved in a contorted form, where our psychological and social – as well as intellectual – dependence on digital networked devices seems paradoxically to engage our minds and do the thinking for us. These devices have become an essential tool in what Armin Beverungen and others have called the "organizational" tendency of media. In their power to shape our lives in the most subtle yet profound ways, these devices exemplify and amplify "the material and technological conditioning and structuring of experience, agency and interaction."[5]

To take one example, in many ways these devices function as an extension of (or substitute for) our memory as we delegate details to them that previously would have been absorbed and accessed through our brain's hippocampus.[6] Equipped with an unfathomable array of apps for nearly ever purpose one can imagine, they produce a "modularity of extended cognition," according to Nick Srnicek. "What unites these apps is their offloading of specific cognitive processes into a handheld central interface (which is today commonly a mobile phone, but in the future may include augmented-reality glasses and other wearable technologies)."[7] These devices can also function as a foil, continually responding to our actions in ways that process our choices and produce suitable reactions, fostering a sense of interpersonal interaction with the object itself. Even as the Internet of Things produces larger, denser ambient networked environments that we may traverse and inhabit, it appears that our reliance on these portable media objects will not diminish anytime soon, as they establish small, seemingly manageable individualized interfaces between us and vast, complex, and often intimidating data flows and telecommunications infrastructures. They bring the immensity of the internet down to a hand-held scale. Indeed, it is often through these pocketable devices that we access and interact with wider networks of objects, as with Apple CarPlay and Android Auto, which allow a personal media device to interact with a car's smart technology. Under such circumstances, these portable devices function as our digital doppelgänger, making us – and our behaviour and inclinations – identifiable to our smart surroundings. They also let us feel that we still have the situation literally in hand, that physical and material control (i.e., we can always shut the device off, put it to sleep, leave it in a drawer, or even smash it with a hammer) can equal control over all the data and information that these objects gather, process, store, and transmit. This sense of control produced by having the object in hand may counter trends toward "invisible" or "disappearing" computing, where networks and our interactions with them blend seamlessly into the environment. This may bear enduring significance not only as we navigate the Internet of Things but also as we increasingly interact with artificial intelligence that adapts to us as individuals while taking on more human-like characteristics of address and interaction. Just as we can cut a call with a friend or lover in anger, we presumably can turn off our AI companion if we want some distance.

In examining this intimate, engaged, yet paradoxical everyday relationship with portable networked devices – especially smartphones, as their most prevalent and complex form[8] – this book asks the following questions:

In what ways do we interact with our personal, portable networked media devices as though they were independent beings with their own needs? How do their manifold properties, such as size, shape, texture, sound, and mechanical and electronic components and capacities, to say nothing of their operating systems, encourage, support, or necessitate these interactions based on normative assumptions about users and usage? And to what extent could these material and informational transactions amount to a personal relationship between us and our devices, where we feel the device *needs* us as much as we need it? This book attempts to answer these questions through consideration of contemporary design norms, media practices, and social attitudes as well as by investigating the multiple genealogies in the evolution of personal media as a social and economic concept since the latter decades of the twentieth century. These deeply personal, networked objects did not simply surface at an opportune moment but represent the progressive interlacing of diverse technical and social components. As Edward Constant wrote in the early days of science and technology studies (STS), "If [technological knowledge] is to be expressed as a tactile, functional artifact, it must be mixed with both base matter and other varieties of technological knowledge … This circumstance implies the cooperation of adherents of multiple communities of practitioners in the creation of any complex system."[9] In the making of these media devices, "cooperation" has sometimes been explicit and sustained, but more often it has been coincidental, intermittent, and even haphazard. Indeed, the beginnings of many "new" approaches and affordances of contemporary media technologies can be traced to diverse and sometimes divergent episodes of media creation, adaptation, or rejection drawn from recent history. Some of these – for example, the development of graphical user interfaces (GUI), the personalized soundtrack of the iPod, and the aesthetics of selfies – are readily invoked by researchers in discussions of today's media environments. Yet others – such as the system alerts of Tamagotchi toys, the competition between resistive and capacitive screens, and the creation of silicon "skins" as device cases – have garnered less attention.

In considering networked interactivity and situational processes of social data this book draws on concepts, methodologies, and research from anthropology, linguistics, sociology, psychology, and cultural studies, as well as other fields. It employs long-standing theories of reference and recognition in interpersonal and object-person relations from George Herbert

Mead, Erving Goffman, Charles S. Peirce, Roman Jakobson, D.W. Winnicott, Vilém Flusser, and Alfred Gell that have been infrequently applied toward understanding contemporary media, particularly in the material circumstances of mobile device use.[10] These theories are brought into dialogue with theories of interface and data, media ecology, and performativity from Wendy Hui Kyong Chun, Sherry Turkle, Christina Dunbar-Hester, Safiya Umoja Noble, and Mikael Wiberg, among others.[11]

Two theoretical approaches, media archaeology and media genealogy, strongly shaped the research process and methodology of this undertaking. Emerging out of the heady days of "new media" research at the start of this century, media archaeology attempts to destabilize narratives of novelty in contemporary media. With a footing in interdisciplinarity, it emphasizes instead the diversity of historical media forms and practices, demonstrating how they may engage issues and experiences that are often considered unique to today's ubiquitous, data-driven electronic systems and habits. "Media archaeologists have challenged the rejection of history by modern media culture and theory alike by pointing out hitherto unnoticed continuities and ruptures," state theorists Erkki Huhtamo and Jussi Parikka.[12] Working within a media archaeological framework requires moving beyond the narrow histories of specific portable networked devices or features to find correspondences or affinities in earlier media configurations or practices. Embarking on such a research endeavour often requires excavating untapped or underutilized historical sources. Examples cited in the following pages include popular media forms that frequently elude scholarly scrutiny, such as print and audiovisual advertising, manufacturer guides and manuals, computer and consumer electronics periodicals, archived social media forums, and even product packaging (i.e., the box in which the device lands in consumers' hands, which can powerfully frame the device and the user's expectations before the first physical interaction).[13]

While media archaeology may find areas of affinity or overlap across diverse media artifacts and practices in regard to form and action, media genealogy analyzes the function of power in these relationships. It asks how the media ecosystem may represent the expansion, circulation, or consolidation of economic, social, and political forces. "Archeological investigation examines collections of historical accounts," explain media scholars Clemens Apprich and Götz Bachmann, while "genealogical investigation focuses on precisely this dynamic process, around the transformation from one discursive formation to another."[14] Exploring technological affordances and patterns of use from a genealogical perspective allows us to consider not only the discursive development of the personal as a concept in everyday media but also how this personal media can contribute to building, sustaining, and intensifying networks of power. Within this lens, the personal is not simply a concept for describing certain types of media use and engagement; it becomes a means of leveraging use for the perpetuation and expansion of processes of economic, social, and political exploitation and inequality. The intimacy the user develops with the device, for example, becomes an affective and discursive pathway to the greater dependency and exploitation of the user as a source of monetization, profit, and asset building. Technology appears to grant some power to the individual with one hand, while taking more power away with the other.

Both media archaeology and media genealogy extend from the work of historian and philosopher Michel Foucault. Foucault adopted archaeology as a means of mapping transformations in discursive patterns. However, he later transitioned to genealogy as a means of examining non-discursive elements, such as knowledge and power, and how these function through material forms.[15] To an extent, the neediness of media described here – requiring attention and data creation – represents these non-discursive elements.

While recognizing the diversity of potential uses of and interactions with devices, as well as how these uses and interactions are strongly shaped by social, cultural, and political contexts, this study primarily considers a Western context, with some notable exceptions. For example, chapter 4 engages smartphone image culture in South and Southeast Asia and chapter 6 explores the development and use of digital pets in Japan. Nevertheless, it is worth noting that many of the interface elements and products analyzed in these pages either have been designed within Western contexts (e.g., Silicon Valley), rely heavily on Western design (e.g., Samsung phones running Google's Android operating system), or are targeted at Western markets. Industry decisions and control over user data are overwhelmingly concentrated in places like Mountain View, Menlo Park, and Cupertino, all in California, and Redmond, in Washington.[16] As such, examining these technological properties and practices alongside the cultural assumptions and socio-economic infrastructures of Western contexts not only sheds light on their ideological roots but also suggests how these properties and practices may encourage or require certain user behaviours over others, despite deep social and cultural differences among users.

In the same vein, it is important to acknowledge that the interfaces, affordances, and systems considered here also assume a normative user. In other words, the elements designed to bond user with device carry cultural assumptions that can marginalize already marginalized populations based on race, gender, or other factors, and also entail physical assumptions that can marginalize users based on ability or age. Sociologist Jenny L. Davis points out that "mechanisms of affordance indicate that technologies *request*, *demand*, *encourage*, *discourage*, *refuse*, and *allow* particular lines of action and social dynamics."[17] Just as Anita Say Chan, Brandeis Marshall, Cathy O'Neil, Lisa Nakamura, and others have shown how systemic inequalities persist in the functioning of digitally based communication networks, especially within privatized, profit-driven systems, these inequalities can also be found in the ways our devices are designed and interact with us on the simplest levels.[18] For example, facial recognition features can lose accuracy with racial and gender differences, the relatively limited range of available phone sizes can produce different challenges across populations based on the hand sizes of users, and skin sensitivity to haptic cues, which often diminishes with age, can affect the usability of certain features for older populations.[19]

Can Media Be "Needy"?

It is not only useful but perhaps even necessary to think of the user-device experience today in terms of a personal relationship, susceptible to some of the same conditions of social responsivity that guide human-to-human interactions.[20] We may tend to think of our digitally based social relationships as taking place *through* devices, rather than *with* them, construing the object merely as a frame or window for our interactions with people, data, algorithms, platforms, and networks.[21] User interface theorists Lars-Erik Janlert and Erik Stolterman claim that we "'see through' interfaces into an underlying meaningful state of affairs and development; they form sense-making models of what they perceive and experience, and those rather than superficial phenomena of the interface, such as the traffic of pixels and key presses, are what drive and guide their interaction."[22] What makes this media interaction personal, however, is not just the information that is exchanged but also how media behave – and can urge us to behave – at a material level. Psychologist Michelle Drouin calls the smartphone "probably the most demanding entity in my current world," explaining that "through my responsiveness to my phone's bids, I have nurtured it as well. But it's not only responsiveness that's solidified our relationship. I carefully wipe its screen to remove smudges (social grooming). I carry it with me everywhere I go in either my purse, hand, or pocket (skin-to-screen bonding). I get nervous if I cannot find it (separation anxiety). We are bonded, and I am smitten."[23]

These interactions and all sorts of other networked activities – from fitness and exercise monitoring to casual game playing – always come down to a physical relationship between us and the device. In other words, a significant aspect of our "sense-making" with these devices may be making sense of – and from – the conditions of the body-object exchange. Through selection and organization of materials and physical properties, these devices facilitate what user interface theorist Mikael Wiberg calls "a particular thread of interaction," which can produce specific psychological and affective qualities.[24] We may watch the device, listen to it, tap it, shake it, tilt it, stroke it. Sometimes these actions may occur to watch a video or listen to music or play a game or send a text. Other times it may be simply for the pleasure or reassurance of interacting with the device as a companion across the many contexts of our daily lives, as when we scroll through feeds that may not be of much consequence to us, tap the surface to wake up the screen, swipe back and forth across windows of icons, or experiment with taking selfies that will never make it to our social media accounts. Sometimes we may clutch the device like a comfort object, or turn it in our hands, long after we have finished our watching and tapping, in the same way a child holds a stuffed animal or an adult might casually hold the hand of someone dear to them.[25] We could say we hold these devices even when they are off, but – other than when their battery dies – when are they ever really off? When not in use they continually throw multiple stimuli our way – fluctuations in light, emissions of sound, and even vibration – to appeal to sight, hearing, and the haptic. Even setting a daily schedule with the Do Not Disturb feature on your smartphone – say, for your nightly sleeping hours – paradoxically can trigger a push notification every time the phone enters that mode.

Through networked software features as diverse as fingerprint scanning, facial recognition, location identification, and push notifications, the device interface becomes a multi-layered process of interaction that draws us in both physically and psychologically. As anthropologist Daniel Miller points out, our possessions can act on us as powerfully as we act on them. "We too are stuff," he notes, "and our use and identification with material culture provides a capacity for enhancing, just as much as for submerging, our humanity."[26] More succinctly, digital media designer Alan Kay explains, "learning to use tools reshapes us."[27] Through its stream of suggestions, updates, reminders, and alerts generated by algorithms underpinned by machine learning, the portable, networked device is a constant, nuanced presence in our lives, contributing to, and fundamentally shaping, our daily physical and social activities. Maintaining this presence of the device requires that we are behaviourally conditioned to regularly recognize – and subsequently act upon – the device to convert our being into a datafied image of ourself entwined in deep neural network processes of commodification and monetization.[28] Augmented by such factors as locative technologies that can detect and track our movements, the device interface's synthesis of data can produce a finely tuned, predictive response that adapts to our physical and digital wanderings in real time, constantly assessing and affirming our existence by situating us within a system of values and exchanges.[29]

Exploiting the changing valences of "friends" and "followers," of "liking" and "loving," as have developed in social media to describe sets of actions and information structures rather than deep emotional or affective ties, the device's interface positions this animated object as our most faithful friend or follower, something – or someone – focused on us and our needs. It is a fundamental component of what Zizi Papacharissi calls "the networked self," Brian Massumi terms "the self-network," and Lee Rainie and Barry Wellman dub "networked individualism."[30] This position is augmented by apps that personalize interaction with users while urging them in turn to pay attention to others – to friend, follow, or like other users, products, or content. In this way, our relationships with other people ultimately become one aspect of our relationship with the device. As Rainie and Wellman remark, "In incorporating gadgets into their lives, people have changed the ways they interact with each other. They have become increasingly networked as individuals, rather than embedded in groups."[31]

Psychologist Margaret Morris claims that this reliance on devices and networks amounts to an alliance between user and technology. "This alliance begins when we acquire or access something, perhaps a new device, service, or data, and evolves as the technology challenges us and we challenge it," Morris states. "We bring the technology into social situations it wasn't designed for. We draw on it to negotiate the limitations we see in ourselves."[32] While we may access information and communicate across a variety of apps, these tasks are united in the body of the device and coordinated by its actions.

Even as all of this points to the device as an emergent independent subject in our lives, as our most astute interlocutor and unflagging confidante, we must recognize that it never fully achieves this. Despite our devices being such strong players in the performance of daily life, we typically do not have personifying names for most of them, nor do we describe them in personal terms. When a smartphone or watch breaks or malfunctions, we abandon or exchange it for another device with relative ease, as long as we can migrate data and settings (more and more of which are stored in cloud computing structures). This ambiguity may contribute to what has made these portable networked devices such a compelling and successful component of our everyday social existence. It allows them to function as an adaptable foil – even as they amount to an extension – of ourselves. They may not be us, but they become a part of who we are.

This can set our experience of these devices apart from that of other networked devices and interfaces. Consider, for example, voice interactive household devices at the centre of Apple HomePod, Google Nest, and Amazon Echo. These and similar technologies often create characters like the even-tempered, smooth-voiced Siri or Alexa, which are meant to mediate as anthropomorphized agents between us and the information we seek. While such efforts aim at making networked interaction more like an interpersonal relationship, they can be experienced as an additional layer interceding between us and the network. They are also prefab, stock personifications, meaning that ultimately there is little that is personal about them. They pretty much sound alike everywhere, though they are crafted as individuals with specific voices and names. As such, these anthropomorphized aspects to interface may actually limit the technology's affective impact. Siri or Alexa is not only not us but also seems more or less the same for everyone. Neither of them is any more our friend than they are our neighbour's, and typically neither of them acknowledges us unless we address them directly. In addition to these distancing qualities, voice interactive virtual assistants also do not afford the amount of privacy between user and device found with hand-held or wearable devices. Commands and questions must be said aloud, for example, making them potentially audible to others.

Given these conditions, can we call the networked devices of our daily lives "needy," as the title of this book asserts? That term is typically applied to people or pets, not objects of plastic, glass, and metal. It is clear that in the twenty-first century we need these devices to accomplish many of the most basic tasks of daily life, turning to them again and again. Each year, as more services and activities move to the internet and in-person alternatives dry up, the many options of online life become requirements. But how would our devices have *needs* that only we could fulfill? How would those needs become a fundamental symptom or condition of their (and thus, our) being?

Being needy – or "neediness" – means to lack something. *Merriam-Webster* defines neediness as "being in want." The term is often invoked to refer to material lack. Those that do not have adequate housing or food, for example, historically have been described as "the needy." (A synonym for needy frequently used when there is material lack is "impoverished.") Our personal media devices may be needy in their want of things. They are technologically rich, but data poor. Imagine the moment we acquire a new device to replace an existing one. The first steps after turning it on are importing and synching. We "autofill" the device with our existing data, because without this the device is of limited use and relevance to us. If we cannot import data or synch the device, then we must slowly feed it bits of information – phone numbers, account usernames, etc. – to personalize it. From these first moments, these devices are highly dependent on our habits and actions in shaping what they are; they mean (and do) very little on their own. In short, they are reliant on us, on our attention to them, to become uniquely crafted objects.

Merriam-Webster also defines neediness as "marked by want of affection, attention, or emotional support."[33] Everyone requires affection, attention, and emotional support on a regular basis. Neediness in this regard typically means *excessive* demand for attention, affection, and security. The term is most frequently applied in this way in the context of close, personal relationships where emotional and psychological stakes are highest. The *Oxford English Dictionary*, for example, defines neediness "with reference to spiritual or emotional needs" but also identifies it as "excessive emotional or psychological reliance on another person (typically a partner or close relative)."[34] Neediness not only implies dependency, then, but also the inordinate solicitation of attention and intervention. Needy people require frequent acknowledgment and comforting. For example, young children may be called needy for the amount of attention and encouragement they usually require. Adults may also be called needy when requiring frequent emotional support or reassurance. The word is often negative and can be pejorative. No one likes being called needy.

As this book will demonstrate, not only are our devices data poor, their configurations and affordances also require regular attention and care to ensure their well-being. Compare your phone, for example, to a conventional landline, a television, or a radio. If you left any of those objects alone for a week – whether on or off – they would be no different when you returned to them. Leave your phone untouched for a week and you return to a device that likely requires an hour of your attention to get it back in shape, from recharging the battery to deleting backed-up notifications and running system updates. Our electronics do not have emotional needs, of course, nor will they for the foreseeable future. Yet they seem to crave our recognition and interaction, harbouring all manner of ways to get our attention. Often triggered by their independent, networked exchanges, they frequently alert us to changes in the content they receive or in their own condition. Sometimes these solicitations are important or even urgent. Often, however, they can seem unnecessarily frequent or excessive. We may ignore them at our own risk, as a reluctance to act will only spur greater solicitation.

Initially, these notifications were the direct result of people we know trying to make contact through the network. Cellphones derived from pagers, small wireless devices that could register phone calls and display incoming phone numbers for the user to return the call from a payphone or landline. For years cellphones functioned similarly, registering texts or calls from specific phone numbers. With the development of smartphones and their apps and networked data flows, however, notifications and updates have exploded. Beyond signalling the incoming messages of people we know, they have become a means to build engagement with apps and platforms to maximize personal data extraction and monetize use. However, these frequent attempts to access the user must hone to a fine line to encourage engagement without triggering frustration. This is where device neediness comes into play. The device's solicitations may be frequent, but they must pique user interest, getting them to pick up the device, unlock it, and scroll rather than turn off notifications or silence them with Do Not Disturb mode. In fact, when this pattern of solicitation works most effectively, users may pick up their devices even when not notified, just to check if anything has changed or if there is a problem.[35]

It is important to note that this neediness of the device may be felt more acutely by those who are isolated, marginalized, or otherwise socially vulnerable. That is, such users may become more dependent on the device and its interactivity as a means of building a sense of social interaction and inclusion. Responding to alerts or scrolling can give the user a sense of social engagement (seeing what others are doing by actively consuming their content) entwined with physical engagement in the manipulation of the device's affordances to access and consume material. In moments or periods of extreme isolation, the personal networked device may hold as strong a presence in the user's life as would another living being (a pet or a person).

What Are "Personal" Media?

With today's emphasis on media use and content as personalized processes that include the collecting and sharing of information on individuals through their networked interactions, it is important to ask precisely what is meant when we call media "personal." The term "personal media" suggests a particular relationship, one that in turn can be shaped and explained in multiple ways. At its base, the term describes a relationship between individual users, the devices and networks they access, and their goals and behaviour in interacting with these devices.

We could call all media personal at some level. Each eventually reaches, interacts with, and affects an individual reader, listener, or viewer.[36] However, there is a specific historical development of the idea of personal media as encompassing certain objects, systems, and contexts specifically centred on the individual and often less on interactions with other people than with the objects and systems themselves. This epistemological and material evolution is significant in tracing how our perception of what constitutes the personal has transformed over time. Most important, it demonstrates how the idea of the personal, in relation to media, has shifted from tightly circumscribed and limited frames to ubiquitous computing, expansive information flows, machine learning, and even artificial intelligence. In this shift, the parameters of personal exchange have moved from person-to-person interaction to person-device interaction. Personal media today, while still facilitating interpersonal communication between individuals in all sorts of ways, also engage their users when no such communication is taking place, essentially becoming an actor in their own right.[37] Interaction with the device can be an end in itself, producing an intrapersonal relationship where the user's emphasis is in communicating with the device, rather than anyone the device might access. Computer historian Laine Nooney has observed, "What makes a computer 'personal' today tends to be defined by a level of *user intimacy*," noting that we might include other devices, such as smartphones and tablets, under the term "personal computer."[38] It is important to note that while the person-to-person relationship may entail multiple daily exchanges with multiple actors who may or may not convey the information exchanged to larger networks, the person-device relationship involves multiple exchanges with a single actor that typically conveys any and all information or data gathered to larger networks for processing and analysis.

Broadly speaking, personal media as a historical concept initially shifted from an emphasis on the person to an emphasis on media that facilitated interpersonal exchanges, before then moving to an emphasis on media hardware designed for individual use. In other words, from an original connotation tied closely to the body as a material instrument capable of making and conveying meaning, it has passed through the development of various media technologies to again rest close to the body in the material ties between contemporary users and their portable networked devices. It reshapes this individual use of devices into something of an interpersonal exchange, regardless of whether this interaction is directly tied to communication with other users. As such, this trajectory parallels the paradox that lies at the heart of the term "personal media" itself. The *Oxford English Dictionary* defines "personal" as generally meaning both "of, relating to, concerning, or affecting a person as a private individual" and "individual, private; one's own."[39] This sets the word in opposition to "media," since a medium is "an intermediate agency, instrument, or channel."[40] In other words, a medium is something that functions *between* individuals or entities, that necessarily extends beyond the strictly personal, and must be shared, all of which makes it a suitable vehicle for communication and the exchange of signs or information. Personal media can be simultaneously contained to the self and extend beyond the self to reach others. This aptly describes the current state of individualized portable device use, where personal media can seem as much a means of turning in on the self as a means of reaching out to others.

The occasional use of the term "personal media" in previous centuries meant something very different, however. Accordingly, it can be insightful to trace the historical progression of the idea since the rise of industrialization and mass media. In nineteenth-century usage personal media could imply the individual subject bound into its materiality – the person and their body – as an agent of communication. This is the case with the term's use in British and American religious texts of the period. An 1846 essay on Christian ministries in *The Eclectic Review*, for example, states that "*personal influence* is one of the most important modes of divine renewing agency. All revelation is personal … And the reasons of it are doubtless among the reasons wherefore it is ordained that 'holy men of God' alone should preach the gospel. Truths are very different things as they are exhibited through different personal media, and clothed with different personal attributes."[41]

The foregoing example implies that the same message can have different impacts depending on who is presenting it and how they present themselves as well as the message they transmit. Similarly, an article on spirituality and selflessness published in the *Newchurchman* at about the same time explains that "the personal medium here is for the sake of introducing the principle, which is still distinct from the personal medium, and is the Lord himself as a principle existing distinctly from the person through whom he flows."[42] Writing on prophecy and proselytizing later in the century, American religious scholar Samuel Harris would use "personal medium" and "human medium" interchangeably in deeming the individual "the only adequate agency for communicating God's revelation."[43] Such Western, Christian understandings of "personal media," though far removed from today's popular secular usage, nevertheless can be helpful in exploring the development of personal digital technologies to the extent that our successful adoption of these technologies often rests on a close – and sometimes seemingly indistinguishable – relationship between the body and the device.

The invention of electromagnetic and photographic technologies in the mid-nineteenth century fostered the spread of "mass" media and precipitated the dissociation of "medium" from the human body. An individual could potentially communicate with many others simultaneously and over great distances through these new, industrial media. Despite this, however, on the rare occasion that "personal media" was invoked in relation to other media well into the twentieth century, it could continue to signify exchanges between individuals. "We must distinguish here between formal mass media on one hand, and informal personal media on the other," states a mid-twentieth-century American periodical on trademarks and patents. "The former includes such sources as magazines, newspapers, radio, television, pamphlets, etc., while the latter refers to *persons* who provide information and views to their associates in a direct, face-to-face manner."[44]

Nevertheless, there are also examples of this term applying not to individual exchanges but to the individual's use of mass media. A 1967 advertising industry journal states that "media usage is more personal than a family activity. This is emphasized as media vehicles become more specialized and audiences more selective. Magazines, radio and newspapers are all personal media ... television (with the help of the second set) is rapidly becoming one."[45] Here personal media can disrupt the face-to-face exchange of family activities as individuals choose to interact with the medium – including its material object – rather than with others present in their surroundings. This reflects Marshall McLuhan's theory of media (developed at that time) as a reshaping of the social by the material conditions and contexts of the medium itself.[46] A public relations handbook of a few years later suggests that "personal media include those forms of communication used by individuals in direct contact with one another – face-to-face, by telephone, or by mail. Direct personal exchange is involved."[47] As some of these examples imply, "personal media" has often been interchangeable with "interpersonal media," particularly when placed in contrast to "mass media." Indeed, "interpersonal media" was the more common expression in the twentieth century, though "personal media" emerged in the 1960s and 1970s. Communication theorist Wilbur Schramm, for example, refers to the relationship between "mass and personal" media in his 1973 book *Men, Messages, and Media*.[48]

During the mid-twentieth-century struggle between "interpersonal" and "personal" in business and academic communication research circles, technological advances allowing for the reduction in size of different communication devices and tools – especially the camera, the radio, the television, and the hi-fi stereo – would produce a new definition of personal media as a class of communication devices intended primarily or exclusively for individual use. Although "pocket cameras" existed by the turn of the twentieth century, most of these devices and their accompanying language of the personal and private only began to emerge in the years following World War II.[49] Radio Corporation of America marketed its RCA Victor "Personal" Radio in 1951 as a portable, book-sized device that "is like holding a band in your hand."[50] A few years later, "pocket radios" such as the Dyna-Mite Pocket Radio and Tinytone Pocket Personal Radio were advertised specifically as "personal" devices (see figure 0.1).[51] Western Radio told the consumer that its Tinytone would let you "listen in private while you walk" or ride in a vehicle. Through its plastic ear plug, "you alone listen anytime, anywhere without anyone else knowing you are hearing radio music, sports, news, weather, etc."[52] In this example, "personal" relates to the private, intimate relationship between the user and the device, even when they are surrounded by others. By 1966 one American manufacturer would classify itself as "a leader in personal electronics" by offering a range of products, including clock, transistor, and short-wave radios, as well as walkie-talkies and portable phonographs.[53]

Although the term "personal electronics" continued to be used through the 1970s, it was only in the 1980s that it would emerge as a commonly recognized category of consumer products, with the success of the Sony Walkman and similar devices for the portable consumption of music through earphones. (Indeed, it is a testament to the "private" nature of the Walkman that it was not equipped with a speaker for ambient listening but only with an output jack, recalling the privacy Western Radio had touted with the Tinytone earplug.)

We can observe across these examples that "personal media" could have different – even opposing – meanings, depending on the context. Prior to the idea of mass media, it would seem, personal media was seen primarily as a close, physical exchange between people sharing the same time and

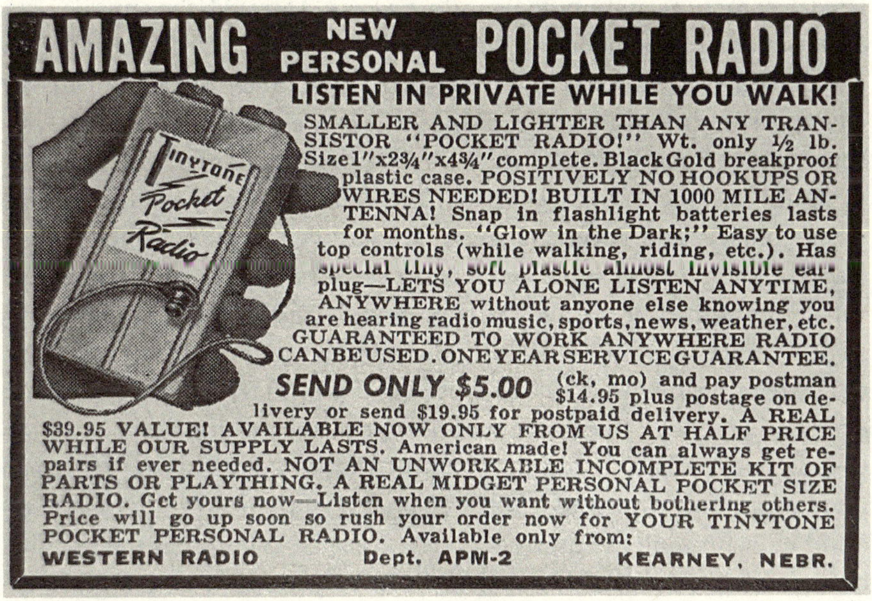

Figure 0.1
An advertisement for the Tinytone Pocket Personal Radio published in *Popular Mechanics* in January 1957.

space. With the onset of mass media, the exchange could still be between identifiable individuals, though it no longer necessarily *required* physical proximity, or it could be between an individual and a media device to the exclusion of others. In digitally networked, platform-based media, the term "personal media" has encompassed technologically supported exchanges that might take place between individuals but frequently include others (sometimes millions of them, in the case of the most popular social media accounts) and corporate data-gathering operations.[54]

In theorizing personal media today, Nancy Thumim contends that the term refers to the combination of "technologies that facilitate one-to-many and many-to-many communication and the content that people produce in that communication."[55] Seeing it as closely related to ideas of social media, participatory media, and citizen media, Thumim places the production of shared content firmly at its centre. Similarly, theorist Marika Lüders explains in her analysis of personal media's characteristics that mass and interpersonal media now intermingle within the same technologies and telecommunication systems and are accessed through the same devices. Lüders defines personal media as "tools for interpersonal communication and personalized expression," which at the time of her research primarily encompassed "mobile phones, email, Instant Messenger, homepages, private weblogs (blogs), online profiles and photo-sharing services."[56] Though some of these examples may be dated, this definition easily extends to more recent objects and products such as wearables (smartwatches, fitness trackers, and the like) and social media apps. In emphasizing the interpersonal communication capabilities of devices and networked platforms, Lüders (much like Thumim) omits the personal connotations of the user-device relationship itself, however, even as this is integral to the experience of digital media as a personal practice. Nevertheless, the main assertion that digital media have "destabilized the traditional dichotomy between mass communication and (inter)personal communication" remains relevant in examining the user-device relationship. It indicates the opening of a space within which "personal media" can operate as a meaningful term describing conditions at the intersection of communication and material interactions afforded by contemporary digital devices.[57]

This intersection of communication with material interactions relates to what media scholar Terje Rasmussen has called the "personalization" of contemporary media. "By personalisation I mean the reorganization of technology according to the expectations of persons," Rasmussen states, explaining that personalization involves not only "personalized connectivity" through security and authentication functions and "personalized services" such as accounts for shopping and sharing but also "devices and their design."[58] Taking a sociological "lifeworld" approach in exploring the significance of personalized media in the everyday, Rasmussen nevertheless focuses on the processes of networked interpersonal communication and the content of exchange as the salient aspects of personal media at the expense of sustained consideration of the material conditions of media interactivity, particularly as they concern device design and functionality. In emphasizing writing, talking, and watching as the principal "meaning-constituting sensorial practices" of personal media, for example, Rasmussen neglects the critical role of touch and wider physical movements, both significant to interactivity with many devices and tightly entwined with the foregoing practices.[59]

To fully seize and appreciate the richness of the term "personal media" as it may apply to contemporary technological and cultural conditions we must venture beyond these limitations. We must consider how our devices today can be personal media in their portability or functionality for sharing and experiencing content as well as in the extent to which they are "of the person" (to recall the *Oxford English Dictionary*'s description). This qualification is significant in multiple ways.[60] First, these devices reflect the person in their configuration and organization. Aside from the hardware and basic functions of the operating system, these devices are highly personalized in their behaviour and content. Pick up someone's smartphone and, once past the personalized barrier of a security setting or password, you will find the choices, tastes, and activities of the owner at every turn. There will be a selection of apps downloaded by the owner to address their specific needs, interests, and desires. The icons for these apps may be displayed over a background photo taken by the owner or an image or design they've chosen from the device's wallpaper options. Many other additional functions of the device, including the brightness of the screen, the types and frequency of push notifications, and the melodies of alerts and ring tones, may be chosen or altered by the owner. We often look beyond these function and performance settings when we consider the personal nature of these devices, however, to focus on the significant amount of information and data these devices record and store about their user. From contact lists, programmed alerts and reminders (such as alarms), route preferences, and stored usage information to the trove of text messages, photographs, videos, and audio recordings, these devices represent our lifestyle and behaviour in innumerable ways.[61]

As a result of the information, networks, and tools that these devices harbour and represent, it is perhaps little surprise they have become "of the person" as physically intimate components of our lived self. Much like clothing, they become an integral part of our material being, accompanying our bodies throughout the day, across activities and spaces. As Norman Medoff and Barbara Kaye state, "The smartphone has become our communication hub and security blanket."[62] Misplacing or losing one's portable smart device can induce feelings of incompleteness, vulnerability, or exposure, and one might feel a deep sense of personal violation if it is stolen or confiscated.[63] Symptoms of withdrawal can occur when one's device is not at hand or no longer functioning, producing a condition known as nomophobia.[64] And there is some evidence that carrying and interacting with these devices on a daily basis may be changing our bodies based on repeated patterns of interaction, such as "text neck" from bending the head while viewing the smartphone screen or reduced sleep from close exposure to a screen at night.[65]

What is most compelling and challenging in thinking about contemporary networked media devices such as smartphones and watches as personal media is the extent to which they can embody *all* these definitions of the personal. They have the capacity to send and receive data, to store information and recordings, and to communicate with others individually or in numbers. And all of this is achieved with an object that is typically owned and operated by a single individual and kept on or near their body most of the day and night.

A Path through Personal Media and Their Needs

The chapters that follow demonstrate how our portable media devices have come to embody the personal in ways outlined above by instilling need as a fundamental condition of encounter and interaction. To varying degrees, each chapter explores the origins and development of a different key characteristic of the personal media object. These characteristics, developed in different contexts and technologies, coalesce in the contemporary device. They bear ideological presumptions about typical users and standard usage, and this book attempts to point these out.

Chapter 1 revisits the era of build-it-yourself microcomputer kits in mid-1970s North America through a critical lens. It explores the tactile, corporeal relationship that defined not only the handicraft assembly of these personal devices by their owners but also the subsequent interactivity and display. Offered as an alternative example of how intimacy can function in user-device relationships, the chapter also uncovers the role sexism and gender bias played in the cultural framing of these material transactions by their (typically) male owners, thereby placing heteronormative gender stereotypes at the centre of that relationship. These early personal computers – often customized in their configuration, controls, and casings

– were sometimes portrayed in hobbyist magazines as either ideal social counterparts or destructive elements in the owner's wider social relationships and familial responsibilities.

Chapter 2 approaches the development of physical interactions with portable digital devices in relation to theories of gesture and performance. It situates pointing as the most basic communicative gesture creating a simulated, shared space between user and device. The chapter explains how this intimacy, initially established through the mouse and onscreen arrow from the 1960s to the 1980s, was lost with many early hand-held touch screen devices, such as Palm's PalmPilot and Apple's Newton. The stylus and script recognition features of those devices shifted emphasis away from interpersonal gesturing, creating distance with more formal sign systems in user-device touch interaction. The distance would collapse, however, with direct-touch smartphone screens of the 2000s that further enhanced spatial recognition of the user-device relationship through geolocative capabilities that made device and user representationally identical through location sharing. From pointing to the device, the device now pointed to the user within networked environments, potentially undermining privacy while reinforcing the close relationship – and even collapsing the identity – between the device and its owner.

Chapter 3 considers the intimacy of mobile media devices through touch and grip. While touch screen interfaces have been instrumental in building intimacy, the chapter argues this close haptic relationship was established with the iPod. Revisiting iPod design and culture, this chapter notes the significance of grip, touch, and contact surface in establishing intimacy in the user-device relationship. Nestled in the palm and manipulated through the touch sensitivity of the click wheel, the iPod became one with the user, yet it was also promoted as an independent body through the proliferation of "skins" – and even "tattoos" – to cover its surface. This skin would become integrated into the aesthetics of the iPhone's iOS by representing the screen surface as a reactive membrane subject to the pull and pressure of the finger through visuals of tightening and lightening akin to the play of epidermal tissue.

Chapter 4 considers the visuality of the user-device relationship through mobile optical systems of recognition. Examining practices around selfie production and circulation as potent forms of face-to-face physical encounter and acknowledgment between user and device, it considers the user-device relationship through theories of mimicry, narcissism, and the extension of the self into the object. This is compounded by face-based game apps and selfie toys for children, which increasingly place the user's face at the centre of any interactions with the device, much as our daily physical interactions with others rely heavily on facial cues.

Chapter 5 extends the inquiry into facial confrontations and interactions with our devices by examining the increasingly common features of device-level facial recognition and attention awareness systems. Facial recognition locks such as Face ID place mutual user-device recognition almost on the same level as person-to-person meetings (whether physical or through videoconferencing apps), where recognizing and remembering the face in front of us is the basic building block of making and maintaining social relationships. Acknowledgment of the user's face, and perhaps even their movements and expressions through other awareness features such as emotion recognition, allows the device to emerge as a savvy, nuanced companion. Through these features the device can potentially adjust its solicitations and reactions to the state or "mood" of the user, while also extracting valuable affective data for app developers and device manufacturers.

Chapter 6 examines how networked interactions facilitated by the device frequently hinge on constant recognition and solicitation of the user. Through default settings such as push notifications, information is framed as part of the work of the device to act as an alert and helpful intermediary that nevertheless craves response. Wearable fitness trackers and smartwatch health features represent perhaps the most extensive application of this system to the material conditions of physical interaction between user and device as they urge users to make subtle changes to their bodies. This recalls the circumstances around the digital toy Tamagotchi in the 1990s. The controversies surrounding Tamagotchi's release in terms of the dangers of intimacy with devices are examined here as a perhaps unexpected, but strongly appropriate, early example of the update-centric relationship between users and their devices today. Just as Tamagotchi required the user's frequent attention and action to keep the device "healthy," the wearable seems to require the same today in ostensibly helping the user stay healthy.

CHAPTER 1

Building the "Perfectly" Personal

The development of personal media in the digital era, following the examples of analogue media mentioned in the introduction, may appear a simple progression from the creation of graphical user interfaces for personal computers (i.e., the desktop or laptop screen display of icons and a mobile pointer) to the rise of personal digital assistants and mobile, internet-based devices such as smartphones and watches. Yet personal digital media have encompassed a much wider range of practices, interfaces, and applications along several paths. They have belonged to differing cultural contexts and reflected a variety of belief systems, invoking the personal in multiple, sometimes contradictory, ways. As historian Laine Nooney states, for example, "We've been told, over and over again … that personal computing was, from the moment of its invention, instantly recognized as a revolutionary technology and eagerly taken up by the American public. This is not true."[1]

The circumstances and understandings of personal digital media surrounding the introduction of computers into homes in North America in the mid-1970s brought a remarkable shift in thinking around digital computing machines as personal objects and tools. The development of personal computers from Commodore, Compaq, Tandy, Apple, IBM, and other companies is a well-known origin story of personal digital media, famously codified by *Time* magazine's unconventional decision in 1982 to change its "person of the year" award to "machine of the year" in bestowing the honour on the personal computer under the headline "The Computer Moves In."[2] Yet prior to the adoption of these out-of-the-box, plug-and-play PCs, the digital computer had already entered the private, domestic sphere as home hobby kits that promised an intimate experience of the object in requiring users to manipulate and connect components within the device itself to produce a functioning machine. These digital devices – and the practices surrounding them – cultivated a highly tactile and physical form of personal media that, by necessity, transformed the device into a deeply individualized, even uniquely constructed, object.

This emphasis on close physical contact and multiple forms of interactivity aligns with the more recent personal media considered in this book, even as it deviates in obvious ways. In research that spans much of this historical trajectory, Sherry Turkle has stated, "When digital technologies first came onto the consumer market in the form of personal computers they were objects for psychological projection. Computers – programmable and customizable – came to be experienced as a 'second self.' In the early twenty-first century, such language does not go far enough; our new intimacy with communications devices compels us to speak of a new state of the self, itself."[3] This chapter takes up Turkle's challenge in reckoning with the gaps and overlaps between these moments.

The mid-twentieth-century transformation of computing from massive, collectively used machines housed in corporate headquarters, university labs, and government agencies to tabletop machines owned and operated by individuals in domestic settings is a critical stage in the historical path to contemporary personal media. Sometimes referred to as an "electric brain" in post–World War II popular culture, the compact, portable computers envisioned in the 1950s and 1960s and rapidly developed in the 1970s and 1980s were construed as capable of producing interactive, potentially interpersonal machine-human experiences unlike any other invention.[4] Computers of the 1950s and 1960s were typically enormous systems kept at a distance from those who might use them. As journalist Mark Freuenfelder writes, "Companies that could afford computers kept them locked away from the employees, who could only peer through plate glass into the computer room … Even the people who used computers to solve problems weren't allowed to touch them. Instead, they handed a stack of punched cards to one of the technicians."[5]

Before the mid-1970s, the term "personal computer" was rarely encountered. When it did appear, it typically figured in futuristic visions. "While it will be entirely feasible to obtain an education at home, via one's own personal computer," a 1964 article in *The New Scientist* forecasted, "human nature will not have changed, and there will still be a need for schools with laboratories, classrooms and individual teachers to motivate the students."[6] Personal computing pioneer Alan Kay employed the term in 1968 for his conception of a "powerful notebook computer." Kay recalls, "I called it a 'personal computer' then, but I was thinking *intimacy*."[7] Here Kay appears to refer to the psychological qualities of the user-device interaction produced by the object's modest physical size and increased portability (in addition to its design for individual use), rather than the nature of work that could be accomplished on it. As we shall see, the original intimacy of the personal computer – experienced through hobby kits in the 1970s – would hinge on small-scale and precise interactions between the kit owner and the computer's many physical parts, rather than the device's very modest computing power.[8]

Hackers, Homes, and Hobbies

Rather than "personal computer," the term "microcomputer" was more commonly used through much of the 1970s when referring to small, personally owned machines. Alternative terms included "small computers," "home computers," and "hobby computers."[9] The prefix "micro" derives from the microprocessors made of integrated circuits on silicon chips that had begun entering the consumer market with Intel in the early 1970s. Microprocessors made home-based computing feasible. The prefix also arose from the need to differentiate these computers from refrigerator-sized "minicomputers," such as the PDP series from Digital Equipment Corporation. Equipped with chip processors rather than transistors, microcomputers represented a substantial reduction in the size and price of computer hardware. Microcomputers functioned as "personal" computers not only because individuals could now buy their own small computers to have at home or in the office but also because the assembly and proper functioning of the technology was often wholly dependent on the owner. These activities produced a personal relationship with the device that subsequent pre-assembled computers would lack.

In describing the possibility for home-built and accessible computers as early as the mid-1950s, mathematician and inventor Edmund Berkeley emphasized the importance of interacting with computers beyond their "capacity for useful work." Berkeley designed a basic electromechanical home computer in 1950 called "Simon" specifically to encourage more leisurely interactions between non-specialists and computing devices. "To abandon this capacity [for work], in fact, is to give us some necessary freedom. We become free to play with the machine, and to tinker with it," Berkeley stated.[10] As Berkeley's words suggest, the path from mainframe to PC was not simply a technological one, where improvements in processing, circuitry, and memory afforded continual reductions in size and cost while potentially increasing speed and efficiency. The path to the personal computer was also cultural. Like other media before it, the personal computer would go through what historians Lisa Gitelman and Geoffrey Pingree have called the "identity crisis" of media when they are new. "Their place is at first ill defined, and their ultimate meanings or functions are shaped over time by that society's existing habits of media use ... by shared desires for new uses, and by the slow process of adaptation between the two," Gitelman and Pingree explain.[11]

Shrinking size and cost intersected in the latter half of the twentieth century with new social dynamics and changing beliefs surrounding the relationships between people, media, and machines. From the mid-1960s, off-peak time-sharing on mainframes at research and academic sites produced a new class of computer users. Eventually known as "hackers," these users treated the computer as a versatile, interactive, and even joyful object with which one could develop and play games, create works of art, or simply explore the possibilities of coding and programming. Hacker and *Whole Earth Catalog* publisher Stewart Brand would describe these users as "computer bums" who freed these machines from their institutional servitude to create interactive programs of pure enjoyment, such as the computer game *Spacewar*. "It was an administrative headache," Stewart claims. "It was merely delightful."[12] More recently, historian Tung-Hui Hu has claimed that institutions had introduced user logins to remedy this "headache," allowing administrators to identify and monitor individual relationships with the computer. "Crucially, the user was not yet personal in the sense of personal computing; rather, this process made a user's personhood synonymous with his or her usage," Hu states.[13] This process has ramifications for contemporary perceptions of networked media use, where users as individual, living beings are barely differentiated from the contents, activity, and location of their portable smart devices. The countercultural ideologies of liberation – both for people and their computers – that developed among hackers also had links to psychotropic drugs, such as LSD. This vision was embodied by Brand's New Communalism, which emphasized holistic personal development and the ethics of community sharing, and Ted Nelson's *Computer Lib,* and their shared promise of the potential for expanding minds and enriching lives in part by building new creative relationships with machines, communications devices, and information systems.[14]

Many accounts of the emergence of personal computing and personal computers have emphasized hacker culture's imagining of the computer liberated by individuals as a "smart," interactive device for creative production to the detriment of computer kit hobbyists in the lineage of Edmund Berkeley, who literally constructed the first personal computers in their homes.[15] For example, *What the Dormouse Said*, John Markoff's book on counterculture and the personal computer industry, states, "Personal computers that were designed for and belonged to single individuals would emerge initially in concert with a counterculture that rejected authority and believed the human spirit would triumph over corporate technology, not be subject to it."[16] Focusing on "homebrew" computing and its associated regional clubs (especially California's Homebrew Computer Club where industry pioneers such as Steve Jobs and Steve Wozniak mixed with social activists including Fred Moore), this narrative accent on countercultural liberation ignores the ways that personal computing developed within the exceedingly conventional social spheres of the suburban tract house and nuclear family. Based in the home – not the club or the computer lab – hobbyist adoption would impact interpersonal relationships within family contexts through intimate connection between user and device based in physical processes of assembly, maintenance, and improvement. If hackers and homebrew clubs sought to wrest computing from the power dynamics of the military-industrial complex, hobbyists sought to reconcile it with the power dynamics of normative social structures like class, gender, and marriage. This radically changes the genealogical conditions of personal media at a key moment in their development and promotion.

Even when hobbyists have been given their due in histories of digital media, little has been said about the ideological underpinnings or social implications of the material culture of hobby computing as it related to everyday life and interpersonal relationships.[17] How did hobby computer building and programming play out in the day-to-day of the domestic sphere, for example? And what might this tell us about the development and role of personal digital media more broadly? Revisiting discussions and accounts of hobby computing from that period – as will be done here – can help provide answers to such questions and enrich our understanding of the material underpinnings of both early and contemporary personal digital media use. Situated outside the antagonism between hackers and institutional authorities, the do-it-yourself and hobbyist movements that thrived in America after World War II peacefully coexisted alongside liberal democratic economic expansionism. Through efforts such as Berkeley's Simon, 1950s analogue computer kits including the GENIAC and the Heathkit EC-1, 1960s digital kits including the Minivac 601, and a slew of 1970s microprocessor-based kits including the Mark-8, the SCELBI 8H and 8B, the KIM-1, the Heathkit H-8 and H-11, as well as the highly popular Altair 8800 (see figure 1.1), the individualized and home-based human-computer relationship would emerge from deeply material and physical maker culture.

This social phenomenon in the domestic sphere was less about rejecting institutional hierarchies and corporate strategies than developing complementary creative spaces from and within them. Indeed, in the initial transition from large-scale corporate computing to home computing in the 1970s, the personal and intimate relationship that developed between user and machine did not involve the interface metaphors of graphical user interfaces or the "friendly" software that was being developed by Alan Kay and others at Xerox's Palo Alto Research Center (PARC) at the time (and that would become fundamental to personal computers a decade later, as seen in chapter 2). Instead, the relationship emerged from the hands-on and sometimes dirty or painful work of manipulating the computer as a complex three-dimensional object. Although PARC management may have dismissed hobby kit computers as "toys," for example, at least one PARC

Figure 1.1
The Altair 8800 microcomputer, manufactured by Micro Instrumentation Telemetry Systems (MITS) in 1975 and sold primarily as a kit to be assembled by the owner.

programmer, Larry Tessler, recognized that these devices were “something really important,” since while they might not be powerful machines, they fully represented the idea of a personal computing device with which owners could interact in myriad, gratifying ways.[18]

The short-lived kit era of personal digital media – roughly spanning from 1975 to 1977 – produced alternate parameters for the personal in digital culture. These parameters remain significant when considering the strong bodily component of today’s relationships between people and their digital devices – what user interface theorist Mikael Wiberg has called “tangible computing” in the turn toward materially based interaction design.[19] Kit-based computer culture required a close physical connection that included an awareness of nearly every material component of the machine, something that lay largely outside the interests of computer liberation ideologies but that made the kit device and its actions a highly tangible presence. The owner alone was responsible not only for the computer’s care and maintenance but also for its very coming into existence as a responsive, “thinking” device. These circumstances would disappear almost entirely by the close of the 1970s with the development of out-of-the-box, fully assembled and integrated desktop “appliance” computers. Yet in this short period these conditions allowed the development of certain assumptions around personal computing (especially concerning gender) that continue to affect understandings of, and relationships with, digital devices.

While the computer liberation ideas of Brand, Nelson, and others outlined what a computer could be and how it would interact with individuals in newfound ways, the success of kit-based computing demonstrates the role that standardization played in the foundation of intimacy between the user and the digital device when digital media first became a significant presence in the private sphere. A February 1975 *Computer Hobbyist* reader survey found, for example, that most readers relied on commercial kits rather than homebrew (i.e., made from scratch) machines: 39 per cent of *Computer Hobbyist*'s respondents owned a Mark-8, 19 per cent owned an Altair 8800, and 12 per cent owned a SCELBI 8008. Another 37 per cent planned to acquire an Altair 8800, which was the first affordable microprocessor-based kit and a now-legendary product that would become "the grit around which the pearl of the personal-computer industry grew," according to computer historians Martin Campbell-Kelly and William Asprey.[20] In contrast, 8 per cent of *Computer Hobbyist*'s respondents owned a homebrew computer with an 8008 chip, 6 per cent with a TTL CPU, and 2 per cent with an 8080 chip.[21] While some respondents reported owning multiple devices, the prevalence of kit-based computing in this early 1975 survey – before rapid growth in kit manufacturers and the diversification of products – may be meaningful for understanding the physical relationship between user and device in today's personal media contexts. User-device interaction today is forged in personal habit and preference, yet it occurs within rigid frames of standardized hardware, operating structures, and telecommunications networks. Despite overlaps with homebrew computing, kit computing was a more routinized and conventional option. If the word "homebrew" connoted experimentation and production outside formal structures, kit computing belonged to the pages of mass media hobby and amateur technology publications such as *Popular Electronics*, *Electronic News*, and *Radio Electronics*.[22] It catered to home electronics enthusiasts who were not countercultural or revolutionary but typically middle-class, suburban, white male professionals. These were what sociologist William Whyte had described in the 1950s as "organizational men." An organizational man, according to Whyte, benefitted from a lower- or middle-management or research post in America's growing post-war corporate culture, which often offered economic stability at the expense of individualism and creativity.[23]

Kit marketing – even in the 1970s – made little claim to ideological or social progress, but rather highlighted entertainment value or ease of use.[24] Hobbyist magazine writing about kit assembly echoed this. "What are you going to do with your computer?" asked a reviewer of kits and assembly practices in 1976, "because there isn't much real need for one, other than for fun and games."[25] Campbell-Kelly and Asprey describe the typical kit computer owner as wanting to "explore its inner complexity, experiment with computer games, and hook it up to other electronic gadgets."[26] One of the earliest examples of a commercial computer kit, the GENIAC (designed by Berkeley in 1955), reflected this perspective. It was marketed as a home "construction kit" of components and books for "designing and building your own experimental computers."[27] The GENIAC's manual illustrated ways to assemble thirty different "small electric brain machines" from materials provided to create the intimate experience of "equipment that you can take into your own hands, play with, and do exciting things with."[28] Minus "electric brains," the same language could be used to tout a smartphone or tablet today, as marketing frequently depicts the joys of user-device interaction.

In studying the social significance of hobbies in twentieth-century America, historian Steven Gelber has distinguished two principal strains of "craft" hobbies – kit-based and do-it-yourself – both of which are relevant to understanding the characteristics of microcomputer kit culture. Kits – for everything from leatherwork to model planes – simulated industrial shop labour by requiring limited skill and discouraging individual creativity. Kits were comprehensive, containing all necessary parts, detailed instructions, and sometimes even the tools. "There were no preliminary steps, no planning or organizing, no thinking about the process. In other words, the hobbyists did not have to engage the craft intellectually. Everything came to them," Gelber explains.[29] Do-it-yourself (DIY) crafts, on the other hand, required creativity and diverse manual skills. Often organized around home maintenance and improvement, from building furniture to creating decor or remodelling rooms, they entailed research, planning, and sourcing and gathering necessary materials, as well as improvising and adapting to the requirements of the particular project and environment.

The American DIY movement paralleled the rise of middle-class suburbs after World War II and played a critical role in establishing stable gender norms after the war had disrupted workspace and domestic roles for men and women. Suburbia's emphasis on home life and nuclear families put men in a "no-win situation" where domestic social routines of gardening and watching television appeared to diminish masculinity, yet men were expected to head the household and contribute to every aspect of its success. (Of course, suburbia put women in similar straits, by emphasizing homemaking and motherhood while distancing them from social and professional opportunities that had arisen during the war.) DIY home projects "permitted the suburban father to stay at home without feeling emasculated or being subsumed into an undifferentiated entity with his wife," Gelber states. "The hammer, saw, and quarter-inch electric drill became the emblems of the new masculinity."[30] While DIY projects could involve the whole family, DIY culture centred on the male head-of-household as a handyman and often involved demarcating masculine workspaces within the home, allowing men to claim garages, attics, and basements as their own studios and workshops.[31]

In considering the personal computing possibilities of the 1970s it would appear that microcomputer hobby kits adhered to Gelber's kit category, while homebrew computing embraced a DIY approach. Kits brought the required materials and step-by-step instructions to the doorstep. On the face of it, the owner would need only to pay attention and put in the time to have their computer. Homebrew computing, on the contrary, would be more improvisational and imaginative as the owner sought out information and materials from various sources to piece together their own creation. This is not how it transpired, however. History is rarely so neat. Even a cursory consideration of microcomputer kit culture demonstrates that kit building paradoxically bore significant traits of *both* of Gelber's categories. Transforming a box of kit components into a fully functioning computer was a laborious process of wiring, soldering, testing, adjusting, replacing, and even improvising and jerry-rigging. Although some computer kits included all components, many lacked one or more key parts. The basic Altair 8800 kit, for example, lacked a power supply. Most kits included only a token amount of memory: enough to turn them on but not enough to accomplish much else.[32] Other kits left it to the owner to source parts, as with the Mark-8 kit, which amounted to a circuit board and a manual. Some-

Figure 1.2
A depiction of the removal of excess soldering, published as part of an article on microcomputer kit building in *Byte* in March 1977.

times requiring weeks of assembly work – in part because components might be shipped separately or prove defective – these projects could take over a basement corner, den, or spare bedroom. Almost without exception, assemblers would need to learn soldering, sometimes finding their initial work so poor in quality that they would start from scratch halfway into assembly (see figure 1.2).

A *Creative Computing* article on assembling the Altair 8800 describes a scenario where the builder must regularly go off-script and endure frustration: "There are some problems in building the 8800, sometimes due to information lacking in the manual, sometimes due to what seems to be poor mechanical design, and sometimes because of a lack of thoroughness by the manufacturer in checking out the parts lists." In particular, soldering the sixty-six three-foot wires was challenging: "No matter how careful the builder is, several are bound to pop off," the article warned.[33]

One of the first periodicals dedicated to home computing, the irreverently titled *Dr. Dobb's Journal of Computer Calisthenics and Orthodontia*, lamented that most kits were "strictly glitchy."[34] A *Dr. Dobb's* article on the challenges of assembling kits and peripherals explained that "the inadequate documentation (and just plain bad writing) that comes with almost all personal computing products and the poor workmanship and parts of a few, will make you prematurely wise."[35] From soldering bus lines to adding sockets for additional RAM, cleaning boards with solvent, and checking work with a magnifying glass to find solder splashes, successfully building a microcomputer entailed close, diligent work, and a little luck.

The many descriptions of idiosyncratic and complicated assembly processes suggest, however, that part of the satisfaction of possessing these computers at home would derive from the ingenuity that emerged from the interactive processes of assembling and troubleshooting. As a *Byte* article on hobby kits explained, "the field of personal computing as it is now known essentially centers around the building, testing, and troubleshooting of computer kits. Many individuals with a 'computer hobbyist' approach to the field are electronic types who enjoy kit building and consider their work with the equipment to be the main focus of their interests."[36] In fact, since kits often included scant memory and no peripherals (e.g., keyboards, screens, or printers), the finished device would do little more than calculate simple mathematical equations or produce sequences of blinking lights (like you might find on a string of LED holiday lights today).

This careful, extensive attention required by kit-based microcomputers brought the hobby close to what science and technology scholar Rachel Maines calls "hedonized technology," since the uses of the computer may have been less interesting or engaging than the processes of assembly and maintenance. According to Maines, "Any technology that privileges the pleasures of production over the value and/or significance of the product can be a hedonizing technology."[37] In building microcomputers from kits, owners and users often gained as much satisfaction from what they had made as from what they could do with it. When Maines describes hedonizing as "the appreciation of good tools that are enjoyable to handle, the joys of process, and the irrelevance of the product that characterize technologies of pleasure," we can see how the microcomputer kit occupied a liminal space. Every kit owner's aim was certainly to put together a working computer system; otherwise, one would have nothing more than a heap of soldered wires, boards, and panels. However, the pleasure – at least as presented in home computing periodicals of the time – was as much in finding novel and sometimes even elegant workarounds and shortcuts towards producing a functioning machine. Of course, with the arrival of the desktop PC this inside-out aspect of computer interactivity and intimacy would largely disappear as handling and interaction would stop at the superficial process of engaging and manipulating pre-assembled interfaces of manufactured hardware and coded software.

A significant aspect of kit computers before the integration of peripherals, such as screens and keyboards, was the physical intensity of the manipulation of the interface as well. While peripherals created distance between the computer and the interface (distance that will be explored in chapter 2 through the increasingly important procedural and symbolic role of pointing), microcomputers such as the Altair 8800 required direct manipulation through front panel switches (visible in figure 1.1). Computer historian Paul Ceruzzi elaborates, "One had to flick the toggle switches for each program step, then deposit that number into a memory location, then repeat that for the next step, and so on ... until the whole program (less than 356 bytes long!) was in memory. Bruised fingers from flipping the small toggle switches were the least of the frustrations."[38] In other words, literally every bit of a program might be manipulated by hand as each 1 and 0 was determined by a finger movement. Hand-loading Bill Gates and Paul Allen's BASIC for the Altair 8800 (after installing added memory) would be "a matter of flipping the switches over 30,000 times without an error"![39] Though it is doubtful anyone ever attempted that feat (tape drive peripherals would obviate the need), doing even the most rudimentary programming on an Altair or similar machine as it was originally designed was an arduous process that further underscored the close relationship between the body of the device and the body of the user.[40] In fact, this level of tactile device interactivity, inputting directly on the front panel of the device with one's fingers (rather than a stylus or a keyboard), would not be matched until the proliferation of consumer touch screen computing in the twenty-first century.

These potential frustrations, however, ultimately opened onto the possibility of deep personal satisfaction from making something by oneself. An article in *Byte* entitled "Assembling Programs by Hand" explained that "you build your one of a kind computer from an assemblage of parts and components liberally mixed with wire wrap wire."[41] A contributor to *Kilobaud* (another of the many hobbyist magazines that rarely make it into histories of the period) stated, "One of the most interesting and rewarding areas of the personal computer hobby is that of designing and building custom interfaces." The writer added that "aside from the sheer pleasure and satisfaction that comes with seeing your new design work, there is the possibility of interfacing something that has never been interfaced."[42] This sense of pioneering achievement could be repeated in the subsequent challenges of programming the device.

Through these painstaking efforts – from matching parts to making tiny connections to rooting out errors in assembly to decrypting typewritten instructions bearing lists of part numbers – the process of assembling and operating a kit-based microcomputer became an exceedingly *individualized* and *intimate* process. Participants acquired an intensive, hands-on knowledge of every aspect of the components and systems of the object they built. When the work was done and the device blinked its lights and ran simple games, the owner was not just the assembler but in many ways the creator of the machine, with all its shortcomings (e.g., sloppy soldering or uneven mounting) as well as its clever improvisations and modifications.

The user-device relationship forged by the microcomputer kit was therefore twofold: intimate contact at the level of material assembly, maintenance, and improvement and embellishment, on the one hand, and a sense of "interpersonal" interactivity with the "thinking" device, on the other. A *Kilobaud* article on the singular virtues of hobby computers explained, "The keyword is *personal.* The value of our hobbies is internal to and inseparable from ourselves. Our hobbies are a part of us, expressing our being." It exhorted microcomputer hobbyists, "When asked what your recently assembled microcomputer does, don't be so quick to apologize."[43] In a study of the nature of diverse digital interactions and interfaces, Lars-Erik Janlert and Erik Stolterman warn that "perfectly personalized, individually tailored interfaces on artifacts have some drawbacks… for instance, it might mean that you can't borrow your neighbor's equipment."[44] When considering standardization and the interchangeability of devices, such personalization becomes a liability. But in the sphere of kit computing, imperfections of microcomputers made them "perfectly" personal precisely because often only the owner knew how to make their device run properly, knew exactly what it could do, and could tell if it had achieved it. Nooney states that "privileged politics of possession was a centerpiece of electronics hobbyist vernacular."[45] Indeed, most important in the circumstances here described was that the device was "one's own," a part of the owner because they assembled it. In addition, it could "recognize" and respond to its owner like an animated being in subsequent interactions through programs and coding. Accordingly, it could emerge as more than an object or possession, akin to a being or presence that only the owner fully understood. In fact, as detailed below, personal computing magazines of the period reflected this sentiment repeatedly in articles encompassing kit computer assembly and maintenance, casting the kit computer as an animated being that threatened to destabilize middle-class households and heteronormative relationships.

Dates, Machine Talk, and Widows

Based on the names of computer hobbyist magazine writers and subscribers in the US in the mid-1970s, the vast majority were men. Early issues of *The Computer Hobbyist*, for example, regularly published the names and addresses of new subscribers. In a census conducted for this book, no new subscriber names were identifiably female-gendered, while 83 per cent had typically male-gendered first names and 17 per cent had initials or names that might be applied to either gender (e.g., Terry, Dana, Lee).[46] Sexism was frequent and unabashed in this overwhelmingly masculine environment. It emanated from corporate computer culture and academic computer science programs, but it also had been prevalent in amateur electronics culture throughout the post-war period. Media theorist Christina Dunbar-Hester terms this "technical masculinity" and explains, "Electronics tinkering was a remarkably stable elite masculine hobby during the twentieth century, offering suburban men and boys both a masculine space within the domesticity of the home and training for white-collar technical professions. But by the last decades of the twentieth century, the object of tinkering had begun to shift away from radio towards computers."[47]

The consumer microcomputer kit commodified a virulent masculinity at play in computing culture, allowing men outside the industry to feel a personal connection to – and power over – the computer as a man's toy. Historian Nathan Ensmenger writes about the development of masculine computing culture in university computer labs in the 1960s and 1970s and its contribution to the figure of the "computer bum" elaborated by Brand.

Ensmenger asserts that this masculine culture continued when computing shifted to microcomputers:

> Place matters, even in the history of a technological genre that claims to make place irrelevant. In this case, it was the university computer labs, the sheltered, unsupervised, and subsidized environments in which the burgeoning computer hacker culture became inextricably linked with the cultural practices of adolescent masculinity. Later, as the locus of hacker activity shifted from the university mainframe to the household personal computer, these practices were recreated in other masculine spaces, such as bedrooms, basements, and dormitories.[48]

Ensmenger links computing in home spaces to the development and rebellious appeal of youth (often teen) hacker culture. Dunbar-Hester refers to this as "geek" culture marked by non-normative, yet nevertheless sexist, masculinity. Primary source evidence from the period suggests, however, that this masculine gendering of computer spaces outside the lab and office was – at least at the time of microcomputer kits – as much an accomplishment of middle-aged, straitlaced working men. Ensmenger, like Dunbar-Hester, ties the "male-dominated computer subculture" of hobbyists into a longer trajectory of ham radio and hobby electronics through the twentieth century. Indeed, amateur radio publications of the 1970s incorporated computing into their pages with the similar sexist tone found in computing magazines. "To understand computers is to love them" opened one article in an amateur radio magazine in 1975: "they are billed as the World's Greatest Toy, and this is not much an exaggeration, young long-haired blonds notwithstanding."[49]

It is ironic, however, to call computer assembly and maintenance a masculine pursuit. The intense labour to detect and correct material problems in kit-based systems resembled the reality of early large-scale computer development, when technicians and programmers had to get their hands dirty resolving circuit snags and replacing defective parts on a regular basis. This work of programming and physically maintaining early digital computers during and immediately after World War II was primarily done by women programmers, technicians, and operators until they were systematically forced out of these roles by research institutions and the computer industry.[50] Indeed, as industrial and commercial computing became the domain of men (the "computer priesthood," as Ted Nelson would call it),[51] personal computing initially followed suit. Computers themselves were now men's work, even though it was often women tasked with assembling them in plants in the US and elsewhere.[52] The Altair microcomputer was no exception. While men were assembling Altair kits at home to create their own personal computers, the manufacturer's main plant in New Mexico employed sixty people, 95 per cent women (according to a 1977 report in the company's newsletter), who machine-pressed components on circuit boards. For orders of fully assembled Altairs, all components were initially hand-soldered by these workers. Even after components could be soldered by machine, customized units – such as those to be adapted to run on foreign currents – still required partial hand assembly at the plant.[53]

Considering these circumstances, it is not surprising that sexism permeated early computer hobbyist magazines. It appeared not only in feature articles on microcomputers, but also in other sections of these publications. *Creative Computing* emulated *Playboy* in its first year, for example, by including a "centrefold poster" of ASCII art in each issue. Although subjects included *Star Trek*'s Mr Spock and the *Enterprise*, its inaugural centrefold featured the face of a tabby cat, producing a readily recognizable visual pun on female genitalia.[54] In another issue, a story about a computer monster ostensibly written by the eight-year-old daughter of a technology executive, entitled "Daddy and His Computer," was accompanied by a short bio of the girl that included her age, weight, height, and marital status ("single").[55] Such visual and textual jokes – though cringe-inducing today – signalled a context comfortably dominated by heteronormative, cis male perspectives.

Creative Computing offered games, art, cartoons, fiction, and other material related to computers and technology, yet a sexualized male outlook also informed coverage of building and interacting with microcomputers, which was the principal content of magazines such as *Kilobaud* and *Byte*. Perhaps unsurprisingly, in this context the computer became a fetishized object of male sexual fantasy, as when *Kilobaud* editors ran an article on diagnostic routines under the title "Chasing Those Naughty Bits."[56] As an adaptive machine that could react to the user and potentially engage in the exchange of all sorts of information, the microcomputer was easily anthropomorphized. Descriptions of home microcomputer building in hobbyist magazines sometimes described the process of creation in terms worthy of Pygmalion, the mythological artist of ancient Greece who sculpted a representation of a woman that then came to life. Like that myth, hobbyist magazine writers sometimes cast their object in human terms, as though they had built a being rather than a machine. "If you just bought or built a computer and if you're new to computing, maybe you're wondering why this inscrutable device is giving you the LED stare-down," begins a *Computer Notes* article entitled "My Computer Just Stares at Me …" It continues, "Why doesn't it DO something? Well, it's probably waiting for you to break the ice."[57] Equipment that stopped functioning properly, on the other hand, might require "an autopsy."[58] And, while often produced for comic effect, narratives suggesting strong emotional ties between hobbyists and their responsive calculating objects were common.

The anthropomorphized microcomputer was frequently gendered as female and subsequently sexualized. *Byte* would publish an article about a man gradually losing control of his home computer to an intrusive drinking buddy, for example, under the title "Having a 'Private Affair' with Your Computer."[59] Some articles went as far as describing how the relationship with the machine could blight a hobbyist's interpersonal and affective relationships with those closest to them (especially women). It could disrupt a household, as was suggested by hobbyist magazine articles from both gender perspectives, which usually depicted the computer as a man's absorbing plaything to the potential regret of the woman in his life.[60]

Turkle has written that microcomputer hobbyists "preferred to work close to the computer hardware; they enjoyed the sense of nothing standing between themselves and the 'body' of the machine."[61] A 1975, first-person account in *Byte* about acquiring and assembling an Altair 8800 sets the scene of this close man-machine relationship.[62] Describing the moment the package of components arrived and "I had the Altair in my hot little hands," the writer recounts his wife's dismay at how little he got for $500. "Undaunted, I shooed her out and locked myself in the back room all weekend soldering PC boards. It took three weekends to complete the assembly."[63] The remainder of the article explores the potential pitfalls of the assembly process that unfolded during these weekends. Overall, the piece serves as a guide for anyone attempting to assemble an Altair, yet it also provides a glimpse into microcomputer culture as a masculine domain, where women are pushed aside so men can become closely acquainted – and develop relationships – with the machines they build in their private, gendered domestic spaces.

Even after assembly, this close relationship would continue. "Jack and the Machine Talk (or, The Making of an Assembler)," is a *Byte* article ostensibly about creating a satisfactory programming language to communicate with the Altair, yet it reads like a piece of pin-up magazine fiction. The article is presented as a series of conversations between the owner and a computer whose lights are "flickering seductively." When the computer explains that it awaits his commands, it states, "My Teletype interface is itching for the touch of your fingers on my keyboard!" It protests that "operations are part of my hardware and I like my internal arrangements as they are!" Jack counters, "I'm not about to touch your little body so don't worry," though elsewhere he reminds the machine that "I soldered every one of your connections."[64]

Other contributions were more direct in their presentation of the microcomputer as an objectified woman under a male user's power. A *Byte* report on the configuration and capabilities of MOS Technology's KIM-1 microcomputer ran under the title, "A Date with KIM." The author explains that "the name KIM ... [is] a pleasant change from the manufacturer's name followed by a number," and concludes his piece with the advice, "Make a date with KIM – you'll enjoy it!"[65] Another article on adjusting processing speeds for KIM bore the title "True Confessions: How I Relate to KIM."[66] Capitalizing on the feminine connotations of "Kim" as a nickname for "Kimberly," a popular first name among young women at the time, writers played with ways of describing the user-device relationship in material terms commonly associated with dating and seduction.[67] An article entitled "Giving KIM Some Fancy Jewels" describes ways of "dressing her up a bit" by covering her "naked board." It warns that "delicacy and discretion with KIM are requirements" when altering the machine.[68] "A New Dress for KIM" similarly describes ways of making new bodies for the microcomputer. This piece is worth citing at length to convey the extent that masculine fantasizing could suffuse DIY practices and social contexts around microcomputing. The writer explains:

> At first I was reluctant to take KIM out in public because she was so small and homely compared to other systems of her age. [...] Then, one evening, while talking to a friend whose IMSAI was drawing considerable attention, as usual, it occurred to me that it wasn't his central processing unit's IQ that set it apart from my humble KIM. No, it was the way that it was dressed that did so much toward creating the image of great sophistication and power. I resolved that very evening to give my KIM the same advantages that her peers had; after all, who wants to be accused of neglecting loved ones? If she was to be ooo'd and aaah'd over, then she'd have to be dressed up before I took her out again. Although, I must say honestly that I doubted that her 8.5 by 11 by 5/16ths dimensions would ever win her a spot on the centerfold of *Byte*.[69]

This description of KIM casts the device as a homely, needy girlfriend, "humble" and "neglected." The owner expresses feeling a duty to take care of her, to attend to these needs. Of course, in its misogynist reasoning, taking care of the device means taking care of the owner's ego in assuring that other computer enthusiasts will "ooh and aah" over his trophy object.

Running alongside this stream of male fixation and sexualized fantasizing around home-built or modified computers were occasional articles meant to offer a woman's perspective on the new relationships blossoming between men and their computing devices. "My Friend Is a Computer Junkie" ran as a reflective, back-page essay in *Kilobaud*. The male editor's lead asks female readers: "Gather around, girls, and see if there aren't portions of Sheila's tale that you can relate to. I say 'portions' because it's doubtful that your man could be anywhere near as hooked (or hopeless) as the one in this article."[70] Sheila describes a live-in male friend who had been "lots of fun to be with. We spent hours talking late into the night, or sunny days sailing off the California coast, or weekends partying with friends. Our friendship was warm and close." Then he revealed a secret: "He told me wistfully that what he really wanted was a computer of his very own." She continues, "He ran across a magazine that advertised 'a computer kit' and sent off a check for the beginning of his dream's realization and for what would become my nightmare." Like the *Byte* writer who "shoos away" his wife to be alone with his Altair in a locked room, from the moment the kit arrives, this idyllic relationship devolves as the male friend rarely emerges from "the cave" where he keeps his computer. When Sheila ducks her head in she catches "a rambling stream of conversation already in progress – with the computer."[71]

In another issue of *Kilobaud* – indeed, the magazine's first issue – a writer describes her status as a "computer widow" since her husband started building his microcomputer.[72] "I sometimes wish that I were as pampered and well cared for as his equipment," she quips. "I guess it should be understandable that all this equipment would require his seemingly constant attention, but there are more things being neglected around our house than just me." The author mentions ignored children and half-finished home improvement projects, concluding that solace may only come from organizing a "Computer Widow's Club for all of us neglected wives."[73]

These contemporary accounts of differing gender perspectives and stereotypes as they intersect through the relationship between microcomputer hobbyists and their devices reinforce the idea, presented earlier, that the "personal" in personal computing within kit culture existed at two levels: building the computer as a personal creation and interacting with the device as a personal relationship. Not only could it be fetishized by its owners, but it could also diminish – and perhaps even replace – domestic interpersonal relationships between a user and their partner or family. This early example of the gendering of digital devices and the dynamics of relationships with these devices is notable for how it projects existing social structures and underlying biases into user-device interactions. And it remains germane to today's relationships with personal media. A 2019 UNESCO report on gender divisions in digital industries and technologies, for example, found that smart speaker personae such as Alexa and Siri perpetuate damaging stereotypes of women as docile and subservient. Developed principally by teams of male engineers, most voice assistants have "assumed uniformly subservient feminine personas, and ... many of the so-called 'Easter eggs' in these products – humorous or unexpected replies to specific questions – often reinforce the assistant's female projection or reference movies, music and television shows popular with men."[74] Media theorist Safiya Umoja Noble has noted that users often adopt abrupt attitudes in interacting with these assistants, which can suggest that "the role of women, girls, and people who are gendered female [is] to respond on demand."[75] While there is no direct connection between the male sexism of microcomputer culture and these voice assistants, the actions and words of hobbyists in explaining the relationship between user and device in the mid-1970s in many ways lay the foundation for the casual sexism and gender bias that they encapsulate. And as these gendered interfaces become increasingly common, the potential social harm of their biases can become more extensive.[76]

From Handiwork to Hand Signals

How else might the relatively brief, kit-computing episode of digital media history inform contemporary digital media use and, more specifically, the idea of networked digital media as personal? Like many of our interactions with media today, these accounts of kit-based microcomputers suggest that they often produced a physically and psychologically involved relationship with the digital object that could unduly impact a user's relationships with others. The Altair and similar microcomputers did not facilitate interpersonal communication with other people (at least not directly, since they did nonetheless bring into being a host of specialist magazines, amateur clubs, and computer fairs). Instead, they were premised on communicating with the device itself by developing languages and programs that one would painstakingly enter into the machine's limited memory in hope of an intelligible response. As a user undertook this effort, they could gain satisfaction in those moments when they felt the computer understood them and was able to formulate a response meaningful only to the user within the parameters of these interactions.

When we consider our relationships with devices today, these aspects of intimacy, and the potential impact on our relationships with those around us, are still present. As our personal digital devices extract our data as the basis for shaping personalized responses, they in some way mimic – although on a *much* more sophisticated level – the simple back and forth that began with microcomputer kits. Just as we may sometimes engage with our portable smart devices for the sheer pleasure of physical, multisensory interaction with a responsive object, the microcomputer offered the possibility of interacting with a personal, animated device that seemed to recognize the user's presence and efforts. In this regard microcomputers and our contemporary smart devices share some of the traits of hedonizing technology described by Maines in placing as much emphasis on the process of making something happen as on what actually happens. The kit computer became in many respects that first "smart" object that people lived and played with in their homes and private spaces, and these objects seemed to need their users just as their users seemed to need them. On those occasions when others might attempt to intervene or use these objects themselves, owners could get jealous and protective.

Within a couple of years, however, personal computers developed from these basic kits into fully assembled, comprehensive appliances for word processing, budgeting, composing, and visual design, in part because a range of peripherals and subsystems – including keyboards, screens, drives, and printers – were already being manufactured.[77] "It was just a matter of putting the pieces together," Campbell-Kelly and Asprey state, so that "by the fall of 1977 … the personal computer had been defined physically as an artifact."[78] The shift to computers "that you simply plug in, and they work," as one guide explained at the time, brought relief to some hobbyists. An advertisement for the Commodore Personal Electronic Transactor (PET), for example, hinted that users could now devote their computer interactions to mental tasks and abstract problems, without worrying about building or configuring hardware (see figure 1.3).[79]

But these changes incited resistance from other hobbyists. Shortly after the release of the Commodore PET, the Tandy TRS-80, and the Apple II – all appearing in 1977 – *Kilobaud* published an article entitled "It's Your Hobby! The Critics Be Hanged" that extolled the unique pleasures of home computer building, despite the lack of useful applications for most hobby kits of the time.[80] By 1982 – when *Time* named the personal computer its "machine of the year" – *Interface Age* asked its readers, "Whatever Happened to Computer Hobbyists?"[81] It concluded that, while computer hobbyists still existed, kits were now rare and computer hobbyists had largely been replaced by "consumers" of computers. "The two couldn't be more dissimilar," the magazine explained. "The consumer's interest is in what the machine can do for him rather than in the machine itself, how it operates and how to program it."[82]

An article entitled "The Ultimate Personal Computer," published in *Kilobaud* in fall 1977, laid out the conditions of this shift from hobbyist to consumer in examining the interactive potential and requirements for personal computing on a broader scale.[83] Its author, organizational psychologist Lawrence Zeitlin, argued that most people wanted a personal computer to

Figure 1.3

An advertisement for the Commodore Personal Electronic Transactor (PET) emphasizing computational power over hardware and interactivity, published in *Scientific American* in September 1979.

help them with their memory (e.g., schedules, lists, budgets, and phone numbers) more than anything else. In attaining this, he explained, they also hoped to be able to "communicate to the computer as they would to another person in a natural spoken language and receive a similar auditory response."[84] Zeitlin predicted the development of small digital implants for this task – a prediction that has been made many times since in other contexts (witness the recent implant experiments of Synchron, Neuralink, and other brain-computer interface companies). Implants aside, however, Zeitlin delineated a sharp divide between ideas that foreshadowed the basic aspects of the personal computers that would soon enter the market and the existing properties of the microcomputers written about elsewhere in that issue of *Kilobaud* as devices to be built, altered, augmented, and customized (and for which the personal had less to do with memory or "natural" communication than it did the intensely physical, material building, maintaining and manipulating of the object and system).[85]

Zeitlin correctly identified the two elements that became part not only of personal computing in the years that immediately followed but also of today's personal media: (extended) memory and simulated social interaction. This interaction with portable digital devices is typically mediated through multiple material properties and affordances: object size, texture, and hardness, sound levels and sequences, light intensity and fluctuation, and so on. However, at its base, the interpersonal user-device relationship continues to rely heavily on one of the most basic vehicles – indeed, perhaps *the* most basic vehicle – of interpersonal communication: the extended, pointing finger. The ideological roots and cultural implications of this choice – as well as how it plays out as a physical action in contemporary user-device contexts – are to be explored in the next chapter. It is not the "spoken" language stipulated by Zeitlin, to be sure, but a gesture that seems such a natural part of communication that it is hard to imagine human interaction without it.[86]

Pointing and clicking would lower barriers to interaction and understanding, allowing for a wide range of computer owners and users, while also suggesting an intimacy with the machine as the responsive recipient of all this pointing. The intimacy of the minute, material assembly of digital devices would now be left entirely to far-off assembly houses usually staffed by women of colour who would remain entirely out of the sight and mind of buyer and user. The new intimacy that emerged from the interplay of pointing and response suggested the computer was not a device one made or perfected, but rather a pre-existing subject with which one could converse.

As many digital media today are reducing or abandoning pointing-based interfaces for other forms of material interactivity, however, we can return to the intensely physical nature of microcomputer kit culture as an early and instructive example of the deep materiality of digital interaction. In this early period, effective maintenance of, and interaction with, the digital device required a variety of physical interventions and actions. When Mikael Wiberg states that "the history of computing illustrates the separation made between the physical and the digital world," it is imperative to remember, recover, and reinforce these alternative lineages of material interaction as indicative of long-standing and on-going material relationships between people and their devices.[87] Doing so should also allow us to access the cultural assumptions that have been bound into that material interactivity – around beliefs of class, gender, and race, for example – and consider their relationship to contemporary bias in the design, implementation, and adaptation of today's materially interactive digital systems. Just as kit culture reinforced some assumptions of what a computer could be while overturning others, it also maintained certain ideas about the individual's relationship to media devices while nevertheless broaching new possibilities, particularly in framing the user-device dynamic as one interpersonal relationship among others.

CHAPTER 2

You Are Here

Our relationship to our most personal media devices – those we keep with us throughout our day – is a constant two-way exchange of location detection and recognition. The device is always localizing us in space as it keeps contact with the network – Wi-Fi, cellphone beacons, even satellites. At the same time, we are always keeping tabs on it, whether it is by our side, in our pocket, or strapped to our wrist. When we lose track of where it is, we may resort to "find my phone" features to reunite with it. It is not simply about ensuring we do not lose an object that is costly to replace. Between the personal settings, the data storage, and our dependence on it to engage with the world, misplacing the device even for a short time can leave *us* feeling lost. This conscious, constant state of situatedness between device and user is a significant component of what makes our media feel personal. The device's location becomes *our* location, its presence in the network becomes *our* presence. We comprehend where we are by identifying where it is – for instance, as a moving point on a navigational app's interactive map. And our relationship with the device is a constant state of recognizing and reinforcing the location-based perspective of the other as it emerges within the frame of the screen. We point to it (and the information on its screen) and it points back at us.

Dependence on pointing as a principal means of exchange and recognition emerged in personal computing systems in the last decades of the twentieth century, famously embodied in the desktop mouse. However, such pointing-based systems developed alongside competing efforts to design handwriting-based interfaces as another, primary means of communicating with personal computing devices. The turn-of-the-century competition between pointing and writing in user-device interactions strongly shaped what personal media would become – and how it would be understood – in the years that followed. Pointing-based systems like the mouse and cursor receive regular attention in histories of digital media and culture as *the* breakthrough to widespread, popular computing. Handwriting-based systems, however, have largely been forgotten, leaving a rich area for further historical inquiry. Both systems are taken up in the pages that follow, not only as competing means of media interactivity but also as symbolic systems that intersect with the self and the circulation of power in significant, but differing, ways.

As seen in chapter 1, intimacy emerged in the early years of personal digital computing media in astonishing fashion. During the kit era, users of microcomputers had complete access to – and responsibility over – the assembly and interoperability of all components and accessories. Once electronics companies produced fully assembled machines at accessible prices, however, this parts-based interaction between user and hardware disappeared for most home computer users. Initially, interactivity with out-of-the-box computers returned largely to the parameters of terminal-based, mainframe computer interactivity: keyboard-based text exchanges between computer and user through a host of learned commands. Hewlett-Packard's HP-85 personal computer, for example, was an all-in-one machine with a screen display, printer, tape reader, and keyboard built into a single casing "about the size of an electric typewriter … [and] as easy to carry as your attaché case," as company advertisements claimed (see figure 2.1).[1]

A 1980 *Hewlett-Packard Journal* editorial introducing the HP-85 as the company's first personal computer remarked, "What makes a computer 'personal'? Mainly the cost has to be low enough," but "compactness is also important."[2] Like most personal computers at that time (the Commodore PET, the Tandy TRS-80, and the Compucolor II among them), it could be carried and moved easily by an individual, but further bodily interaction in communicating with the device was limited to typed instructions and

Figure 2.1
The Hewlett Packard HP-85 personal computer, released in 1980 and marketed as a portable device.

keypad commands. With Apple's introduction of mouse-based graphical user interfaces – first with Lisa in 1983, then with Macintosh in 1984 – pointing at the screen, either directly or indirectly, established itself as a principal means of interacting with personal computers, obviating the need for learning written prompts.

Although the mouse had been integral to the Xerox Alto desktop computer since 1973, Apple's marketing success of the much cheaper Macintosh would make this peripheral an expected feature of subsequent personal computers. Most desktop computers today still include them. Pointing and clicking (and eventually pointing and tapping) became the foundation of device interactivity, although other modes of communication, such as speech recognition, have remained in use. If for no other reason, the utter simplicity and seeming inevitably of pointing as the basic user-device interaction merits scrutiny here, especially given its sustained pre-eminence in personal media interactivity. As such, this chapter tackles several questions: How does the act of pointing establish a physical relationship between the user and the device? What affective weight may it bear in its psychological dimensions? How does it differ from similar ways of interfacing, particularly manual, writing-based systems where users trace words with their finger or stylus? Finally, how might these differences reinforce the affective significance of user-device relationships based mainly on pointing? Exploring both the conditions and connotations of these related – but competing – ways of interacting produces a nuanced picture of the stakes of the gesture of pointing. Applying ideas from psychology, linguistics, physiology, and haptics demonstrates that pointing's simplicity is deceptive. Although the physical act may be easy and obvious, its bearing on our sense of self, our belonging, and our agency and expression can be complicated.

The Object(s) of Pointing

The history of modern screen media is replete with devices and operations that incorporate pointing as an essential component. Perhaps the most enduring example is not the mouse – made popular only in the 1980s – but the television remote control. Around for nearly the whole history of consumer television, remote controls have harnessed ultrasound and infrared light to allow hand-held, distance control of television sets since the early 1950s.[3] "Remotes" transformed what is often a shared household device – a television screen in a common living area – into a personalized object that recognizes and responds to the gestures and commands of a single user. For Space Command remote TV tuning in 1957, Zenith employed the tagline "Nothing between you and the set but space!" to underline the new, more intimate relationship between the individual and television produced through this affordance.[4] Early remotes were connected to a television set by a cable and therefore did not need to be pointed at the television, since the signal travelled solely through the cord. They also did not control separate areas of the screen, so did not require any spatial referencing between device and screen coordinates or corresponding screen objects. As such, the remote could sit on an armrest or behind a vase or ashtray while the viewer operated it. Later remotes, functioning through sound or light waves passing between the device and the television set, required direct pointing free of intervening barriers. Although the remote control would become a pointing device, there was no corresponding visual affirmation of that act on the screen, other than the specific change attempted (the set turning on, the channel changing, etc.). Rather than the screen or any corresponding screen objects, the remote control would be pointed toward – and interacting with – a signal receiver on the set. This receiver would often be in a spot near the screen – perhaps by the control panel or buttons. In the case of cable television from the 1970s onwards, the remote would need to be pointed at the cable box and not at the set at all. Another salient feature when comparing the remote to a pointing-based computing control such as a mouse would be how the hand generally clutches the device like it would the handle of a tool. The fingers do not necessarily point toward the screen or device, but rather the thumb depresses a button on the remote control's face.

Like television, pointing as a part of computing interfaces has existed from the early development of electronic computers in the aftermath of World War II. Although keyboard-based commands predominated through the 1970s as the standard mode of real-time user interaction, screen-based methods developed in a few highly specialized computing sectors. The Semi-Automatic Ground Environment (SAGE) networked computer system developed by the US military and MIT to intercept intercontinental air attacks, for example, relied on a "light gun" that operators pointed at cathode ray tube (CRT) radar screens to input data quickly (see figure 2.2). The system was developed as a simple and effective means of locating and tracking aircraft to prevent a possible Soviet airstrike on Canada or the US.

In another field of computing, the early graphic design system Sketchpad, created by Ivan Sutherland as an MIT graduate student in the 1960s, used a "light pen" and onscreen crosshairs to point at depicted elements and send commands to the computer. Sutherland described the light pen as a "demonstrative input for pointing to existing picture parts to make changes."[5] By the turn of this century, Sketchpad would be hailed as "the graphical ancestor of today's human-computer interaction and computer graphics, and much of new media in general."[6] However, the light pen had only limited applications over that period, in part because of the muscle discomfort produced by holding a pen in mid-air for extended periods of screen interaction.

From the 1960s these input devices, as well as desktop stylus pads and track ball devices such as the mouse, contended as practical means for computer users to interact with their machines.[7] The greatest shift would

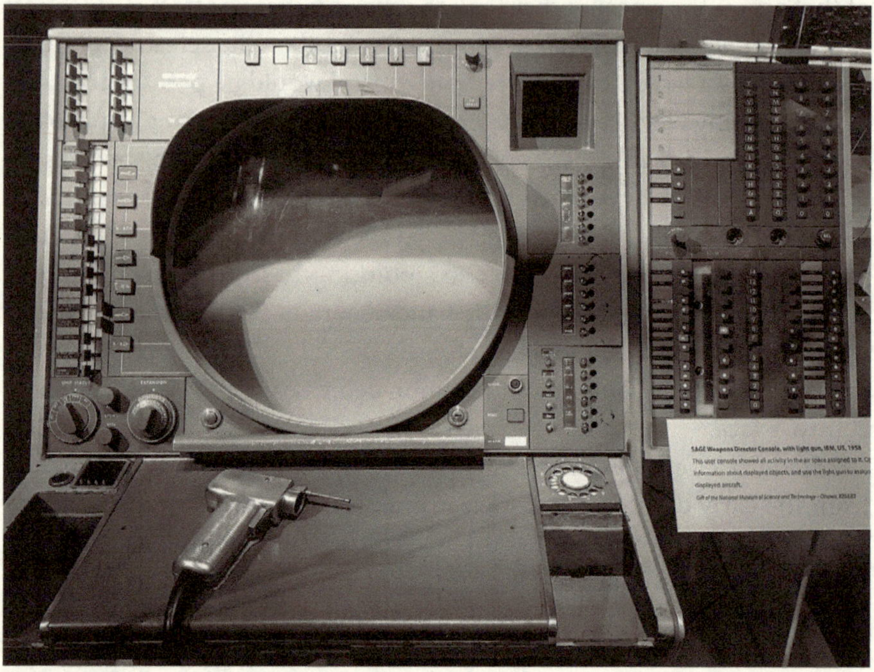

Figure 2.2
A Semi-Automatic Ground Environment (SAGE) computer console with its light gun resting in front of the screen, as displayed in the Computer History Museum, Mountain View, California.

involve the mouse and onscreen pointer, invented in 1963–64 by Douglas Engelbart at the Stanford Research Institute (SRI). This interface accessory was further developed at Xerox's Palo Alto Research Center, primarily with the graphical user interfaces of the Alto computer in 1973 and the Star 8010 Information System in 1981, and it would become key for Apple Computer's Lisa and Macintosh computers in 1983–84. The mouse is so familiar and common even in today's touch screen-dominated world that it is difficult to step back and scrutinize it as a cultural artifact of ideological significance. Yet making this effort allows us to appreciate how the mouse taps into basic conditions of human language and psychology to deeply entwine computer and user beyond the level of input and commands. It may help explain why the mouse may have been the single greatest step in the development of affective relationships between users and their computing devices.

Figure 2.3
A corded computer mouse with two input buttons and a scroll wheel.

To start, a mouse is a small (usually about 12 cm × 6 cm × 4 cm) oval or rectangular hand-held tabletop device (see figure 2.3). Originally, it was mounted on wheels or a ball; today, it often tracks movement through LED or laser emitters and sensors. Usually made of plastic, most versions through the early 2000s included a cord extending from the front end to connect to the computer (this appendage contributed to its resemblance to a rodent). Contemporary versions of the mouse tend to be cordless, relying on Bluetooth or USB receivers to communicate. The horizontal motion of the mouse – over a flat surface beside the computer and detected by the rolling ball, LED, or laser – will move its corresponding onscreen pointer.[8]

Engelbart developed the mouse as a breakthrough component of what he had already described in 1962 as a system of "humans interacting with computers, in… an intimate personal sense."[9] Yet the mouse, and other pointing devices at that time, often allowed only two actions: drawing images on the screen or selecting pre-assigned quadrants on the screen to initiate specific commands. In drawing mode, the screen functioned much like a sheet of paper. With a light pen, for example, the pen's signal might cause the brightness of the screen to reduce wherever the pen passed, producing visible lines. Alternately, the screen would display specific command buttons that the user could then choose through pointing. "These buttons can be treated as programmable push buttons," remarks one survey of such devices from 1967.[10] Later, pointing would encompass a much larger range of actions and effects, such as moving elements around the display or increasing and decreasing their size.

So why was pointing a long-standing dream of computing from the 1950s into the 1980s? And why, once generally adopted, has it remained a resilient computing practice for nearly a half century? If nothing else, its combination of versatility and simplicity in interfaces is matched by universal application across human contexts and experiences. Pointing things out, after all, is routine in making our way through the world and having meaningful exchanges with others. As such, this may be the one interactive component of computing that requires virtually no explanation or training, regardless of user or environment. At the same time, through its similarity to everyday pointing in interpersonal exchanges, it can imply a dialogic relationship with the machine and help develop empathy in user-device contexts. Pointing also gives a sense of power or command, as objects in an environment are prioritized or endowed with special value and meaning by the gesture. When a person points, they may feel in control.

Just as pointing has held a place in modern computing nearly from the outset, it is a human gesture that develops in a person's earliest stages of communication and sociability. (It even exists among other animals, such as chimpanzees and dogs.) Pointing is one of the first actions that connects each of us to the wider world. As infants we develop from bodily contact and touch as primary means of interaction and exploration to gesturing with our hands to assert our position and perception in the environment. As linguist Aliyah Morgenstern states, pointing "is one of the first gestures that enters children's productive repertoire ... [and] is considered a developmental cognitive and social milestone, as well as one of the first forms of communication used as humankind developed and thus a basic tool for cooperation."[11]

Unlike many bodily actions or gestures, pointing is almost always a communicative act based on "joint attention" between the pointing person and another. In fact, the term "index finger" derives from this correlation, building on the definition of the index as something that "leads one to a particular fact or conclusion."[12] The index finger, alternatively called the "pointer," has related names in other languages. In German it is the *Zeigefinger* (showing finger). In Tamil – one of the world's oldest continuously spoken languages – it is ஆள்காட்டி விரல் (*aalkaatti viral*) which translates as "person-showing" or "person-pointing" finger. As these names imply, pointing conveys meaning through the presence of others. "Showing" is meaningless as a solipsistic act. Remote control technologies aside, we never point at things around us when we are alone. We point in the presence of others, to establish relations that are always specific to the context. When we point in front of us, for example, the gesture means "this" or "that." It could refer to a chair, a ball, a building on fire, a ship on the horizon, or any other visually recognizable thing, depending on our spatial placement among objects and elements.

In his nineteenth-century theory of the index, philosopher Charles S. Peirce explained that pointing "is in dynamical (including spatial) connection both with the individual object, on the one hand, and with the senses or memory of the person for whom it serves as a sign, on the other hand."[13] Applied to the current context, Peirce's "person" could be the computer as much as the user. Pointing is deictic, like demonstrative pronouns such as "this" or "that." It requires a frame of reference and is wholly dependent on context for its meaning. Whenever we encounter a pointing finger – whether a person's hand in physical space or a depiction in an image or text, we inevitably refer to what lies directly ahead of the finger – physically proximate – as the referent of that gesture. Writing about how the index functions within media environments, film theorist Mary Ann Doane explains that "the index as shifter (or *deixis*) forces language to adhere to the spatiotemporal frame of its articulation." Doane notes that within the study of art and aesthetics there is "a formal logic of the index – that of indication and connectivity."[14] The index not only points out but also builds a connection – a connection between pointing and the object pointed at, as well as a connection between they who are pointing and those who receive that message. Pointing's reliance on the specific spatiotemporal frame of the event pushes this sense of connectivity since, in another context, the pointing can refer to something else entirely. In fact, Doane argues that the index "implies an emptiness, a hollowness that can only be filled in specific, contingent, always mutating conditions."[15] In a computing context, the indexicality of pointing both *opens* a space for interaction and *fills* that space with meaning.

The Point of a Mouse

Computer historian Paul Ceruzzi explains that computing's mouse-and-pointer configuration relies on hand-eye coordination developed over thousands of years to produce a "superior method of interacting with a computer that [does] not strain a user's symbolic reasoning abilities."[16] A mouse typically includes only one or two buttons and perhaps a scroll wheel on top, positioned to be under the fingertip, to be depressed to interact with elements indicated by the onscreen pointer. Often, the user's index finger is outstretched atop the mouse, creating a correspondence between the pointing hand and the onscreen pointing arrow (see figure 2.4). Research into embodiment with tools suggests that, under some circumstances, the brain will apprehend the tool as an integral component of the body, rather than as a discrete object.[17] This is especially true of tools that extend the pointing potential of the body. A study that asked participants to estimate the distance of a spot several inches away from the fingertip, for example, found that participants believed the spot was closer to them if they held an outstretched pointing device (a conductor's baton). In other words, the tool made them feel closer, as though it was a continuation of the body itself.[18]

Through the movements of the mouse and corresponding onscreen pointer, the user indicates things to the machine and the machine responds. When viewing the pointer as an extension of self, this event can resemble an interpersonal relationship as the machine processes pointing as a meaningful gesture that can change with the specifics of context. For example, pointing at the centre of the screen can mean very different things as the "this" or "that" of the arrow refers to whatever is displayed at the centre in that moment – a window, an icon, a prompt, and so on. In these cases, the user is not pointing at the centre, per se, but rather at what is

Figure 2.4
An example of customary hand positioning while manipulating a mouse.

displayed there. It is this locative aspect of user and device interacting in and through a specific, shared space that emerges in the mouse and has endured in our relationship with most touch screen personal devices today.

How might seeing the real-time correspondence between one's index finger extended across a moving mouse and the diagonal arrow moving on the screen produce the sensation of real-time interaction with another being? Morgenstern writes that "pointing can only be paired with a function when it is analyzed in association with the conversational content, the affordances of the situation, other multimodal cues (e.g., gaze, facial expression, vocal productions, words/signs), and the interlocutor's response."[19] When Engelbart demonstrated the basic workings of a tracking-ball-based graphical user interface in 1968, he explained it was like having "a computer that was alive for you all day and was… instantly responsive to every action you had." He described the tracking ball as "a device to move that tracking spot and *you're in the tracking spot*."[20] An early user of Lisa – Apple's first mouse-equipped product – wrote, "What is remarkable is the way in which a person using the Lisa mouse can quickly and effortlessly glide through complex *conversations* with the machine in a most natural way." They remarked, "Once it is up and running, you will be tempted to start playing with Lisa instead of dutifully going through the interactive tutorial."[21] As another writer stated upon the release of Lisa's successor, the Macintosh, "Mac is a friendly little devil" with an "approachable demeanor."[22] While reviewers' enthusiasm for these machines – as with many product reviews – may have been influenced by promotional access, advertising buys, and the like, it is significant that they were comfortable invoking "conversations" and "demeanor" when writing about a machine plugged into a wall. In her work on the relationship between computers and the self, Sherry Turkle also invokes "conversations" in describing the Macintosh, explaining that through such features as the pointer "people were encouraged to interact with technology in something resembling the way they interact with other people. We project complexity onto people; the Macintosh design encouraged the projection of complexity onto the machine."[23]

These descriptions of the social and potentially affective qualities of conversation and play produced through pointing in user-computer interactions align with research in childhood development of communication and language skills, where pointing involves both exchange and play. Research suggests that infants and toddlers first develop imperative pointing (pointing as a means of acquiring) but that this is soon supplemented by declarative pointing (pointing to show and share). "Declarative pointing reveals an understanding of others as intentional agents who possess independent psychological states," explains one study. "Declarative communication and reading intentions share a common mechanism that enables the child to appreciate the other person's psychological experience in relation to an object or event of common interest."[24] In other words, very early in our lives pointing arrives as a means for us to engage with others through objects.

Graphical user interfaces on personal computers offer the same opportunity. Turkle argues that a mouse-based interface made computer use superficial.[25] That is, by interacting with surface simulations users became less aware of (and perhaps less interested in) the device's inner workings and operations. Indeed, the superficiality of pointing – a communicative act that literally calls attention to the surface of things – played the central role, diverting users' attention away from the processes of computing to the screen-based "personality" of the computer. Indicating and selecting onscreen "objects" through pointing produces a sense of sharing and interaction with the device. At a psychological level, it might seem for the user that they are sharing their perspective with the device, and the device is recognizing the user's moves and preferences, without the sense of the user necessarily *ordering* the device to execute actions, as would be the case with text-based commands. As the pointer moves across the screen and objects may become brighter or change in other subtle ways without any other action or command taking place, the device seems to be signalling to the user, "I see (or feel) what you're doing" or "I follow you." This process of graphically (and by extension, aurally or haptically) recognizing and reflecting user presence even when the user has not yet made a selection or command has become key to user interaction with subsequent devices, such as touch screen phones.

Ironically, an industry analyst quoted in a 1988 *New York Times* article on graphical user interfaces and the ubiquity of the mouse in personal computing at that time would state, "Users don't care about hardware; it's inherently boring… To make a computer different it boils down to software that gives it a personality and feel."[26] Less than a decade after it came to the market, it seems, the mouse had become "boring." Yet perhaps the most fundamental component imbuing the computer with "personality and feel" for the user, as infant gestural research suggests, was this hardware that translated a physical action into a corresponding screen presence of similar gestural valence. The computer appeared to "possess [an] independent psychological state" because pointing – both physically in the outstretched finger on the mouse, and symbolically in the pixelated arrow – was meaningful. In reality, it was hardware in conjunction with software that produced these perceptions and sensations.

Manipulation

The quality of touch is built into mouse-based systems through depictions of grabbing and dragging screen "desktop" items by depressing and holding down the button (or buttons) atop the mouse. In writing about the development of Lisa and Macintosh, technology journalist Steven Levy describes a sense of "direct manipulation" in the use of the mouse to interact with and change displayed information. "The ability to open a file simply by moving a mouse – *sticking one's hand in cyberspace* – and selecting an icon was amazing."[27] In considering this sense of reaching into the space of the screen, it is important to realize that the user manipulates the mouse on the table or desk beside the monitor and keyboard, normally outside the direct path of vision. In this regard, the onscreen pointer becomes the finger for the user. Indeed, as just mentioned, under certain onscreen circumstances of grabbing and dragging, the pointer transforms into an image of a hand.[28]

If pointing is one of our first acts of symbolic interaction and communication with others – acquired well before we begin to speak – how might this correlate to the sense of touch? Looking back at the development of pointing in early childhood, research in cognitive psychology suggests that symbolic gesture pointing emerges from touch. "Children use a prototypical pointing hand shape to explore objects tactually from as early as 6 months, and as the frequency of pointing gestures increases from around 9 months of age, the frequency of this kind of exploratory touch decreases, suggesting that pointing is somehow 'taking over' from touch," one study concludes.[29] This evolution is noteworthy when considering the intimate and affective aspects of touch-based interfaces, where pointing becomes a common practice, though it may be tied to other motions and other digits (most notably the thumb). In fact, how one points to objects even as an adult may still be informed by the gesture's development in early touch. "Although adults and older children are able to interpret pointing gestures as arrows," cognitive psychologist Cathal O'Madagain and others explain, "from infancy to adulthood, pointing gestures are oriented toward their target not as arrows but instead as though they were attempts to touch that target … The wrist is rotated in a pointing gesture as it would be were the producer attempting to touch the target."[30] If we recognize traces of touch in the human development of pointing, we might say that in the development of computing there is a trace of earlier indicative mechanisms, such as the mouse and pointer, in today's touch interfaces.

The combination of pointing and touching with the finger as acts that connect the body and the self closely to the objects and beings with which they interact suggests that the touch screen – as well as touch sensitivity in other parts of a device – may be indispensable to generating emotional and psychological connection. In this regard, the early development of touch screen portable devices, such as EO's Communicator and Apple's Newton

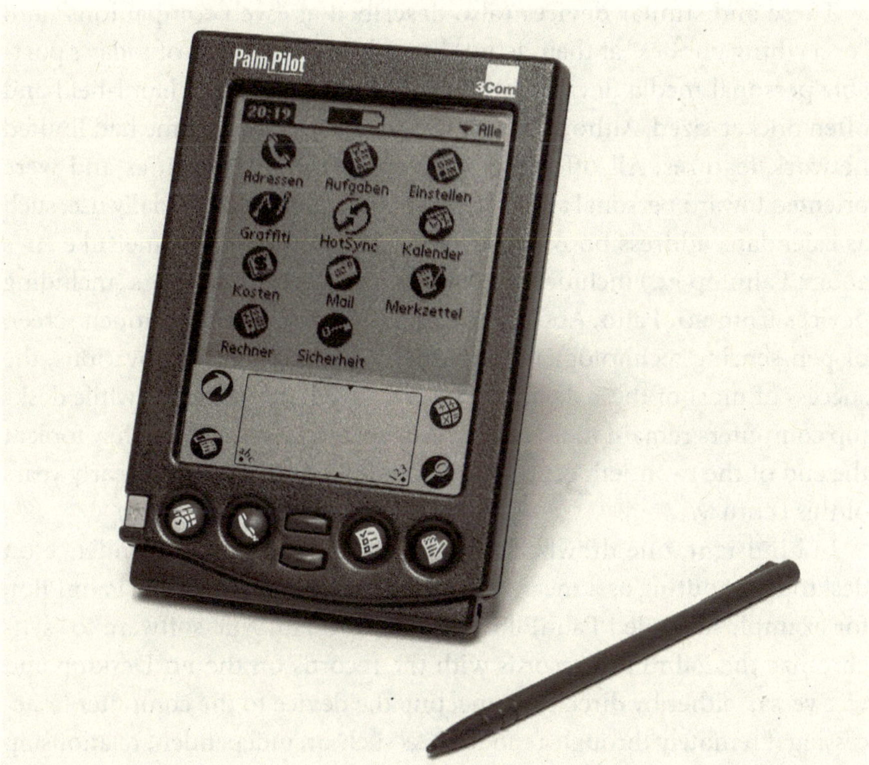

Figure 2.5
A PalmPilot 1000 with its stylus. The lower screen includes an open space for inputting letter and symbol strokes with the stylus.

MessagePad in 1993, U.S. Robotics' PalmPilot in 1996, and Handspring's Visor in 1999, would seem a significant step in hand-held alternatives to personal computers in the last years of the twentieth century (see figure 2.5). Indeed, while cellphone sales were soaring in North America, the market for these personal digital assistants (PDAS) was also robust, with over four million sold in 1998 (mostly in North America) and expectations for that number to quadruple by 2003.[31] PalmPilot alone accounted for about half of sales. "In retrospect, the Pilot will be seen as a turning point in the migration of computation from desktop machines to handheld devices," commented an MIT-based tech reviewer in heralding a "handheld revolution" in 1997. "Soon, many of us will spend more time interacting with our handheld devices than with our desktop computers.[32]

These and similar devices (also described as "web companions" and "everything phones" at their debut) brought many aspects of today's portable personal media devices into circulation.[33] They were hand-held and often pocket-sized. Although most were not telephonic, some had limited network features. All offered diverse computing capabilities and were oriented toward personal and interpersonal applications for daily use, such as calendars, address books, to-do lists, and messaging. Some (like HP's 200LX Palmtop PC) included small keyboards, but many others (including devices from EO, Palm, Apple, Philips, and Sharp) relied on touch screen or pen-sensing technology for data input. Despite their innovations, the success of most of these devices was short-lived. Interestingly, while desktop computers remain to this day in essentially the same form they took at the end of the twentieth century, PDAS did not last beyond the early years of this century.

In hindsight, one drawback of many PDAS was their dependence on desktop computing as a means of updating and synching. The PalmPilot, for example, included PalmPilot Desktop and HotSync software to "synchronize the PalmPilot records with the records on the PC Desktop and vice versa," either by directly connecting the device to the computer or accessing it remotely through a modem. As such, an independent relationship between user and device was impossible; the device's relationship to the computer always intervened to shape the device for the user. While handy, PDAS mostly remained an office peripheral, tied to the exigencies of the workplace rather than the whimsy of personal lifestyle. (As such, they tended to be sold in office supply stores rather than computer shops.)[34] There was also not much to them for play, for creativity, or for the fun of interacting with the device itself. For hand-held electronic fun, users were more likely to turn their attention to gaming devices like the Nintendo Game Boy or Sega Game Gear.

Hand-held, touch screen smart devices would not become widespread until the 2010s, and then only through the vector of the cellphone – another competing device of the 1990s – in its transformation to the smartphone. If touch screen today means a screen sensitive to the finger (whether by pressure or electric conductivity), in the development of touch screens this intimacy of the touch of the hand was mitigated as other forms of pointing were prioritized. PDAS struggled to exploit the nuances of touch and the ways it could build intimacy and affect into the user's relationship with the animated object. Typically, pointing and other screen actions were accomplished with a stylus, which meant inserting an additional object (however diminutive and unassuming) between the user and the smart device. As explained in *PalmPilot: The Ultimate Guide*, "There's nothing magical about the stylus included with the device – it's not magnetic, or electrostatic, or otherwise gimmicked. The PalmPilot can't tell whether it's being touched by the stylus, or, say, your fingernail (although unless you've got some kind of rare genetic condition, the stylus is probably more precise than your fingernail)."[35]

The Stylus and Writing

The PalmPilot and other PDAs offered the tantalizing possibility of haptic intimacy between the finger and the screen, without fully delivering.[36] In guides, manuals, reviews, and discussions, the screen is not "touched" on these devices, but "tapped." The preferred means of contact with the screen for most of these devices was the stylus, not the hand (see figure 2.6). Deriving from the Latin word for both "style" and "spike" or "stake," a stylus is defined as "an instrument for writing, marking, or incising."[37] The term has been used to describe tools for pressing symbols into clay tablets in ancient Babylonia, cutting and reading grooves in gramophone records, and indenting or scratching signals into paper.[38] The stylus did not evolve as a means of interaction or indication – it was never a pointer – but as an instrument meant to permanently change the surface of an object so that it could be read by people or machines at a later date, sometimes using the stylus as the means of reading (as with the "needle" stylus on a turntable). While styli were often made of hard materials, such as bone or metal, the PDA touch screen stylus would have a metal or plastic shaft with a soft plastic or synthetic rubber tip to prevent scratching the screen. "Grasp it in your fingers as you would a pen or pencil," the PalmPilot manual advised users. "Always use the point of the stylus for tapping, or making strokes on the PalmPilot screen. Never use an actual pen, pencil or other sharp object to write on the PalmPilot screen."[39]

In giving this advice to avoid screen damage, the PalmPilot manual listed three user actions associated with the stylus: tapping, stroking, and *writing*. Handwriting recognition was a major component of many PDAs, including

Figure 2.6
Using a stylus to interact with Apple's Newton MessagePad.

the PalmPilot and Newton. The device would adjust to the idiosyncrasies of the user's script through calibration and practice sessions, allowing for the relatively quick and accurate conversion of stylus strokes into type. Indeed, when the Newton's advertising touted "Newton is personal… Newton is intelligent, Newton learns about you, understands you," the claim rested mainly on the device's ability to adapt to different styles of handwriting.[40] Media scholars José van Dijck and Sonja Neef describe handwriting as "an absolutely individual and non-exchangeable sign, almost as unique as fingerprints or other biometrical data." Handwriting is a deeply personal trait – bearing the presumed unique authenticity of the autograph that van Dijck and Neef call "the 'auratic' dimension of handwriting" – that is nevertheless rooted in, and shaped by, cultural conventions (e.g., standard writing implements and shared symbol systems and languages).[41] As such, handwriting encapsulates the everyday tensions between agency and normative embodiment identified by theorist Carrie Noland. "*Gestures*, learned techniques of the body, are the means by which cultural conditioning is simultaneously embodied and put to the test," Noland asserts.[42]

Like the PalmPilot, the Newton was designed to recognize the learned techniques of an individual's handwriting through the idiosyncrasies of gesture. However, the Newton's adaptability to different styles of handwriting was limited. Apple conceded the point in its introductory videos for the Newton, which included tips on how users might write more neatly for the software. Apple's eight-minute "Welcome to Newton" video from 1993 claims that "Newton actually learns how you write … [and] will fine-tune itself to your handwriting." Yet the video includes a sequence entitled "Handwriting Tips," where the presenter suggests users must fine-tune themselves to the Newton, explaining that "some people find that it takes a little bit of practice." The tips, presented with visual examples, include reducing pauses in the middle of words, avoiding rapidly correcting errors while writing, leaving space between words ("even exaggerat[ing] it a little bit"), and writing "as simply and neatly as you can [in making] your o's look like o's and your a's look like a's." The presenter concludes the section by explaining that "it's common sense, really."[43]

These and other writing constraints fuelled one of the major criticisms of the Newton during its five-year existence. "You'll need to practice with the shape of letters and with timing," warned an otherwise glowing review upon the Newton's launch, stating flatly that "Newton isn't trainable: your handwriting must conform to its range of standard preferences."[44] While a user's handwriting might be unique, the Newton could not recognize this uniqueness: the user was forced to suppress the distinctiveness of their writing to adhere to the hardware and software limits of the device's recognition system. Education scholar Lesley Gourlay makes a similar argument about handwriting and textual technologies as a historical pattern. In examining handwriting's connotations of intimacy, Gourley points to medieval copyists and the limitations imposed by standardization. "Although it is undeniable that the intimacy and direct visually-observable trace of the writer's hand is lost when writing is converted to print," Gourley states, "it is worth noting that while manuscripts of the medieval period were produced by hand, many did not resemble everyday handwriting as such, but instead were stylized, and relatively standardized in their presentation of text."[45]

Given this potential split between writing and intimacy due to system requirements, Gourley argues that genre may play a role in linking handwriting to the intimacy of the text. "A handwritten letter is likely to appear more intimate than an expertly-produced illuminated manuscript," Gourley claims, "although both are technically produced by hand."[46] The emphasis on stylus and script recognition in personal digital devices of the 1990s shifted the user's focus from the interpersonal gesturing of pointing and "grabbing" to tools of recording. In exploring writing's relationship to contemporary visual media across cultures, Jeff Rice identifies the intersection of writing textuality and graphics as going back to Sutherland's 1963 Sketchpad drawing system and its light pen. Calling it a "personal, graphic manipulation program," Rice claims Sketchpad "equated writing with visual expression" through the manipulation of symbols with the light pen. "Sketchpad reconfigured the writing space from paper to the visual screen."[47] Sutherland himself saw the light pen interface of Sketchpad as a means of moving from "writing letters to … conferring with our computers," as it replaced written commands with pointing and selecting.[48] Yet, with the advent of the stylus in the 1990s, pointing was translated into another register of meaning that moved away from the immediacy generally associated with the gesture. The stylus touching the surface was only the beginning of meaning-making, rather than a communicative act in itself. Indeed, devoted PalmPilot users even resorted to ballpoint pens in place of the stylus, despite Palm advising against it, making a connection between tool and inscription reaching beyond the specific frame of digital interface to encompass writing more generally.[49]

As one PalmPilot reviewer wrote, the "handwriting-recognition feature is a little awkward, and the marks for punctuation and commands aren't intuitive. I had to constantly look these up while I used the machine."[50] Like the Newton, the PalmPilot required users to alter their writing habits for better "stroke" recognition. Palm produced the "Graffiti Alphabet" for its devices and affixed stickers of the alphabet to the back of the casing (see figure 2.7). Writing an "A" with Palm's Graffiti recognition software, for example, required making what looks like an upward arrow.

Different parts of the screen would be dedicated to writing letters and numbers, so the script conversion would not confuse an "S" with a "5" or a "T" with a "7," since each of these pairs entailed virtually the same stylus strokes. Initial reviews of writing-recognition PDAS may have marvelled at the possibility of a device recognizing and converting the idiosyncrasies of individual writing. "Handwriting recognition in an intelligent assistant is a vital step toward making machines conform to human needs, standards,

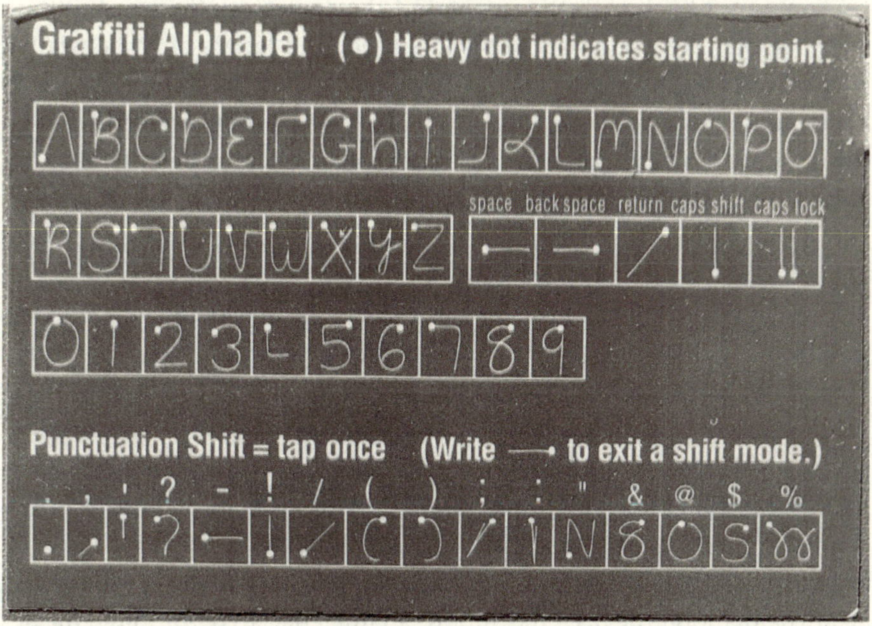

Figure 2.7
The Graffiti Alphabet writing chart affixed to the back of the PalmPilot.

and styles, rather than the other way around," claimed one review.[51] Yet, in practice, these systems required users to adapt the movements of their bodies and alter the physical subtleties of a communication system they had learned in the first weeks of grade school, suggesting the power ultimately lay with the device and not the user.

Such behavioural constraints distanced the user from the immediacy of touch recognition as a means of uniting user and device around basic conditions of bodily proximity. In considering writing within a wider exploration of the role of gesture in our lives, philosopher Vilém Flusser theorized that "the structure of our gesture of writing … gives a form to (informs) a whole dimension of our existence in the world." This is so fundamental to our standing in the world that, according to Flusser, "To alter one single aspect of this accidental structure, for example, to suggest writing in reversible directions as the ancients did, would mean to change our way of being in the world."[52] The writing recognition systems of the Newton and PalmPilot required just such a destabilizing and potentially alienating shift. Imagine, for example, the intimacy of the game of tracing letters on someone's back with the finger and their guessing the word. But, in place of the finger, a dowel or stick is used, and letters must be written in new, unconventional ways. A game of contact and familiarity, of minds meeting through bodily sensation, changes into a (self-)conscious operation of tasks. These differences parallel, in some ways, the difference between our physical and psychological relationship with touch screens today and the relationships between user and device produced through the interfaces of stylus-based PDAs.

Even in those rare circumstances where screens were designed for finger-based touch recognition, the stylus was not far away. In 1994, IBM introduced the Simon Personal Communicator, a hand-held, touch screen PDA that included most of the features found in Apple and Palm products of the 1990s. However, the Simon also had telephonic and wireless data exchange capacities for making phone calls, sending email, and faxing documents, making it one of the first smartphones.[53] "You now have total personal communications – including your cellular phone – in one small, hand-held, mobile device," the Simon's manual declared. Although the device allowed interaction through finger contact on the screen, IBM recommended using a stylus. "You can touch a feature using either the stylus that came with this product or your finger," the manual explained, though subsequent instructions throughout the manual described interactions taking place only by means of the stylus – "move the cursor… directly by touching the screen with the stylus" or "as you slide your stylus, the number highlights."[54] As the Simon was only ever available in the southeastern US (through a partnership with telecommunications company BellSouth) and appeared on the market after stylus-based touch screen devices such as the Newton, it gained scant media attention. The few references to the device in the mainstream press made little mention of the touch screen, let alone the possibility of using a finger as the means of interfacing with it.[55]

When the iPhone was introduced in 2007, however, Steve Jobs was quick to extoll the device's touch screen capabilities while dismissing the stylus as a reliable user option. "Who wants a stylus? You have to get them and put them away and you lose them. Yuck. Nobody wants a stylus … We're going to use the best pointing device in the world … We're going to use our fingers."[56] The special role of the finger not only as indicator but also as point of *contact* between device face and the user's body will be explored at length in the next chapter. But what seems clear in the current context is that the move to finger-based touch screen interaction also removed the complex and sometimes frustrating mechanisms of writing that haunted the stylus.[57] Of course, it is important to recognize that the stylus can be – and still is – used by many to interact with their phone or tablet. It is especially useful, and even necessary, for users with skin conditions or motor function impairments that may prevent effective contact, pressure or targeting with the finger. Nevertheless, in these cases, the stylus serves mainly as a substitute for the finger and generally is not required for device functioning, nor does it entail learning special strokes or new symbols to be able to communicate with the device.

Of course, it is tempting to read the failure of stylus-based interfaces as inevitable alongside the success of finger-based touch interactivity. As Jobs said, why use a stylus when you can use your finger? The same could be said about eating, however, and still we find silverware, chopsticks, and other devices for manipulating and picking up food in many homes around the world. To be clear, both stylus and finger as interfacing tools require disciplining of the body. Devices are configured to interpret certain gestures in specific ways, whether executed with a stylus or a finger. Algorithms are developed to allow a certain leniency in detecting and determining gestures, yet these algorithms will nevertheless follow certain standards and require users to adapt if they want to use these devices effectively. If we see the exercise of power systems in the disciplining of user handwriting with PDAs, for example, that process continues in any "intuitive" interface where the user must pick up the rules of the game and often subtly change their movements until they become "natural." We rarely recognize this process, except when we must change devices and find our muscle memory now produces different results. That we may adapt to a new device in a matter of days – or even hours – does not diminish its disciplining power but merely renders this process less palpable in our daily lives.

Geolocation Points Back

Portable personal media have shifted pointing-based interactions from the micro to encompass the macro. Users still experience a psychologically intimate relationship with the device through pointing and being understood by the device as both share the same situational awareness. However, these devices also tap into ambient telecommunications and data networks – satellite navigation systems, cellular towers, and Wi-Fi routers – as locative media to pinpoint and situate the user as a moving spot on the globe, both for the user and others. Indeed, Engelbart's offhand remark during his 1968 demonstration of the mouse, that "you're *in* the tracking spot" on screen, aptly describes how location and interaction have evolved in computing.[58] While we continue to point with our finger to indicate specific onscreen spaces and objects to the device, the device now points back at us in many apps and features by continually and accurately indicating our location in the world down to a few metres. The pointing arrow is no longer our finger; it's the device's "finger," indicating its awareness of our unique physical presence. This interplay of pointing – and that sense of continual device awareness of our presence – can strengthen our attachment to the device as intimately linked to our being. Significant work has been done on locative media and the user's relationship to the environment, yet less attention has been paid to changes in the user's relationship to the device itself through locative features.[59]

Geolocation, or phone tracking, involves an array of technologies, some housed in networks, some housed in the device. Networks can triangulate the strength of device signals to neighbouring cellular towers to narrow location down to several metres in infrastructure-dense environments, such as cities. Global Positioning System (GPS) activation on the device can pinpoint location with even greater accuracy. When GPS tracking is turned on, the device becomes a GPS receiver, calculating its position by collecting signals from geopositioning satellites overhead. A device's location systems will often draw on both GPS data and cellular tower signals, however, as well as crowd-sourced Wi-Fi hotspots, to build as accurate a picture as possible of the device's position in the environment.[60]

The US government authorized civilian applications of GPS satellites in 1999, clearing the way for GPS use in personal media devices. This step spurred production of dedicated portable navigation devices for driving and hiking by companies such as Garmin, Trimble, and Panasonic. Only in 2005, after several technological and infrastructural advances, including cheaper, more sensitive device antennas and cellular tower-enhanced location data transmission (to supplement satellites and conserve battery power), did GPS become readily available in cellphones and smartphones. Over the next four years, more GPS receivers were installed in phones (three to five hundred million) than had been manufactured over the entire quarter-century history of GPS prior to 2005.[61]

Phone-based GPS was initially promoted as a safety and route-finding feature, supplied in part to satisfy US requirements that cellphones have accurate geolocation data for emergency services responding to 911 calls. Position data was used primarily in relation to navigational systems. Nokia called its GPS systems Walk and Drive to emphasize their role in route-finding. Such systems merely pointed out the user's position and movement within the static environment of a preloaded program (a map), extending the pointer-screen-mouse relationship of the desktop computer, although here the mouse, pointer, and screen all converged in the phone. Holding the phone steady in your hand and moving the phone across the terrain around you as you walked would move your point on the onscreen map.

Although this system may have appeared closed, sharing your position with the network through the device's GPS introduced the possibility of sharing with others. Phone manufacturers seized on this as a potential tool for greater interpersonal communication and intimacy. Even as late as 2012, a manual for a GPS-equipped phone from Austrian manufacturer Emporia suggested that users could share their phone's GPS data with a circle of friends. "These contacts are defined in your *Friends list*. Do not worry: numbers that are not on this list cannot determine your position."[62] Under these circumstances, GPS was transformed into a personal social network, providing constant information on the movements of people known to the user, as well as sharing the user's movements with them. Importantly, this information was not archived or applied toward other purposes by the device or software providers. Today, this is rarely the case with apps that use localization.

Google's development of Android as a mobile operating system marked a turning point in this process. A year after Android's 2008 introduction, phones running Android from manufacturers such as HTC and Motorola included Google Latitude, an app tied to Google Maps that allowed users to share their location with others. Latitude would access a device's GPS capabilities as well as cellular tower and Wi-Fi signal information to generate relatively accurate location information, but users also could disable this and manually enter a location. The draw of Latitude was its real-time mapping of the user in relation to friends, colleagues, and acquaintances gleaned from the user's Gmail contacts list and other sources. Latitude had replaced Dodgeball, a previous Google location sharing service that relied on manual location entry. While Dodgeball required users to point themselves out on the map, Latitude automatically pointed them out to others.[63] Like the mouse-computer interface, the point represented the user on the screen in such a system, but here the user did not independently control the point in interacting with the device. The device as a whole became a networked pointer that constantly pointed back at the user for others to see.

Apple's iPhones were not originally equipped with GPS, although third-party apps were developed to simulate GPS by collecting and analyzing other transmission data.[64] Built-in GPS capability arrived with the iPhone 3G in 2008. In 2010–11 Apple offered Find My iPhone and Find My Friends as location-based features, eventually bundling them into the "Find My" app. Find My represents a complex system of spatial relations in the Internet of Things between users and their objects in the construction of networked identity. Find My allows the user to share their iPhone's location with friends and use the iPhone to find their other connected Apple devices (such as a MacBook laptop or an AirTag key chain) through Bluetooth short-range wireless capabilities (see figure 2.8).

Samsung's Find My Mobile and Google's Find My Device function similarly. However, Find My also enhances user location options by continuing to indicate the device's whereabouts even when the device has no network or is powered off or erased. Find My relies on the global proliferation of Apple devices to form a network of interacting objects, allowing nearby Apple devices to detect and indicate the presence of the user's device via Bluetooth, even if the device is not interacting with a cellular or Wi-Fi network. As Apple explains, "If your missing device can't connect to the internet or has little to no battery life, the Find My app can still help you track it down using the Find My network – hundreds of millions of iPhone, iPad, and Mac devices around the world. Nearby devices securely send the location of your missing device to iCloud, then you can see where it is in the Find My app."[65] Find My also provides greater accuracy in locating the user by bundling location across devices, such as the iPhone and Apple Watch. If a user has Find My activated on both devices and they are proximate – e.g., one on the wrist, the other in a pocket – their location will be

Figure 2.8
Apple's depiction of the Find My interface for locating networked objects.

determined by the iPhone. However, should the user move away from their phone, user location will be detected through the watch's movement.

In these examples of the intercommunication of diverse objects that emerged with the Internet of Things, the object is sometimes identified as the object and sometimes as the owner. When I get into a rental car, for example, I may be able to synch my smartphone with the car's media system through Bluetooth, finding "Stephen's phone" or similar terms among the options in the system connections. When I share my location with my friends, however, they may see a point on the map marked only as "Stephen," not "Stephen's phone." This alternation lies at the heart of our identification with – and even as – these networked objects. As our relationship to these devices becomes more intertwined, there may come a day when all these instances will bear only a name as a label (e.g., "Stephen") belying the communicating object. As a tool, the device would no longer be construed as an extension of self but would become entirely absorbed within the self for all social intents and purposes.

Making these apps meaningful requires keeping geolocation features permanently activated, however. Selective activation diminishes their effectiveness. For example, if a device is misplaced while geolocation is off, the feature cannot be activated remotely and is of no use in retrieving the object. This perceived need for permanent activation produces valuable corporate and institutional data for building detailed profiles of users and their lifestyles in tracking where, when, and how they circulate. By accessing, recording, analyzing, and potentially sharing such data, corporations and other entities can influence and monetize users in new ways. They can personalize not only product offers (such as advertising and in-app purchase opportunities) but also the whole user experience, by adjusting app and device interfaces and content. As a building block of surveillance capitalism, locative capabilities become a way for corporations, governments, and other organizations to situate the user in the world, and also in relation to products and services both online and off. Where once only we the user may have had access to our GPS data to help us get somewhere, now others also use the same data to take us somewhere. As early as 2007, a tech writer covering geopositioning in mobile phones speculated that it presents "all sorts of possibilities for advertisers, who would love to have you walking past a store and seeing their deals popping up on your screen."[66] Google's entry into the cellphone business with Android also raised concerns at the time. "If Android merges location and calling data with that gathered by search engines, Google will be able to retain more detailed information on users," explained a *New Scientist* article, quoting data privacy advocate Simon Davies that "Android has the potential to be a privacy Chernobyl."[67]

In essence, enhanced spatial recognition of the user-device relationship through these networked geolocative capabilities makes the device and user representationally identical. This merges the interpersonal (between device and user) with the personal (device *as* user). Embedded in geolocative technologies such as satellite navigation systems, the device shows us where we are, placing us in any number of representations of locations. In reality, these technologies only detect the device and its signalling. There is no direct correlation to the user's body. Yet we equate these technologies with showing us where we are. These devices have become such a presence in our lives, such constant companions, that we may not differentiate the live dot on the map from ourselves. And, of course, we only see them locating us when we are in their close presence, interacting with them. Ironically, dystopian narratives of such individual tracking from the late twentieth century – as personal networked devices were just taking hold – often imagined tracking devices as bodily embedded.[68] We would always be tracked, these stories suggested, because our cyborgian bodies themselves would always be reporting our presence to the network. Such tracking has come to fruition, but through the ostensibly voluntary and reversible act of carrying these devices on a near permanent basis. They become fitted to the body *psychologically* to the extent that we may refer to them and those who carry them interchangeably in making spatial judgments. In their physical form and reactive capacities, they also create new relationships with the body, particularly around touch and haptics. This relationship, of the fit of bodies and devices in contact and the potential intimacy that arises, will be explored next.

CHAPTER 3

The Right Touch

It is almost impossible to imagine our interactions with personal networked devices without touch at the centre of the experience. Of course, there are many devices that we may use regularly without touching. Voice interactive devices in the home or car allow access to a range of networked tools and services. And certainly, the basic act of handling our devices is nothing new but rather as old as the first tools of our ancient ancestors. Even when limiting ourselves to the realm of computing, from the early years of computers there were relays to be plugged or unplugged and switches to be toggled up or down. Then there were card punchers and keyboards and magnetic tape reels for programmers and operators to manipulate in various ways. Nevertheless, today our interactions with devices through the myriad sensors of their touch-sensitive surfaces allow the subtlest variations in hand movement and contact to produce an astonishing range of responses and results. Faint contact – or even near-contact – in one direction or another can move objects on the screen, trigger menus or windows, commence or conclude networked transactions, or zoom in or out on images, among many more possibilities. Screen sensitivity to contact has become so acute that even inadvertently grazing the surface with the side of the hand – so lightly that we may not feel any contact – may be sufficient to wake the device from sleep mode and illuminate its screen.

Philosopher Matthew Fulkerson notes that touch may be the most complex of our five senses, since it can involve both bodily awareness and exploratory action. He writes that

> touch often involves exploratory movement, often combined with the use of tools and other intermediaries that seem to extend our awareness beyond our bodies. The world does not come to us in touch; we must reach out and actively engage with the world to learn about it through touch. And we use a diversity of movements: reaching, tapping, rubbing, grabbing, squeezing, pressing, and pulling. These movements are often combined and connected, allowing for more robust information to be extracted from objects we meet.[1]

This chapter explores the affective potential of personal media devices in their exploitation and nuancing of skin contact and touch. It considers how these devices encompass both bodily awareness and exploratory action by simultaneously functioning as an extension of the user's body in the pairing of object and grip, and as an interaction of two proximate bodies through somatosensory cues and haptic response. These pairings – awareness and action, extension and other – can intersect to give the user both a strong sense of agency and a deep dependency on the device. This makes touch capabilities a valuable component in building and extending larger processes of economic and political power, much like earlier tactile objects, such as prayer beads developed in Christianity and Islam to build spiritual devotion and obedience.[2] And the near-constant contact of the smartphone or smartwatch with a user's body can contribute to a feeling of physical incompleteness when the device is missing. As such, touch becomes a key component not only of connectedness and possibility but also of groundedness and presence. That we may not feel safe if we don't physically *feel* the presence of our device points to how power can circulate through the materiality of the object and impact the very core of a user's being. This dependence – underlying any agency the device might afford – recalls Michel Foucault's theorization of power's propagation through the disciplining of the body. As Foucault explained, "Disciplinary coercion establishes in the body the constricting link between an increased aptitude and an increased domination."[3] In mastering awareness and action of touch and touch-based commands, the user may develop a sense of aptitude, yet this comes at the cost of the device's domination as a bodily presence and necessity.

The advent of small, portable, and highly interactive personal devices in the early 2000s set the stage for new physical exchanges with communication devices as these products became attendant to – and closely associated with – the body. While the networked, mobile device emerged as an essential component of selfhood in many contexts, as mentioned previously it also served as a companion with which the self could interact. This dichotomy – of integrated part and independent entity – can be managed and leveraged through the fluctuating objective and subjective perceptual distinctions of touch. While these conditions certainly came into play in striking ways with the major shift to touch screen smartphones in the 2010s, they did not begin there. For example, Apple's development of the iPod a decade earlier prioritized touch and haptic interaction in seminal ways as surface and skin became key to intimacy and interaction with the portable music and video player. The iPod, and related accessories, will serve as a conduit in this chapter to a deeper exploration of the affective potential of tactile and haptic interfaces, and perhaps help explain the dominance of touch screen devices in recent years.

Hand-Held

Significant relationships between the hand and the device have already been explored in previous chapters. In chapter 1, the microcomputer appeared as a handmade object requiring user assembly and even jury-rigging. In chapter 2, the mouse and pointer placed hand gestures at the centre of human-computer interaction. With small, portable media devices such as a smartphone, it is necessary to further explore the significance of the device as a *hand-held* object. As wireless objects that fit in the pocket, weigh less than a bag of potato chips, and can potentially run for days on a single battery charge (depending on use), smartphones may seem obviously designed to remain in the hand for long periods (much longer than the PDAs of the turn of the century) across changing and unpredictable conditions of everyday life. Visit any public place and you are likely to see multiple people with a phone in their hand. In some cases, they will be actively interacting with it; in other cases, they may be "just" holding it. And in the case of smartwatches and fitness trackers, of course, the device will remain in constant contact with the body, whether or not the user is engaging with it.

Reflecting on the smartphone as a hand-held device, scenes from two Hollywood movies come to mind. The first, from *Wall Street*, takes place in 1987. Walking along a beach on New York's Long Island at sunrise, corporate raider Gordon Gekko calls his protege on a cellphone the size of a large brick. The device is a Motorola DynaTac 8000X, the first commercially available cellphone, released in 1984. The phone extends well beyond the length of Gekko's stretched index finger as he holds the phone to his ear. The other scene is from the 2001 comedy *Zoolander*, where self-absorbed fashion model Derek Zoolander can't resist answering his phone, despite being chided by a friend for the disruption. Zoolander's fictional device – lampooning the rapidly decreasing size of phones at the turn of the century – is no larger than a pair of dice. Even when cradled at his fingertips, the phone is nearly hidden by them. While the *Wall Street* scene of Gekko holding a two-pound Motorola DynaTac 8000X to his ear projected luxury and privilege in the convenience of mobile telephony, it would become an internet meme of "cumbersome" convenience, while *Zoolander* satirized the push toward smaller and smaller cellphones that dominated the 2000s, with diminishing returns as the phone shrank to the point of inoperability by human hands. Bookended by these cinematic extremes, phones have mostly fluctuated by millimeters here and there over the past three decades to the point where they rest comfortably within the limits of most hands to cradle them, and most fingers to tap and swipe their surfaces.

Most smartphone models are sized so the average adult can hold and manipulate the device single-handedly. When cellphones were primarily used for phone calls and short texts, single-hand manipulation was a minor concern. Since phones now accommodate a stunning range of content, interactions, and uses, they are far more likely to be held in one hand for long periods of time. We hold our devices in all sorts of circumstances, often while our other hand holds something else – a handrail, a child, a coffee cup, an eating utensil. It feels comfortable enough that we commonly hold it with one hand even when the other is free.[4] Under these circumstances, we may work with the device, accessing and perusing information by moving a finger across the screen. We may also simply clutch the device as we tend to other tasks. These possibilities of extended, intense interaction and long moments of inaction, during which the device is in the hand, differentiate the contemporary phone from some other hand-held communication devices, like the remote control or the walkie-talkie.

Conduciveness to extended holding, whether we are actively interacting with the device or not, can contribute to dependence and intimacy. It is easy to keep the device not just near us but in contact with our skin. An important factor is our grip, or the ongoing relationship between the hand and the device as it is held. The history of hand-held electronic and computing devices spans decades, encompassing pocket calculators, electronic games, and PDAS, in addition to cellphones and even the desktop mouse. In the development of PDAS alongside cellphones in the 1990s, the capacity to be held in one hand would occasionally become a marketing point.[5] However, PDAS were often described at the time as *resting* on the hand, rather than being gripped by encompassing fingers, as though the computer simply moved from one surface – the desktop – to another, smaller and more mobile one. As such, the whole field of hand-held computing in the 1990s was described as "palmtop" computing.[6]

This imagining of the hand-held device and its orientation to the body re-emerged with the iPod as a hand-held electronic music device. Released in 2001, the iPod was marketed as a device that rested firmly – even tightly – in the hand as a listener used it. "It felt good in my hand, like some sort of squashed mobile phone," commented journalist Dylan Jones on his first encounter with the device.[7] Apple's advertising campaigns from 2003 to 2008 suggested this feature was integral to the device's use and appeal (see figure 3.1).

These campaigns featured solitary, silhouetted figures dancing before bright, monotone backgrounds. The small white rectangle of the iPod in the hand, with its earphone cords extending to the figure's head, stood out against these silhouettes and backgrounds. In Apple's audiovisual advertising, these figures danced frenetically, their arms and legs flailing, the earphone cord swinging around the arms, across the chest, and even at the face. Throughout this frenzy, the device remained snug in the hand. Depicting the iPod under these conditions served two purposes. First, it demonstrated that the device, unlike previous portable music players that used cassettes and CDS, could be shaken vigorously without affecting playback quality. Second, it suggested that the iPod could become one with the body in the act of music listening as the device smoothly conformed to every bodily movement, no matter how someone danced.

Figure 3.1
A billboard advertisement for the Apple iPod, Dallas, Texas, 2005.

Nestled in the palm, the device could become part of the user, a material media condition that technology theorist Heidi Rae Cooley has called "fit." Relating the use of hand-held mobile devices to the concept of "tactile vision" through the coordination of hand, eye, and screen, Cooley draws from biomechanics and industrial design in theorizing fit as "the particular relationship between the hand and the MSD [mobile screen device] as a happening, which occurs at the instant of contour when the hand forms to the MSD and the MSD *gives* to the hand."[8] Describing this as the hand and device "becoming one," Cooley explains that fit is not a purposeful act of the hand to engage with the device, but rather "transpires immediately and without volition" as the user grasps the device. In fact, it is the very involuntariness, if you will, of fit "that enables such a dynamic happening between hand and MSD. Interesting to consider in this regard is the fact that increased transmission of haptic information occurs when tactile exploration is not motivated," Cooley explains. "In other words, tactile engagement that is not directed by volitional movement tends to produce an increase in somatosensory input."[9] Just holding the device, Cooley argues, can produce a special relationship between it and the user. Somatosensory input can continue even when the user is not interacting with the device – or its apps – toward some goal.

This situation positions the device as a special object between the self and the outside world that can build reassurance and provide comfort. Here it shares valuable characteristics with the childhood "transitional objects" theorized by psychoanalyst D.W. Winnicott in the mid-twentieth century. In describing the function of transitional objects, Winnicott made a distinction between object-relating and object-usage. Object-relating involves the subject projecting onto the object. This projection is akin to fantasy or illusion and need not be recognized or understood by other people. Object-usage, however, involves everyone (including the user) recognizing the object as a material part of the surrounding world. Crossing the two actions in what Winnicott called a paradox (the object is part of the user, but also not), Winnicott stated "relating can be described in terms of the individual subject, and ... usage cannot be described except in terms of acceptance of the object's independent existence, its property of having been there all the time."[10]

Winnicott researched transitional objects such as teddy bears and security blankets as essential to an infant's process of socialization and entering the world of others, yet his ideas may be applied to our complex relationship with objects throughout our lives. Certain special objects in adulthood can oscillate between these positions. We may project onto them as part of our inner world, while also recognizing their functioning outside of ourselves in relation to the rest of the world. Like the microcomputer hobbyists who anthropomorphized their kit computers in the pages of 1970s home computing magazines, Apple's iPod garnered similar projections from some users after its release in 2001. Since an iPod's hard drive could hold a user's entire personal music library (one thousand songs), intimacy seemed built into the relationship. As Dylan Jones suggested, his iPod had "a two-inch LCD window that lights up superbrightly for exactly two seconds when I touch one of its buttons (I have told it to do this and it does what it's told) ... The light recedes and then jumps back to life; it's winking at me, letting me know it's available and ready. It's willing and able, too, hinting that its vast library is there for the taking" (see figure 3.2).[11]

Several researchers, including Sharif Mowlabocus, have pointed out that personal media devices such as smartphones seem to occupy this transitional space through any number of design and programming features that

Figure 3.2
A sixth-generation iPod, with a touch-sensitive wheel and video playing capabilities.

transform them into trusty, versatile companions.[12] Note how the smartphone as a special object, for example, is often reinforced by users through personalizing accessories like stickers and cases. More will be made of these add-ons below, but it is worth indicating here that many cases – especially those chosen by younger users – tend to zoomorphize the device (see figure 3.3). This aligns the device more closely with, say, the stuffed animals at the heart of Winnicott's study.

Even without such accessories, however, the phone fulfills some of Winnicott's claims, especially as a mobile and hand-held object. Archaeologist Penny Spikins emphasizes the consistent role of touch and portability in such comforting objects across history and cultures. Spikins states that "the very constancy of such objects provides an additional sense of security," while noting that "the boundaries between functional objects and those that provide comfort can also be fluid."[13] This places personal media objects like smartphones in a long line of special objects carried close to the body

Figure 3.3
A phone in a rabbit-ear case by Rabbito Boutique.

that mediate the user's relationship to themselves and their sense of being as well as to the rest of the world. Crossing somatosensory input with fit, the device becomes an intimate presence that can act as a comforting buffer between the user and the outside world. The user can "curl up" with their phone. The user can squeeze their phone in moments of stress or discomfort. What other object can a user interact with under the blanket of their bed, at the counter at work, or in the yard at a family gathering without raising suspicion or concern?

In shaping this intimate, hand-held object, a significant sizing concern arises not only around the possibility of easily grasping the device with one hand but also with being able to use that hand for all device interactions. Of course, there is no single way to hold or handle a smartphone (or tablet). Users are likely to adjust how they grasp and interact with a device across circumstances, making modifications for space, surrounding objects, muscle fatigue, screen reflections, privacy, and so forth. User interface designer Steven Hoober has observed that users more often handle their smartphone with two hands but rely on one thumb for input.[14] The development of larger screen sizes to accommodate the demand for watching videos on phones has made single-hand gripping and manipulation more complicated. Manufacturers have attempted to remedy this with optional settings that change content configuration on the screen. Apple has "reachability mode," which is meant "to lower the top half of the screen so it's within easy reach of your thumb."[15] Phones running Android have "one-handed mode," which works similarly. However, neither of these features is a default setting, nor are they prominently promoted in marketing these devices.[16] "Reachability" is accessed under "Accessibility" and "Touch" in iPhone settings and through "Systems" and "Gestures" with Android.[17]

Foldable phones, such as Samsung's Galaxy Z Fold series, represent another attempt at bridging the gulf between one-handed manipulation and larger screen viewing. When folded, the Galaxy Z Fold is about the size of a standard smartphone, but it can be opened to access a larger screen with dimensions rivalling a tablet.[18] However, despite several years of consumer availability (Samsung released the first Fold in 2019), foldable phones have not made a significant impact on the global smartphone market. Perhaps this relates to their more complex relationship to the hand and body, but it could also derive from their uncertain status between phones and tablets or their pricing at multiples above that of other smartphones.

Surface as Skin

Returning to aspects of grip and touch developed with the iPod, it is important to recognize that, even as this device seemed in many ways to unite with the user's body, it was promoted as an independent body. While the iPod's form and proportions could conform to the hand as an integral part of the body, its sensitive – and even fragile – surface functioned as a zone of diverse interactivity between its body and that of the user.

From the start, the iPod's surface was fetishized by Apple and Apple customers alike. The first iteration of the iPod was sheathed in a white plastic face and stainless-steel back. "It was … not just everyday white but a stunning, luminous, brilliant, attention-getting white," write tech journalists Jeffrey S. Young and William L. Simon.[19] Later versions, including the iPod nano and iPod mini, were faced in aluminum. These metal surfaces, particularly the polished back, were prone to scratching (see figure 3.4).[20] "Without a case, that shiny, mirrored metal back would start attracting scratches and dings as soon as you took it out of the box," recalls *Macworld* writer Christopher Phin. In language that resonates with Winnicott's theory of transitional objects, Phin continues, "But to me, an iPod whose metal case has been dulled by wear and by use is a thing to cherish. As a face lined with wrinkles and bearing the evidence of a life lived can be as beautiful as a child's, so your iPod's ravaged visage is just as lovely as it was when you first prized it from its box."[21]

Apple fetishized the delicate, reflective surface of the iPod by offering engraving on the back of the case for customers purchasing the device through Apple's online store. Engraving distinguished the object as valuable and personal. Apple enthusiast Steven Levy explains in his book on the iPod, "With all your music at hand, in an enclosure to die for, the personal experience of the iPod goes beyond mere listening. It's almost a relationship. So maybe it's understandable that people often cement the relationship by personalizing the iPod itself. This helps explain the popularity of Apple's program that offers free engraving."[22] While potentially

Figure 3.4
The stainless steel back of an iPod, with scratches and an engraved quotation from William Shakespeare's *Hamlet*.

enhancing the object's value for its owner, engraving diminished the object's resale value. "This is the iPod equivalent of a tattoo, so think very carefully, as you're stuck with it," one iPod guide explained in 2004.[23] An engraving industry trade magazine picked up on the trend, noting that "those who really want to 'trick out' their devices are turning to laser engraved tattoos," and that iPods were the leading electronics to be brought to engraving shops for this service. An engraver told the magazine, "[You're] able to take a customer's iPod that millions of people own and make it unique to that customer's tastes. Really, you're tattooing a product in an incredibly personal way for customers."[24]

As the iPod took over the portable music player market – selling one hundred million units in five and a half years[25] – it created a base of unusually loyal users. By 2006, over a thousand accessories were available for the iPod, many tied to the device's case and surface. Levy notes the popularity of "literally dressing the devices, like a doll or a small pampered dog," either with homemade outfits or cases produced by luxury brands such as Prada or Christian Dior.[26] Of note, however, are those products that evoked epidermal connotations of the surface, including (non-engraved) "tattoos" and "skins" for the device.

When Apple partnered with HP in 2004 to develop an iPod that would appeal to PC users, HP's iteration of the device was nearly identical to what users could buy from Apple. To differentiate the product and generate independent profits, however, HP created iPod tattoos that were printable on HP printers. *PC Magazine* described these as "removable skins that wrap around the iPod … [and] personalize the device."[27] Tattoos based on supplied designs or created by the user themselves could be printed on specialized sheets for HP printers. "That would transform your plain white iPod into something that was one of a kind and all the more cool," explains Steve Stoute, whose company collaborated with HP to develop the proprietary product.[28] Other "tattoos" for the iPod included stickers that could be applied to create patterns across the surface, which were more or less permanent modifications to the case. As one product reviewer explained, "stickers may disfigure it for good," an outcome confirmed by at least one tech blogger at the time.[29]

As a form of body modification, tattoos historically have represented one's membership in a group or culture while often also differentiating the self from others. In describing tattooing as a social practice, sociologist

Michael Atkinson identifies it as an example of body redesign projects. "While other types of body projects involve foresight, planning, reflexivity, and self-awareness, redesigning body projects generally involve the highest level of commitment," Atkinson explains. "Redesigning body projects are hyper-expressions of personal understandings about one's cultural location [and are] outwardly displayed according to the (perceived) social reaction elicited in specific contexts of interchange."[30]

Naming these decorative device accessories "tattoos," rather than "appliqués" or "stickers," implies the media object is a body and its surface is skin. It also frames applying and displaying these designs as a potentially subversive and countercultural activity. Through much of the twentieth century, tattoos connotated deviance in Western contexts. They were the realm of sailors, criminals, carnies, and motorcycle gangs. Connotations have changed significantly in the twenty-first century as tattoos have become socially acceptable and even banal consumer items. At the time of the iPod's success this shift to cultural convention was underway, but not complete.

If tattoos, cases, and engraving emphasized the iPod surface as a place for the expression of individual identity – whether that be the identity of the owner or the identity of the object (as with the costuming mentioned by Levy) – the development of "skins" for iPods brought the device's surface into focus as a zone for haptic sensitivity and interaction. At the height of the iPod's popularity, "scores" of third-party companies manufactured skins for the device.[31] Unlike other types of cases, skins were not snap-on frames or envelopes with flaps, but sheer, stretchable protective covers or sleeves made of malleable molded silicon. To enclose the iPod in a skin, the user would pry open the silicon, slip the device through the screen opening, and wriggle the object in the case until it fit snugly.[32] Because they were thin, stretchable, and close-fitting, skins offered the protection of a case while retaining the component of fit so critical to the iPod's identity. Descriptions and reviews of skins in tech magazines referred to their "grippiness" as an asset.[33]

Design theorist Juliette Kristensen has noted that the advent of skins "explicitly connects the iPod to flesh, to being alive."[34] Like the epidermis, some skins even included "heat-ventilation pores" to dissipate the thermal energy produced by the hard drives that differentiated iPods from most other MP3 players.[35] Appreciating the significance of these skins to young iPod users, a 2011 health and hygiene book meant for teenagers approached the subject of human skin through this "techno-focused skin." It claimed an iPod skin not only protects the device but also "tells the outside world something about your personality. In a way, your natural skin does the exact same thing," it asserted.[36]

Like adhesive tattoos, skins were not only a protective layer but also a style choice, coming in any number of motifs and designs. In the anthropomorphism that suffuses descriptions of iPods of the period, one reviewer wrote about a new skin for their iPod: "My iPod mini was living a lie. Though blue on the outside, it had always felt pink on the inside. Perhaps it needed to express itself. Or perhaps it was just tired of being scratched up in my pocket. Either way, I knew it was time to get a case for it."[37] (Indeed, the tone and perspective here is strikingly similar to "A New Dress for KIM," the computer hobbyist article – quoted in chapter 1 – about building customized computer cases nearly three decades earlier!) The gendered aspect of pink and blue casing described in the review also resonates with the account of Connie Guglielmo, a tech reviewer present at Steve Jobs's unveiling of the iPod in October 2001. Guglielmo remembers asking Jobs about adding a case to protect the device. "What for? It fits in your pocket," Guglielmo recalls Jobs responding. After showing Jobs she didn't have pockets and explaining that people might keep them in purses and the like, she claims Jobs walked away without comment. When she got home, she took the matter in hand and sewed a case for the new device.[38]

A Sensitive Touch

In analyzing the iPod's design, user interface researcher Guy Julier emphasizes the special interface of the click wheel in the iPod's "transition from visual appearance, through tactile engagement, to aural immersion."[39] A raised circle on the device's face, the click wheel – like the hard drive – distinguished the iPod from most other portable music devices. As users turned the wheel, the device would scroll through its contents within a category (e.g., artists, albums, songs). The click wheel was mechanical on the first version of the iPod and moved on ball bearings. For the second generation and those that followed, Apple replaced it with a touch-sensitive wheel (see figure 3.2). Developed in partnership with Synaptics, Inc., the new wheel accomplished two things. First, it allowed users to move through categories and options simply by stroking the wheel. The user no longer needed to apply pressure – the lateral movement of a finger in contact with the surface would suffice. Second, the wheel became virtually flush with the device surface.[40] If the surface of the iPod could be skin-like, then the surface was now more similar to living skin as its capacitive technology acted like nerve endings, alerting the device to respond to slight contact and surface movement. Julier explains that "an exchange between human manipulation and electronic responsiveness is embedded into the design of the product via the outer skin of the object and, in particular, via the surface of the click wheel." He asserts this skin-like aspect is further reinforced through silicon skins.[41] In fact, skins typically would have a cut-out for the wheel to allow direct finger contact as human skin would meet the responsive skin of the device itself.

Since the 1990s, touch-based human-computer or human-machine interaction primarily has encompassed two rival configurations of interfacing: resistive and capacitive. Although they may seem similar (even identical) in activating surfaces that recognize and respond to the user's finger contact, resistive and capacitive systems have fundamental differences with strong affective consequences. Resistive systems involve two surface layers of thin, conductive filaments forming a grid. These layers include a resistive film, with a small gap between them and a low electric voltage passing through one layer. When pressure is applied from outside – as with a stylus or a finger pushing down on a screen – the electrified lines make contact with the perpendicular rows of lines below, triggering a circuit. The system identifies the coordinates of this contact on the grid through pulsed signals. Such screens dominated the touch screen electronics market until the early 2010s, being a cheaper and more robust option for consumer and commercial devices. Most touch screen ATMs and electronic games in the 1990s and 2000s, for example, employed resistive screens.[42] Likewise, the touch screen PDAs of the 1990s – from the Communicator and Newton to the PalmPilot and Visor – used resistive systems. In fact, the dominance of the stylus with these PDAs was due, in part, to the firm and precise pressure requirements of these screens.

Today, smartphones, watches, and tablets regularly use capacitive interfaces. Capacitive systems also employ a grid of filaments in layers. The grid parallels low-voltage capacitors. When users touch the top layer of the grid, their bodies create another capacitor, since human skin conducts electricity. The coordinates of this electric signal are recognized by the grid. Capacitive screens are far more sensitive than resistive ones, since they do not require pressure. They also make multi-touch commands (like pinching to zoom) possible. However, they can lose effectiveness when a user wears gloves or the surface gets wet, both of which diminish cutaneous conductivity.

Capacitive sensing would be popularized with the iPhone's touch screen in 2007, channeling nearly all interactivity with the device and its apps through the conductivity of the human finger. Nevertheless, capacitive sensing had already proved itself as a reliable and pleasurable means of user-device interaction with the iPod's click wheel. Part of the pleasure of capacitive screens is the sense that one interacts with an object *through* its surface. That is, at a psychological level, we feel we are tapping the button, link, photo, or keyboard represented on the screen rather than the transparent glass or plastic that covers it. With the iPod, however, the touch-sensitive wheel suggested one was caressing the body of the device to trigger responses and events. The user could adjust the volume or move to the next song with a short, light stroke of the surface that did not even require the user to interact visually with the iPod's small screen.

The electrical conductivity of human skin has been a rich topic of psychophysiological research that explores the correspondence between shifting emotional and psychological states and fluctuations in skin conductance. When our brain responds positively or negatively to outside stimuli like sounds or images, or even certain social circumstances, such as performing before an audience, it can trigger autonomic nervous system arousal. This arousal impacts how conductive the skin may be. In fact, monitoring this electrodermal activity has become a useful tool for evaluating physiological symptoms of psychological processes, measuring attention, habituation, and conditioning, as well as assessing feelings of pleasure, stress, disgust, and sympathy. Electrodermal activity monitoring has been employed to study consumer preferences, aesthetic responses, and even moral decision making.[43] Known as "skin conductance response" (SCR) testing, the procedure detects changes in electrodermal activity as indications of emotional response to outside stimuli such as visual or aural cues. These tests can detect positive, neutral, or negative responses to unconscious stimuli, as when images of potential threats (e.g., snakes, spiders, or enraged faces) are flashed before a subject for as little as thirty milliseconds.[44] To collect this data, SCR tests often involve attaching electrodes to a subject's fingertips or hands to detect slight surface changes.

Skin conductivity, then, is not a stable constant in human physiology. It not only fluctuates with other bodily processes and states but is also tied to (and indicative of) our passing emotions. To build a device whose opaque surface responds to our skin conductivity in minute and certain ways (like lighting up and "winking," as Jones described it) can produce positive physical responses and emotional states in itself.[45] Like petting a small animal, interacting with an iPod by stroking the surface with the side of one's thumb as it conformed to the hand could in itself border on a therapeutic act. Moving the finger along the surface as though caressing ultra-smooth skin is sometimes visually reinforced in touch screen personal media by the aesthetics of apps and operating systems. For example, the iPhone's original graphical user interface animated the screen surface as a reactive skin with the pull and pressure of body contact between user and object, producing visuals of tightening and lightening similar to the physiological changes in epidermal tissue and capillary action under tension and release through intermittent, localized pressure. Referred to as "rubber-banding," Apple's visual effect of the stretching and snapping back of the screen image would occur when scrolled information reached its end and the user's finger would lift from the screen surface. One tech journalist described it as "a stretchy, whimsical snap back effect."[46]

Such characteristics suggest a regular, inter-corporeal intimacy between hand and device. Apple considered rubber-banding so fundamental to the iPhone experience that it filed patent infringement lawsuits against Motorola and Samsung for employing similar interface effects, eventually winning a one-billion-dollar judgment against Samsung.[47] Android operating systems have incorporated their own effects suggestive of the screen image as a flexible and highly sensitive living membrane. Android 12 introduced a stretching effect where, when a user reaches the end of a scroll but continues to drag their finger, the elements on screen (such as a group of icons) will appear to stretch apart vertically or horizontally. Systems prior to Android 12 had an edge-glow effect for this action, which suggested the phenomenon of unequal blood flow in skin capillaries under pressure or tension.[48]

All of these effects visually reinforce what media scholar Alexandra Schneider has called the "becoming skin of the screen" in touch screen devices' production of tactile visuality.[49] Coupled with capacitive sensing, where the slightest touch of the finger is registered, understood, and acknowledged by the device, these effects can produce a strong psychological draw and build dependence on the device as a responsive being. From these small, frequent interactions, the user may infer a similar sensitivity and affective need in the device. That is, its skin seems to behave like our skin, so perhaps its interactive needs are similar to ours (and to those of other living beings). This mimics the processes of "affiliative touch," the pro-social, deliberate skin contact between people that comes from actions like caressing.[50] Affiliative touch is known to reduce stress and negative feelings, and research suggests that its affective power comes from "low-threshold mechanosensitive" fibres in our skin that best respond to a "gentle stroking touch," much like capacitive surfaces.[51]

While logically we see the device as a plastic and glass tool, these micro-interactions (combined with other features, such as facial recognition) can build a sense of the device's mutual, affective need that can be soothing to us, even as it may reinforce dependency that augments power imbalances in data extraction and assetization. It is important to recognize that user-device interaction based on conductance – initiated with the iPod and continuing through so many of our devices today – could also become a pathway to greater biometric data collection. These pleasurable effects of the surface, in essence, not only may distract us from the underlying processes of political and economic power concentration, but they may also contribute to them as data about our bodily conditions and changes are harvested from these superficial moments of contacts. It may not be far-fetched to imagine a future of capacitive devices that will detect and react to touch while measuring and assessing electrodermal activity to determine arousal by screen content and infer mood. Capacitive interfaces potentially open the door to user-device interactions that start with the simple recognition of touch by the screen as a command, but progress into algorithmic evaluation of affective states and psychological conditions based on minute skin conductivity measurements. This, in turn, could reshape device response and interface options to conform to, change, or even capitalize on a user's perceived emotional state for additional data extraction and exploitation.

Along these lines, as early as 1999 researchers at MIT's Media Lab developed the "galvactivator" as a consumer-level "affect-sensing wearable technology" to measure such bodily activity.[52] "The galvactivator has many potentially useful purposes, ranging from self-feedback for stress management, to facilitation of conversation between two people, to new ways of visualizing mass excitement levels in performance situations," the Media Lab's project description stated.[53] Similar assessments could be made by a hand-held or wearable touch-activated device. In any case, what these approaches and activities suggest is that touch-based interaction need not be simply a matter of controlling representations at the surface, but also a process of affect and adjustment expressed through the continual, modulated contact between user and device.

Vibration and Haptic Feedback

Smartphone producers integrate haptic feedback across their systems both to create different effects as users engage with the device and to signal changes in the device apart from the user's direct intervention (e.g., the reception of incoming data, etc.). Haptic feedback notifies the user that a certain operation is activated or complete and also suggests the device is alive. When writing about an LG Android phone's haptics in 2018, a *Verge* reviewer commented that "the vibration motors and actuators are used throughout the system in a fun, playful way – you'll feel cute little bumps when swiping away notifications or adjusting camera settings that enhance your connection to what's going on behind the pixels." The review continues, "Apps become so much more responsive and fun to use that going back to other phones makes you feel like you're holding an inanimate brick. Which you are, of course. But true haptic feedback can do a good job of convincing you otherwise." It concludes, "Once you've used a phone with proper haptics, other devices just feel dead inside."[54]

Haptic feedback is common in many devices and systems. Gaming hardware regularly exploits vibration – synchronized with visuals – to project the user "into" the game. The performativity of these devices belongs to a larger history of haptic feedback in virtual reality systems that came to the fore in the 1990s.[55] Hand-held game controllers provide haptic feedback for any number of game genres. A vibrating controller may simulate recoil in a point-and-shoot game, or collision impact in a racing game, or simply bumping against walls, people, or other boundaries in the corresponding animation. Whatever the case may be, haptic feedback here is principally a synchronized component of screen-depicted game environments. As such, a controller without vibration might make the game environment less realistic or immersive but probably would not bring the gamer to say the controller felt "dead inside," to return to the foregoing description of phone feedback. (Of course, one can play games on a phone that include these game effects. Here the device is both screen and controller – an integrated game environment.)

Vibration as a means of notification developed quite early in the history of networked portable media, first emerging with personal pagers. By and large, the pager as a communication tool and social practice has fallen through the cracks of media history (there is no book-length history of the pager, sadly), yet pagers played a critical role in the development of portable, personal telecommunications. Popular in the 1970s and 1980s, pagers were small devices (about the size of a bar of soap) that would fit in the pocket or be attached to a belt. They allowed users to receive phone notifications and messages while on the move. Given their use in contexts where their buzzing or beeping could be a distraction or interruption, pagers were also designed to vibrate via embedded motors that rotated tiny cylinders to produce vibrations resonating on the surface of the device.[56] In cellphones, vibration features originally were construed as an aid for hearing-impaired users, but eventually became a major component of user-device interaction for all. Whereas sound cues alert not only the device user but also bystanders (unless, of course, the user is using earphones or buds), dissolving the intimate relationship with the device, haptic feedback builds intimacy through inconspicuous bodily interaction that easily excludes those nearby.

Haptic feedback has become diverse and subtle through a range of vibration scales, intensities, durations, and patterns that figure into any number of device features and interactions, creating a nuanced interplay of bodies that can communicate without resorting to visual or aural stimuli. It can also imitate the typical actions of sentient beings. A feature such as

Samsung's "Alert when phone picked up" can represent the phone as a sleeping and waking device. As Samsung describes it, "Set the device to notify you about missed calls and messages by vibrating when you pick it up."[57] While the effect alerts the user to the device's reception of new information, the device's behaviour of rapidly and minutely shaking when lifted by the user replicates the reflexive reactions of living beings when their slumber is abruptly disrupted. It implies the device needs the user to give it attention and calm it. (Recall the definition of neediness cited in the introduction as "marked by want of affection, attention, or emotional support.")[58]

While the user can break the device's somnolent peace at any time, conditions such as "phantom vibration syndrome" can disturb the peace of users as their own bodies have become finely tuned to the haptic cues of these attendant and closely kept devices. Phantom vibration is a perceived haptic cue from a device that is not vibrating and may not even be close by when the sensation occurs. As Sherry Turkle has noted in her interviews with school students, "Even when [their phone] isn't on their person, when it has been banished to the school locker, for instance, they know when their phone is vibrating."[59] The syndrome amounts to "either a misinterpretation of sensory stimuli or, in the absence of sensory stimulation, a tactile hallucination," states a study by Michelle Drouin and others.[60] As an easily recognizable, relatively common occurrence, phantom vibration is a remarkable indication of the way personal media devices can powerfully condition and change our very being. We adapt to our devices, to their properties and affordances, such that certain sensations in the body or physiological changes may be reflexively understood in relation to them, even when they are not at hand. A study of phantom vibration among US university students in 2012, for example, found that nearly 90 per cent of those surveyed had experienced the phenomenon. Additionally, 40 per cent had experienced the phenomenon weekly, and more than a quarter experienced it *every day*. Despite – or perhaps because of – the prevalence of the phenomenon, few respondents were especially concerned. In fact, 91 per cent found it either not bothersome or only a little bothersome.[61] When attached to the wrist, a device's vibration can feel like the body itself alerting the user, similar to the effect of phantom vibration, further confounding the physical and psychological boundary between user and device.

Philosopher Robert Rosenberger has explored the significance of phantom vibration through the theoretical lens of phenomenology as an example of "bodily-perceptual habituation." In their scrutiny of the body-device relationship, earlier phenomenologists Maurice Merleau-Ponty and Don Ihde considered how pre-digital devices such as a cane or eyeglasses could become either an extension or a transparent addition to the body and its sensory capacities.[62] Rosenberger argues that the smartphone functions similarly. It becomes absorbed into the sensory capacity of the body and as such conditions the body for phantom vibration. Rosenberger describes this as a process of "sedimentation" in which "our past experiences build up (like sediment solidifying into rock) to provide a pre-set context of significance through which our experiences occur."[63] While Rosenberger suggests that users interpret the vibration – whether real or imagined – as a "bid for attention posed by another person *through* the vibration of the embodied phone," we could just as easily argue that this haptic feedback can be read as the phone itself seeking attention, since vibration also can be triggered by alerts and notifications from the device, its operating system, and basic app settings not tied to communication with others.[64] Calendar alerts, system update notifications, and low battery warnings are common examples.

In conclusion, across ideas and features of fit, touch, and vibration the personal media devices that accompany us throughout the day simultaneously conform and respond to our body. They can merge into our being, only to differentiate themselves at key moments. This contradiction has become commonplace for us, shaping our psyche and how it perceives stimuli. However, our frequent interactions with these devices as *seeing* beings – loaded with lenses, cameras, and motion sensors – can remind us how these devices remain a presence at an ever-slight remove. Unlike the touch and vibration explored here, vision systems work best at a distance, even a short one. They can instill a sense of surveillance – a looking *at* or a looking *after* the user. These conditions, and how they emerged, will be taken up in the next chapter.

CHAPTER 4

Face to Face

The convergence of the human face and networked digital technologies has become a political and social battleground, with their intersection in personal media devices as a potential ground zero. As the bodily feature that is both the most distinctive and most regularly on view, the face has become the target for intense automated optical and algorithmic scrutiny. This process has taken place in laboratories and institutions, including schools and hospitals, but more and more it has enveloped and permeated other public places, such as retail shops, streets, transportation hubs, and parks.[1] Through machine learning and neural networking, facial detection and recognition systems have become sophisticated enough to isolate the faces of multiple moving people in busy spaces and match them in real time against vast databases of identified individuals. China has been at the forefront of these efforts, installing integrated networks of cameras to track populations. Facial recognition systems have been used effectively in China toward goals as diverse as identifying and fining jaywalkers to systematically tracking ethnic minorities.[2] Social justice movements have included calls to "defund facial recognition" as an increasingly pervasive technology that, in conception, design, and implementation, is fundamentally biased and inextricably bound to systemic racism and its modern development of machine vision to track and oppress individuals and populations.[3]

One of the leading tools in the development, refinement, and promotion of facial recognition systems is not housed in the research centres of governments, universities, media conglomerates, or start-ups, however, but can be found in our pocket or strapped to our wrist. In the camera-equipped smart devices that we regularly use to craft, record, and circulate our image, the ties between personal media devices and the face have become more and more complex. Diverse and dynamic facial recognition and tracking systems exploit and reshape the relationship between personal media and their users, shifting emphasis away from the user's touch or voice to their face as the new frontier of interface development.

Representing the face as a means of personalizing media has a long history in digital interfaces. Apple's "happy Mac" Macintosh icon of the 1980s and 1990s was a groundbreaking visual feature in the development of affective bonds between users and their desktop computers. "Waking up" when the unit's power switch was flipped, the screen would reassure the user that all was functioning properly during boot up by displaying the small, centred image of a Macintosh computer with its tiny screen converted into a smiling face (see figure 4.1). In an era when personal computers routinely were turned off when not in use, this waking representation suggested the computer was less a machine than a counterpart or friend. As Steven Levy recalls on first seeing this Macintosh start-up sequence, "Until that moment, when one said a computer screen 'lit up' some literary license was required."[4]

Optical detection systems with the potential for facial recognition also harken back to the earliest days of personal digital media. One of the first peripherals for the Altair 8800 – that legendary microcomputer kit considered in chapter 1 – was the Cyclops Camera from Cromemco. Produced in 1975, the Cyclops generated only a 32x32 pixel image, but the device was not much larger than a canning jar, making it easily portable. Cromemco's catalogue explained that the Cyclops could be used in conjunction with a microcomputer and TV to produce a live camera image. But as an "optical data digitizer," it could also be used for "surveillance or pattern recognition" and "automated control systems."[5] This unites artificial visual recognition with personal digital media (at least in concept, if not very practically) at the dawn of personal computing. A *Popular Electronics* cover story on the Cyclops promoted it for surveillance use in conjunction with the Altair 8800. "The combination could be used to build a security system that

Figure 4.1
The colour Happy Mac icon that appeared on Apple Macintosh computers from 1995 to 2001.

Figure 4.2 *Opposite*
An advertisement for the Cyclops digital camera from Cromemco, published in *Computer Notes* in January 1976.

would operate on the basis of a person's appearance," it explained.[6] This description, though general, suggests the possibility of digital visual recognition tied to the physical markers of the face, just as personal media today regularly employ facial recognition locks and alertness detection systems to identify their users and adjust the interface according to visual cues signalling the degree of interaction. The idea of personal observation, recognition, and analysis is in fact succinctly represented in the marketing of the Cyclops. An advertisement from 1976 (see figure 4.2) depicts Cromemco's diminutive camera alongside a pair of thin-rimmed eyeglasses that the consumer might associate with refinement, scrutiny, and intellectual pursuits. The Cyclops, this pairing suggests, can study and read images as carefully as we might study and read texts. Indeed, expanding on the possibility of its human identification capabilities, *Popular Electronics* suggested that "this approach also opens up a brand new and exciting area … a digital computer that has 'vision.'"[7]

Precedents like the Cyclops remind us that, although the increasing presence of lenses, optical mapping, and motion sensing equipment in personal media is transforming our devices into continuously observing objects, symbolic and technological representations of such capabilities were already in place at the earliest stages of personal digital media development and use. The possibility not only of a seeing device but also one endowed with the power of recognition (whether real or imagined) was bound into the idea of what might make consumer-level digital media even more deeply personal.

With the recent rise of a more visually reciprocal relationship between devices and their users, however, two areas of face-based optical interaction have gained prominence. The first is the production of photographic self-images (i.e., selfies) through a device's optical recording systems. The second is the use of facial recognition and tracking through optical sensing and recording systems to unlock devices and gauge user attention. These areas will be considered across this chapter and the next, since together they illustrate the practical scope and social consequences of such optically powered forms of user-device interactions and data generation. On their own, however, each represents the "seeing" device in a significantly different way. The use of the device for producing photographs of the self, for example, is a deliberately interactive performance. Upon opening the app to take a photo, the user may exercise a strong level of conscious control over the device, even as features embedded in both the app and the device provide varying levels of automated responses and limitations. Employing facial recognition and tracking systems, by contrast, requires significant user decision-making in the interactive process only at the moment of set-up. Thereafter, these systems typically run constantly and require little more effort from the user than aligning their face – intentionally or not – with the field of a device's sensors. Accordingly, awareness of the device's role in the exercise of techno-political power may be masked by the initial wonder of the device "seeing you and only you." The subsequent convenience of its functioning in this physically close encounter can occlude the reality of off-device networked processes and data extraction potentially interceding between user and object as they interact.

These two modes of optically based interaction bear significantly different connotations as well. The selfie is often made to be seen by others, while a facial recognition system is typically construed by the user as a visual interaction limited to the device. Nevertheless, as will be explored here, these practices and supporting technologies have become interrelated in building an affective, complicit relationship between users and their devices. As both modes involve the user facing the device and its optical sensors to capture an image of the user's face, they contribute to an interdependent relationship between device and user based on frequent, personalized recognition and response through face-to-face exchange as the basic condition for more extensive interaction.

Lens, Screen, and Mirror

Among the most common and well-known visual interactions between users and the lens of the personal media device is the production of still- and moving-image selfies. A selfie may be any photographically recorded image of the self that a user takes to represent their life or express their subjectivity.[8] As the genre's name suggests, typically the user figures prominently in the image, with their face a central element. These photographs and short videos may be shared on social media apps and platforms such as Instagram, TikTok, Snapchat, WhatsApp, Discord, or X. One of the most celebrated and disparaged interactive personal media practices, making selfies epitomizes a dialogic unification of user and device in engaging and navigating affective networks. The selfie's popularity, both as a visually creative practice and as a means of social networking through portable digital media, attests to the significance of the user-device relationship as a critical building block of contemporary identity. Since making and sharing selfies first came to mainstream attention in 2013, however, tactics and aesthetics have evolved and expanded in response to shifts in both social and technological affordances.[9] Making selfies can involve elaborate mise en scène, carefully chosen filters and effects, including other people in the frame, and even involving production crews (or at least a friend or two enlisted as assistants) to convey the codes of professional travel, fashion, or documentary photography. For those who have made the selfie part of a more extensively mediated persona for professional reasons or profit – as with celebrities or influencers – production and circulation of these seemingly intimate or offhand images may operate within an elaborate and finely tuned plan of narration, promotion, and marketing.[10]

These possibilities aside, the selfie as it is most commonly imagined remains a self-portrait the user takes by directly manipulating their device and its controls with their hand at the moment of exposure.[11] This type of selfie – perhaps still its most frequent form – can be accomplished by holding the device at more or less arm's length, often at a high angle or eye-level, with the lens turned toward the user (see figure 4.3). Alternatively, it can be made by posing before a mirror while holding the device and angling the lens to capture the user's reflected image. Both types of selfies are common, although the mirror selfie was especially prevalent when devices were equipped only with rear-facing cameras, as this orientation would allow the user to see themselves (and what the lens "sees") at the moment of production. With both types, however, the particular conditions of production – unlike those of photographing other subjects with these devices – can imbue the selfie with an intimate and even improvisational quality. It is as though the aesthetics of the image are worked out at the moment of its taking, through the shifting but physically interconnected spatial relationships between the user and the device in hand.

Media and culture scholars have produced a rich body of work on selfies and their social role. In particular, researchers have examined the significance of the circulation of self-as-image within social media networks and the effect this may have on the construction of the self within wider structures of social power, especially in relation to gender, race, ability, sexual orientation, and socially and politically marginalized identities.[12] Of frequent concern has been the tendency – especially in the early evolution of selfies – to pathologize the practice in targeting those made by women, queer people, and racialized groups with "'damned-if-you-do and damned-if-you-don't' rules of visual [self] display," according to media scholars Theresa Senft and Nancy Baym.[13] The popular media, as well as some scientific scholarship, have maligned making and sharing selfies as trivial, narcissistic, and even dangerous practices, thereby placing practitioners at risk of social reproach that often enforces prevailing social hierarchies and inequalities.[14]

With this tendency in mind, it is imperative to consider the role technological and design innovation in personal, portable media has played not only in the circulation and consumption of selfies but also in the production of selfies as a meaningful user-device interaction. This practice has changed the user's relationship to the device in significant ways while reinforcing intimacy, flexibility, and reciprocity. Most photographic self-images that circulate through social media platforms – it is important to remember – are rooted in the visual and physical interplay between a user

Figure 4.3
A selfie taken with a Redmi Note phone. The phone and outstretched arm can be seen in the background reflection.

and their device to produce a visual representation of the user that they may share with others as a suitable statement about themselves as an individual. "The phenomenon of the selfie … [is] at once representation (a photo), presentation (a performance), and, importantly, materially and affectively entangled," notes photography theorist Katie Warfield.[15] The nature of this exchange at its material, psychological, and performative levels is critical to the semantic value of any image it may produce. And as with other user-device interactions examined in this book, aspects of selfie making draw on previous forms of mediated interaction between personal objects and their owners while opening the way for implementation and adoption of additional interactive technologies – such as facial recognition and attention awareness features – that can deepen the user's affective relationship with the device.

Writing on selfie practices, social media theorist Jessica Maddox has emphasized self-reliance and expression as fundamental aspects of the production process. Makers of selfies have "agency and control in their own image production because they are no longer relying on an extra person (or, outside photographer) to take the picture for them."[16] That loss of interplay as image maker and subject of the gaze merge into one is displaced, however, by the affordances and limitations of the device as a counterpoint to the maker-subject in shaping production. As the user assumes control of the camera to direct the process themselves, the device and its properties – as socially produced materials, structures, and protocols – function as a source of control as well in offering specific possibilities through material design, technological capacities, and processing configurations.[17] Emphasis on this technological, corporeal, and spatial entanglement of devices and users – central to the production of networked images of the self – lies at the heart of recent digital materialist approaches to the significance of selfies within wider considerations of the user-device relationship. As Warfield argues, "In the case of the selfie … the presumed to be separate entities of body, camera, self, space, and image are considered as a whole entangled phenomenon and their boundaries, and thus distinction from one another, emerge from within the phenomenon."[18] Since self extends across body, device, and image, being is rooted in a union of the three. Making selfies becomes a communicative act, both between user and device, and between the user-device pairing and social media embedded in networks branching out from the device. The self thus emerges through interconnectedness, and the selfie is that visual depiction that not only represents the person, but in its subsequent intersection with social media also represents the person's active acknowledgment of – and engagement with – social interactions through ever-present technological objects, affordances, and infrastructures.

Dynamic shifting of point of view becomes a critical physical and psychological component of this integration. Selfies are specifically about negotiating and expanding point of view, both by capturing the selfie maker's point of view and by transmitting it through telecommunications networks. "What distinguishes the selfie from other photographic genres is its ability to enact intersubjectivity – the possibility for difference of perspectives to be created and this difference to be shared between the image creator and the viewer," theorists Sumin Zhao and Michele Zappavigna explain.[19] While the viewer could be anyone in the selfie maker's social media circles who accesses the image, it can be argued – at least in the first instance – that the viewer articulating, participating in, and negotiating this difference is none other than the device looking back from the maker's hand. The selfie is rich in meaning because it can represent and address both the perspective of the self and the perspective of another (the camera, the viewer). As Zhao and Zappavigna contend, even as the makers of selfies may "look inwardly into 'the self,' they also create a means for the self to engage outwardly with the world."[20] And yet, these perspectives are always entangled. The selfie is constantly shifting across these perspectives, within and between images.

Cultural theorist Anirban Baishya emphasizes the fundamental role of a physical connection between user and device within close spatial proximity for producing these intersecting perspectives. "The connection of the hand to the cell phone at the moment of recording makes the selfie a sort of externalized inward look, and the point of view of the selfie is … that of the hand that has been extended the power of sight," Baishya states in examining the political role of the selfie in South Asia. "The point of view of the selfie seems authentic, because it is as if the human body is looking at itself."[21] The device and user are unified through an exchange of gazes, such that the user constantly sees themselves, at least in part, through the presence and perspective of the device and its gaze. This describes a deeply intimate performativity between user and device as the two interact in the production of an image (and sense) of self for the user. It informs as well – as we will see in the next chapter – the affective import of subsequent user-device visual practices based on optical scanning and recognition systems.

These considerations of the shaping of perception and self through the image-making capacities of personal media devices resonate with earlier psychological and sociological theorizations of the formation of the self through exterior representations and perspectives. Acknowledging this link, technology critic Nathan Jurgenson has asserted that "making a selfie mimics the making of a self." Specifically, it "conveys an intimacy akin to looking in the mirror [and] in the tension between mirror view and external view is the self."[22] Working from sociological theories of the development of the self, Jurgenson emphasizes sociologist Charles Horton Cooley's early twentieth-century work on the role of the mirror – as an object both real and imagined – in the psychological construction of the self as a social entity. Cooley's theory of the foundations and functions of the self describes the shaping of personal identity precisely as producing a "looking glass self." Cooley structures this as a three-step process: first, seeing ourselves ("our face, figure, and dress") in the mirror, then imagining "in another's mind some thought of our appearance, manners, aims, deeds, character, friends, and so on," and, finally, being influenced by this imagined perception such that it affects how we perceive ourselves and how we interact with others.[23] Cooley was careful to note the limits of his analogy, declaring that the example of a mirror "hardly suggests the second element, the imagined judgment, which is quite essential." He explained, "the thing that moves us to pride or shame is not the mere mechanical reflection of ourselves, but an imputed sentiment, the imagined effect of this reflection upon another's mind."[24] His theory is useful not only in understanding the potential power of making and sharing selfies but also in considering the potential sense of necessity for doing so within the close, affective relationship that can arise between an individual and their networked device.

Cooley presents the mirror as a static, unchanging object, however, a condition that diverges from the typical circumstances of selfie production and its relationship to the mirror in at least two important ways. First, there are the affordances and dynamic capacities of the device as it represents what is presented before it. That is, while the screen provides an image of the world in front of it, that image is not a simple reflection of light but rather a continually changing computational output converting data retrieved from light sensors into a more or less accurate and readable image of the space and objects present before the lens. Its image may be mirror-like, but it's certainly no mirror, in the strict sense of the term. The image it makes of the object before it amounts to an interpretation by the device, based on the specifications of its hardware *and* the human-written and edited coding of its software. This difference makes the device image something of a fusion of the steps presented by Cooley. We see "our face, figure, and dress" already being interpreted by the device as it calculates and adjusts the image in real time, much like the production "in another's mind [of] some thought of our appearance, manners, aims, deeds, character, friends, and so on."[25]

The second divergence from Cooley's scenario is the shifting spatial relationship between the device and the user in the production of this image, as the two are materially connected in the process of posing and taking photos. The device is not simply an objective, fixed image of a space as one would get with a mirror hanging on a wall, but rather it is intimately involved in the process of self-development and self-exploration as it moves with the hand and functions as an extension of the body that holds and possesses it in rendering the circumstances and perspectives noted by Zhao, Zappavigna, and Baishya. After this visual exploration of self, the device will very likely go back into the user's pocket, remaining a key psychological and material component of their existence, ever accessible and deployable across differing spaces and circumstances over the course of the day, unlike the bathroom or dressing room mirror that remains on the wall after the user leaves that space.

One of the complexities of the selfie, both as a physical practice and a system of representation, is that the "mirroring" of the user can alternate or be compounded as user, screen-device, and reflecting surface converge and intersect. With this in mind, it is invaluable to tease out the differences and similarities between image-making with rear-facing cameras (embedded in the back of the device), which often involves the use of a mirror, and image-making with front-facing cameras (where lens and screen share the same side of the device), which often allows the user to rely solely on the screen image for organizing shots. These varying conditions, produced in part by technological and design constraints, can contribute to the affective potential and qualities of intimacy of selfie production. Although both circumstances produce an overlap between user and device in the production and performance of self, each entails different spatial relationships and visual parameters in shaping it.

Mirror-based images of the self, in their formal aspects and conditions of production, bear significant similarities with earlier forms of photographic self-portraiture, which often employed mirrors and other reflective surfaces (such as windows or water) as a means of simultaneously seeing and executing the image.[26] The prevalence of mirror-reflection selfies in phone-based self-portrait photography of the first years of social media platforms such as Friendster, MySpace, and Facebook derived in large part from the standardized placement of the camera lens on the back casing of most phones before 2010. Aiming the lens directly at the user's body with a rear-facing camera requires turning the screen away from view, depriving the user of seeing both what is in frame and how the device's sensors and processors are interpreting it (e.g., in reproducing light levels, contrast, and colours). Aiming the device at a mirror, however, allows the user to take in the lens' field of view and compose the image within the mirror frame (see figure 4.4).

This configuration may also allow the user access to the image feed in the screen frame, depending on the orientation of the device in relation to the user (e.g., placing the device slightly ahead and to the side of the face for visual access to both the camera's frame and the mirror's frame). Given the general necessity of a fixed mirror for stable mise en scène, these selfies frequently have taken place in those private spaces where mirrors are most common, such as bedrooms or bathrooms. However, they also may take place in semi-private mirrored contexts encountered across the folds of public, shared space, such as fitting rooms, washrooms, or elevators.

The device's place in the circumstances of mirror-based selfies – acting as the seeing, sharing companion of the bathroom, bedroom, or fitting room – gives it an unparalleled access and intimacy in the construction and expression of self, especially as it relates to the pre-existing social production and meanings of everyday, lived spaces.[27] (In fact, this only intensified during the COVID-19 pandemic as people were confined to their living spaces during lockdowns, curfews, and quarantines.) These images testify to the regular, intimate scrutiny of the self as a visual object within the world as well as the place of the networked device as an integral part

Figure 4.4
A selfie taken in a mirror with a rear-facing camera.

of understandings of the personal, the private, and self-identity as these concepts are produced and managed through such visual encounters.

With front-facing cameras the construction of self through the mirror takes on other meanings, however, where the device itself becomes the surface for the user's reflective gaze. The front-facing lens has fundamentally altered the dynamic between user and device in the performativity of the visuality of self, to produce a newfound mediated interaction. Whereas mirror-based self-images could set the body and the device in opposition to the mirror – forming a triangulation of the three – the front-facing camera reduces the relationship to an opposition of device and body within their shared space.

Across all these circumstances, nonetheless, interaction with the device is strongly determined by physical and technological affordances. For instance, the size, curvature, and placement of the camera lens; the size, aspect ratio, pixel density, and reflectivity of the screen; and the size, placement, and sensitivity of the shutter button all play a role. These amount to material concerns, existing above and beyond any software and network particularities (such as image settings, resolution, filters, and data speeds). When considered together as contributing factors to both the process of image making and its potential results, these affordances point to the strong role that the material conditions of the device can play in the shaping of self-perception.

Writing on the materiality of interactivity, interface theorist Mikael Wiberg states that the user-device relationship "is constantly formed and transformed by three intertwined processes." These are processes of interaction, processes of computing, and the "*materiality of interaction* as an ever-changing process that reflects the entanglement of the other two processes."[28] Repeating the techno-social condition of "entanglement" described by Warfield and other digital materialists, Wiberg points out that this shifts interaction away from "any entity-based model of interaction that focuses on the entities of users, computers, and interaction as only being about turn-taking between these two entities."[29] The typical performative conditions of selfie production – its constant, nuanced adjustments involving user, device, digital processing, and space and environment – abundantly reflect Wiberg's claim of the materiality of interaction as indicative of ever-changing entanglement.

The materiality of making selfies, which may in fact add to the appeal of the practice as an exercise in craft and creativity, reflects not only technological entanglement, but affective entanglement. For example, when applied to the process of representing the self through lens-based personal media interactions, Wiberg's theory of interactivity as constant entanglement resonates with Cooley's, Warfield's, and associated theories of the construction of the subjective self. Just as Cooley envisioned the self as emerging from a three-step process (seeing ourselves in the mirror, imagining our impression on others, adjusting "how we see ourselves and how we behave" based on this imagined perception), Wiberg situates the meaning and value of the user-device interaction not only in the production of this interaction (e.g., a digital image) but in the *interaction as production in itself*. This process-based focus in Cooley and Wiberg (and, indeed, Warfield) is significant because it conjoins entanglement and intimacy. Interactions with objects bear aspects of affective relationships linked to establishing and affirming the subject. In the case of a person before a mirror, or a person before their live image on a hand-held screen, the reinforcement of the subject plays out in the entangled processes of the moment, whatever the subsequent material output may be (if any).[30]

This dynamic process of examining and asserting the self as subject through visual and haptic interactions with a portable device has an important and intriguing antecedent in the material culture of visual media and identity with the popularity of the pocket mirror in modern history as a personal, portable, and versatile image-producing accessory. In terms of intimacy with an object designed for self-visualization in public spaces, the development of the selfie as a relationship between the portable device and the face in everyday life – especially through front-facing cameras – benefits from the development and eventual mass implementation of the pocket mirror. An accessory for the wealthy in Europe from the sixteenth to the eighteenth century, industrial techniques of glass production in the nineteenth century made pocket mirrors – along with the comb and the powder compact – a common item for less affluent people to take with them when they left the house.[31] In writing a history of the mirror, Sabine Melchoir-Bonnet cites a fascinating seventeenth-century text that describes an imagined dialogue between a wall mirror and pocket mirror. This early text already identifies the pocket mirror as a special type of mirror specifically aimed at the performativity of representations of self with others in mind. Whereas the wall mirror is presented in the text as an object simply reflecting a stable representation of the space before which it hangs, Melchoir-Bonnet explains that the portable and adjustable aspects of the pocket mirror position it in the dialogue as "the 'spot counselor' … which was incessantly consulted in order to see if 'the face has all that is necessary to please,' and with which the coquette practiced her gestures." Melchoir-Bonnet adds, "The little mirror was left open to accusations of frivolity and lies, whereas the large one was said to speak the truth of a person."[32]

The significance of the difference between the two mirrors in the text lies in their design attributes as well as presumed use. Each surface likely reflects in precisely the same way, and the user's face in one would look much the same in the other (if distances and lighting were equivalent). But the "little mirror" overemphasizes the face and gestures, while the larger mirror seems to speak the truth because it cannot be physically manipulated by the user, thereby representing the user only within static surroundings unaffected by the user's performance. The potential for making fleeting images of the self through a kinetic interaction with the device – incessantly consulted to examine the face or practice gestures – becomes a cause for concern in the text. Indeed, it is the presumed interactivity, where the user seems to shut out their surroundings in the moment to embark on an exchange with the device itself, that is put into question. The "accusations of frivolity and lies" inveighed against the pocket mirror and its user have lived on, with little modification, in popular assessments of selfie making with personal media devices. As media scholar Chris Broodryk explains, "The ubiquity of the selfie has resulted in criticism of the selfie as narcissistic, superficial and frivolous; there are many instances in which a selfie constitutes moments of perceived indulgence, as when subjects take 'duck face' selfies and 'mirror selfies,' all of which may call into question the perceived authenticity of the selfie."[33]

Interestingly, pocket mirrors were carried by both men and women into the early twentieth century. To entice men, advertisers would produce give-away mirrors backed with images of attractive women promoting any number of products.[34] However, by the 1920s the pocket mirror became associated primarily with women and feminine culture, fuelled by the growing market for consumer cosmetics. In 1927, Kodak sought to exploit the feminine connotations of cosmetics and the mirror in the amateur photography market by creating a line of cameras as female fashion accessories for the "style-conscious woman." Kodak offered the Vest Pocket Vanity Kodak with a matching art deco vanity case that – in the "ensemble" version – was fitted with a mirror and held a compact and lipstick holder (see figure 4.5).[35] Rival manufacturer Ansco created the Photo Vanity, a box camera in a mirror-lined case with lipstick, rouge, powder, and a comb. The Photo Vanity camera could take photos through a notch in its cover even when the case was closed. Furthering the association of makeup and mirror with amateur photography, a cosmetics manufacturer of the period

Figure 4.5 The Vanity Kodak Ensemble as depicted on the front page of Eastman Kodak's *Trade Circular* for October 1928. The Ensemble's mirror is mounted in the open lid, while the camera rests in the bottom of the case.

produced a vanity case with a simulated shutter button to open it and a lipstick tube that resembled a film winder.[36]

While such products would meet their end in the austerity of the Depression of the 1930s, they demonstrate early associations in modern material and visual culture between portable cameras and mirrors as everyday media. The Vanity Kodak couples the image of the self – whether the image for the self as reflected in the mirror or the image for others in the fashion statement of this accessory – with the power of the camera as a machine for capturing images of one's world and existence. "It is the ideal accessory – highly useful, highly ornamental and intensely personal in character," declared one Kodak advertisement.[37]

This history of the pocket mirror as a portable visual device for modern female self-examination and expression – coupled at times to the camera as a visual recorder for women – contributes to the history of gender and visual devices that has helped shape both selfie practices and societal responses to them. From a design perspective, contemporary smartphone screens mimic the mirror as a smooth, reflective glass surface. The push toward "all-screen" phones, where the screen occupies the entire surface of the phone and there is minimal indication of other components (e.g., little or no area along the edge with camera lens or other sensors), completes this convergence of camera and mirror.

Incidentally, the resemblance of phone screens to mirrors has been explicitly invoked since the smartphone's beginnings. One of the first published guides to the iPhone noted not only that the device's touch screen would serve as "your mouse, keyboard, dialing pad, and note pad," but that "you can also use it as a mirror when the iPhone is off."[38] After a front-facing camera was added with the iPhone 4 in 2010, another guidebook pointed out the potential use of the new feature both to make selfies and as a mirror. "This camera has lower resolution, no flash or zoom, but … It's handy for self-portraits (or if you find yourself without a mirror and some lettuce in your teeth)."[39]

Front-Facing Cameras, Enchantment, and Gesture

Front-facing cellphone cameras first appeared in Japan in the 1990s, a time when most phone screens were not much larger than a postage stamp. The feature debuted in Western markets in 2003 with phones such as the Sony Ericsson Z1010 and Motorola A835. Although front-facing cameras would fundamentally change the selfie-maker's relationship with their device, they were initially designed for other purposes.[40] The Motorola A920's front-facing camera, for example, was promoted as "a digital, built in video camera" allowing "real time video calls to friends, family or colleagues."[41] When Apple added a front-facing camera to the iPhone 4, it was similarly marketed as hardware for the FaceTime video calling app. At the phone's unveiling, Steve Jobs emphasized its role in FaceTime but made no mention of its potential use as a camera for still photographs.[42] By 2015, however, Apple would include a default – and undeletable – "Selfies" folder in its iPhone photo albums, to the consternation of some users (perhaps due to the negative connotations of the selfie).[43] In concert with iPhone's Face ID facial recognition system, the Selfies folder would automatically house any photos shot with the front-facing camera that included the camera owner's face.[44]

In its adoption for photographing the self, the significance of the front-facing camera shifted from being a component designed to engage with other people in real-time video interactions *through* the device to a means of interacting individually *with* the device. While a user may take selfies with the intention of sharing them with others, that transaction does not necessarily take place at the moment of production. Whether it's a few seconds or a few hours later, uploading the selfie to a social media platform often remains a separate, subsequent step.

When equipped with a front-facing camera, the device's qualities as a mirror bear new significance. In assessing the special properties and effects of apps using camera-based screen images as real-time mirrors (or as windows, when using a rear-facing camera) media and performance theorist Anna Munster underscores their illusory and affective power in uniting device, image, and body.[45] In a real-time feed, the screen does not reflect surrounding space but rather processes it into material that unites the visual and the haptic for the user. This linking of "media, software, and devices as material concentrators and mobilisers of aesthetic forces and relations," according to Munster, contributes to the way "the app on our phone has become a mode for both affecting other technologies and others in general and for the way the phone affects us." The app's linking of the screen image to the user's surroundings produces an "immediate and affective experience; that is, at the level of sensory perception."[46] The device not only makes the image in real time – with the user's intervention, of course – but the real-time image is always a part of the device. That is, the device's image – what the device "sees" – is available to the user in real time, even when the device is pointed back at the self. I see myself *and* I see myself being seen, even as this "being seen" is accomplished *by myself*.

While the front-facing camera's live feed may produce a laterally inversed image to mimic the familiar view of looking at one's self in the mirror – contributing to what Munster calls "optical illusionism that permeates the visual imaginary of apps" – usually any image it records will not be reversed, thus showing the view from the device as an independent point in space, as though the device were another subject watching the user.[47] As Jurgenson writes,

> Some [photo apps] give you the view that someone looking at you would see, but others flip the image so that it looks like what you would see in a mirror … The apps either produce what others usually see when you are among people or what you usually see in the intimacy and privacy of the mirror. The subtle distinction between these views can help illustrate how making a selfie mimics the making of a self … In the tension between mirror view and external view is the self, and, like the self, the selfie traverses that space, puts it into social circulation.[48]

These circumstances of view and interaction are noteworthy in part because they precede, and in fact often do not require, networked actions of the device as a tool of image circulation. Image-based interaction with the device under these conditions reinforces the self through the user-device relationship regardless of the network, though selfie production often involves subsequent transmission. Unfortunately, much theoretical work on selfies has considered them mainly or exclusively as a component of social media, evaluating the significance of the selfie only in terms of its circulation and engagement with other people. This ignores the affective and psychological significance of interaction with the device. A 2018 study of two hundred US university students found, for example, that while documenting memorable moments and interacting with others were primary motivators for taking selfies, the next most frequent motivations were "entertainment," "creative expression," and "passing time."[49] It is unlikely that a user uploads every selfie they make of themselves. Many more selfies are made than ever reach the internet.[50] While often one exemplary selfie from a series will be uploaded as representative of the user's current circumstances or mood, there are also many occasions and circumstances when a user might make selfies with little or no intention of sharing them. What are we to make of such solitary practices? What significance should we afford them when the resulting images are not shared online? Indeed, they testify to the significance of the device as an integral part of everyday understandings of the self regardless of the presence of others, whether physically or through telecommunications networks.

The highly performative interaction between device and user in the production of selfies can suggest an enchantment with – and of – the technological device. Munster identifies "an entire sense of magic permeat[ing] the smart device" through lens-based interactivity. Her descriptions recall work on technology and enchantment by social anthropologist Alfred Gell, who saw a profound interdependency between technological processes and affect.[51] Focusing primarily on art and handicraft, Gell claimed that "the power of art objects stems from the technical processes they objectively embody: the *technology of enchantment* is founded on the *enchantment of technology* ... Art, as a separate kind of technical activity, only carries further, through a kind of involution, the enchantment which is immanent in all kinds of technical activity."[52] For Gell, these objects were a technology of enchantment because they muster certain technical processes to make things that produce affect or emotion in the viewer or user. Art represents the enchantment of technology to the extent that it "achieves its effect via the enchantment cast by its technical means." As illustration, Gell cited the novel example of a matchstick model of a cathedral that he encountered as a child while visiting the European gothic cathedral on which it was based. The matchstick model was part of the technology of enchantment in serving as an "advertisement" for the cathedral – it enhanced the building's value and presence (at least to an eleven-year-old boy). It achieved the effect through the enchantment of technology, which Gell described as "the manner of its coming into being or, rather, the idea which one forms of its coming into being."[53] In other words, how it was made, the processes and tools and state of mind – at least as this is imagined as the viewer observes this technological product – is part of its power and appeal.

Of course, a selfie is a far cry from a matchstick cathedral. Nevertheless, it may garner its power – producing positive or negative reactions, but rarely indifference – based on its enchantment of technology. That is, the means of the selfie's production involves the maker as the subject who, through the affordances of the technology (literally) at hand, can produce their own image. The connection between the user and the device is not only strong, but also all that is required to create the selfie. This can make it – depending on the viewer – an especially powerful or an especially weak image (contributing to the celebration and ridicule that selfies have incurred simultaneously as a genre). The device adjusts to the user's circumstances through auto settings, the device's sensors may react to the user's wave of a hand, and the device displays the user's image so the user may adjust their body or expression or orientation at any moment – device and user become locked in an exploration of technical capacity and image potential all bound into the representation and expression of the self. Given these circumstances, it is easy to imagine both the widespread appeal of making selfies and the frequent derision of the practice as overly self-involved or self-isolating.

Even the advent and adoption of accessories such as the selfie stick reflect this intimacy of the user-device relationship. First developed in Asia, the selfie stick became popular in Western markets in 2014 (see figure 4.6).[54] Denounced at the time as "vanity-promoting" and a "narcisstick,"[55] the selfie stick permits the user greater diversity and flexibility in the production of images, without ceding the device to the grip of others. "If you've been sightseeing recently, you can probably understand why the device is so popular. With the stick, users no longer have to ask strangers to snap a photo of them, nor do they have to settle for a poorly shot selfie that omits key details and, sometimes, parts of the people in the photo," explains one 2015 article.[56] Selfie sticks are often used to make group selfies – their typical three-foot extension widening the lens' visual scope to accommodate more people. However, the stick also facilitates a solitary practice of making selfies with less physical limitations. Rather than diminishing the intimacy of the user-device relationship, the use of the selfie stick would appear on the contrary to insulate that relationship by warding off interference from those nearby. Indeed, in various media descriptions of the selfie stick when it began appearing in the West much was made of the device as off-putting to those in the environment, with little notice from users too involved in their image-making activities.[57] As one travel journalist wrote, "It isn't necessarily that the selfie or the selfie stick is wrong-headed, but it has helped to foster a culture that is obsessed with constant connection, hashtags and followers, seeing the world through a smartphone screen rather than through their own eyes in the moment that they are actually experiencing it."[58]

It is not only critics who have noted this "obsession" with seeing through the device's eye, however. Smartphone marketing also has promoted this trope, often making the "obsessed" user-device-network relationship of selfie production a centrepiece of ad campaigns. The launch video for Samsung's "awesome is for everyone" Galaxy A campaign in 2019, for example,

Figure 4.6
A person taking a photo with a selfie stick.

is a brisk montage of what appears to be user-produced content full of stunts, visual tricks, and in-device effects. At least a half dozen of the participants appear to be holding the device at arm's length as they shoot themselves getting out of bed, standing on a beach, or wearing surreal face paint.[59] A 2018 video advertisement for Google's Pixel 3 includes scenes of a woman swiping through over thirty images of herself from a single selfie session, another woman taking selfies with the device propped on a surface and held at arm's length, and a user's point of view as the user (in this case, a man) takes a selfie with friends by holding the device at arm's length and tapping his finger on the phone frame.[60] A 2019 campaign for the Galaxy S10 features Thai singer Lisa posing and dancing before her device in multiple spaces, the object rarely leaving her hand as she shoots video and still images of herself from different angles. Interspersed with these images are black screens of bold script urging the audience to "own it, create it, shake it."[61] Finally, a video campaign for Gionee phones in 2017 features Bollywood actor Alia Bhatt singing "Welcome to Selfiestan" as it depicts

Figure 4.7
A screen grab from the Apple promotional video "iPhone 11 Slofies – Introducing Slowmo Selfies," 2019.

Bhatt and other people taking selfies across diverse settings – poolside, at the theatre, at the gym, at the office, in the yard.[62] The selfie appears essential to daily life here, no matter where one is or what one is doing.

When Apple introduced the slow-motion selfie – or "slofie" – with the iPhone 11 in 2019, it produced a promotional video that played with the limits of the selfie as an isolating act between user and device.[63] The ad features a young woman taking a selfie as a steady breeze lifts her hair. Presented from the camera's perspective, the ad depicts her slowly shifting her shoulders and subtly turning and tilting her head as her gaze remains fixed on the lens. As the air current becomes too strong, however, forcing her mouth open and her eyes shut, the video cuts to a wide shot of the woman sitting in a bedroom, holding her phone before her, as a boy – likely her younger brother – aims a hairdryer at her (see figure 4.7). She lowers the phone and looks at the boy, adjusts his aim, then raises the phone and returns to shifting poses as she slowly angles the device. The video closes with a shot from just behind the device, with the phone's back surface in focus as the broadly smiling – but out-of-focus – user holds it with one hand. As she moves the phone, the shot moves with her, the phone remaining steady at the centre. While the boy has contributed directly to the image's production, the audience may infer, ultimately it is only the user and the device that – literally – remain in perfect synchronization, as though they have become one in this process.

The performance of the self with and through the personal media device in such dynamic, material interchanges manifests key aspects of symbolic interactionism, a guiding theory of sociological thought. Symbolic interactionism – present in the work of Cooley but developed more extensively in that of sociologists George Herbert Mead and Erving Goffman – situates the self as a product of the interactions and exchanges between an individual and those crossing their path. Following Cooley's lead, Mead asks, "How can an individual get outside himself (experientially) in such a way as to become an object to himself? This is the essential psychological problem of selfhood or of self-consciousness; and its solution is to be found by referring to the process of social conduct or activity in which the given person or individual is implicated."[64] Mead identifies a "conversation of gestures" as basic to this process, describing it as "social intercourse in which one is addressing other persons and at the same time addressing one's self, and in which one controls the address to other persons by the response made to one's own gesture."[65]

While interacting with a device's front-facing camera can replicate the encounter between a user and a mirror, gesture-based interfacing features – as demonstrated in some of the foregoing advertising examples – create a more dynamic, performative relationship that activates the screen image in dramaturgical or conversational ways (to use the terminology of symbolic interactionism).[66] The image becomes a responsive element, an active audience not only presenting what is before the lens but also reacting to it and generating signs for the viewer. This is the case with auto-focus features, which lock onto conspicuous shapes or objects in the field to determine focal length. The process will often be conveyed to the user through frames appearing on the image.

Although such elements may only be a means of predicting likely image qualities when the photograph is made (i.e., signalling to the user what elements will be in focus, adequately lit, etc.), they can also indicate a visual conversation between user and device. This has been most strongly represented in the performativity of features such as LG's Gesture Shot and Samsung's palm trigger for selfies. As seen in chapter 2's analysis of mouse-based desktop computing as interpersonal exchange, bodily gestures are linguistic elements that have often been employed in interface design to build more intimate, affective relationships between users and digital devices. LG's Gesture Shot, introduced with its G3 phones in 2014, would take a photo or series of photos with the front-facing camera if someone within the frame opened their palm and moved their fingers downward in a movement similar to up-and-down waving.[67] As one LG campaign proclaimed, "Wave a 'Hi,' count till 3 and pose!"[68]

Samsung's palm trigger, found in its Galaxy phones, is a similar visual interaction between user and device meant to activate the photographic process. The Galaxy user needs to lift their hand before the camera and wait for the recognition system to detect it as a hand. This starts the camera's timer. In effect, the gesture functions as both a trigger and a sign. As a Samsung instructional video illustrates (see figure 4.8), the palm trigger embeds the conversation of gestures into the image-making process in clear ways suggestive of traditional gestural communication. This Samsung feature produces conditions that imply a friendly wave from the user at their device, which makes the real-time "reflected" image of a wave in return.[69] At the same time that the gesture can be understood as the action that launches the automatic process of taking a photo, it can also read as an acknowledgment of the device's dynamic gaze. This may feed into the perception of the device as a needy object, one that requires positive social reinforcement from the user to bend to their wishes. You wave to the device, much like a social gesture, and the device takes your photo, much like a reciprocal social gesture. This intimation of a social interaction may explain why one tech reviewer called the palm trigger "a neat trick that you can use to start a timed selfie capture in the front camera, even though you might feel embarrassed doing it out in public."[70]

With these triggering features of LG and Samsung devices, the gesture of mediation within the user-device relationship is endowed with the added social valence of everyday face-to-face signs of greeting easily identifiable both at the technological level (i.e., easily detected by the device's sensors) and the semantic level (i.e., as signs of friendship or acknowledgment). Such gestural affordances open up intriguing possibilities for examining and analyzing precisely how the user-device and user-network relationships can overlap and differentiate themselves, producing related – but potentially distinct – affective links and psychological impacts. When the user is attempting to take a photo of themselves waving to their networked audience of followers, for instance, this gesture-based interfacing can cause confusion

Figure 4.8
A screen grab from the "Taking a Selfie by Showing a Palm" instructional video for Galaxy smartphones.

between device and social network. In this case, the first wave is to the device, and the subsequent wave is to the device *and* the presumed viewer of the image. And throughout this process, it must be remembered that the user is always waving to themselves as a "reflected" real-time, screen-borne image. To the outside observer it may appear as an interaction between the user and device that – because the device's lens is turned back on the user – cuts out the surrounding world, even though the image made from this physical performance is often meant to circulate out into the world, engage viewers, and elicit reactions.

Gender, Children, and "Prescriptions of Practice"

Since the 2010s, hundreds of millions of people have made and shared selfies every year. Although research on this photographic genre has encompassed diverse topics, including migrant activism, branding, and even ostomies, scholarly and popular discussions have frequently gravitated toward the practices of young women and girls.[71] Researchers have considered the selfie as an online extension of existing normative gender codes and practices where, for example, increased audience feedback through likes and comments is often tied to the exaggeration of gender norms and bodily display.[72] Indeed, marketing of photographic technologies and selfies typically features women – sometimes celebrities, but often not – as the posers and takers of photographs. Concentrating on women, the female body, and visualizing gender norms binds these perceptions and discussions to wider issues of body surveillance, media objectification, and self-objectification. As Jurgenson states, "Because social photography is about visibility, it's no surprise that it's also deeply gendered and stigmatized."[73] Perceptions of selfie-making as a female pursuit may be linked to the dominate tropes of the genre – private spaces, self-scrutiny of body image, and a perceived superficiality and vanity. In studying "Insta girl" videos made to convey effective selfie techniques for young women, a team of researchers found that "the techniques these tutorials recommend resemble normative feminine poses prevalent in mass media depictions of women, which characterize them as indolent, childish, and sexualized."[74] Media scholar Anne Burns has stated more broadly that "constructed within popular discourse as a trivial type of image, the selfie is predominately associated with a set of negative female stereotypes relating to narcissism, vapidity, and sexual impropriety."[75] Burns continues, "By naturalizing certain knowledge – such as the narcissistic nature of selfies – as 'truth,' the discussion of selfies acts as a subtle yet significant form of social control and a means for maintaining gendered power relations."[76] The open and popular discussion of selfie-taking tips, suggestions, mistakes, and disasters across social media produces what Burns calls a "prescription of practice" that particularly targets young women.[77] These recommendations and warnings can come into play in the moment of making a selfie. Some of them, such as setting and dress, may involve aspects of milieu and the user's physical appearance. Yet others, such as angle, framing, lighting, resolution, and effects, may involve the specifics of the device and its settings.

The emphasis on the user-device relationship in self-imagery – where social media networks may be available but do not appear integral to the process – as a gendered activity manifests itself most starkly (and disturbingly) in the production of selfie toys and electronics for children. The Explore & More Selfie Phone from Skip Hop, for example, is a phone-shaped mirror with light-up filters for toddlers that simulates "Baby's first selfie!" and "encourages self-recognition at playtime," according to the manufacturer. Marketing images for this selfie mirror posted on Skip Hop's website feature six toddlers with clothing cues (such as pink and blue fabrics) that suggest four toddlers are girls and only two are boys.[78] JaRu's Color Me Cutie Cellfie Time Gloss party favours are smartphone-shaped makeup kits with small mirror "screens" that the company recommends for girls aged four and up.[79] The My Pretend Selfie Set of a toy phone and selfie stick from What Kids Want deploys a pink and purple colour scheme with hearts and glitter in situating itself as the "perfect [toy] for any young girl with a fun imagination."[80] The few products whose marketing leans towards boys are also replete with gender stereotypes. The VTech Kidizoom Flix Selfie Camera features a boy on the front of its box, while the device is shaped to look like a one-eyed blue "alien." The back of the box includes several images of boys and girls – all appearing to be White, incidentally – interacting with the toy. These images are placed against a motif of satellites and planets.[81]

If the relevance of the user-device relationship to the assertion of self-identity through the production of selfies – exclusive of networks – is already reflected in these toys, it reaches perhaps its most extensive representation in the development of a fully functional, digital toy like Kidi Secrets Selfie Journal from VTech, meant for children from six to twelve years old (see figure 4.9). A close examination of the design and functioning of the Kidi Secrets Selfie Journal demonstrates how the affective qualities of personal digital devices in the entanglement of identity and the materiality of technology can be targeted at – and nurtured in – the early stages of the development of personality and identity.

The Kidi Secrets Selfie Journal functions much like an oversized smartphone or small tablet, but it does not have network capabilities. It allows users to enter text in calendar entries, listen to music, interact with virtual pets, and take photographs with front- and rear-facing cameras. It even has a facial recognition lock. As a physical object, it is designed as a stereotypical girl's toy in the contemporary aesthetics of the industry. Its plastic shell is a mix of pastels – pink, purple, and blue – with a glitter finish. The front surface is covered with butterflies, hearts, stars, and flowers. A large heart cut-out is moulded into the plastic below the lens. Just as keeping a

Figure 4.9
The Kidi Secrets Selfie Journal from VTech, 2018.

journal – especially as a young person – often has been seen as a girl's pursuit, the design and marketing of the Kidi Secrets Selfie Journal, as with most of the other toys mentioned here, suggest that selfies are, first and foremost, for girls.

Since it has no antenna and does not allow users to upload or share content, this device is premised on the value and interest of exploring one's identity simply through a relationship with the device. "Protect your thoughts and dreams with the Kidi Secrets Selfie Journal," VTech's promotional materials state.[82] The emphasis on this toy's ability to "protect" the child's thinking and imagination, rather than simply record it, suggests it is a necessary step of self-development and integral to the preservation of the child's being. Without this device, one can infer, their thoughts and dreams are somehow left exposed and vulnerable or, worse, inchoate and underdeveloped.

As they mature, young users will undoubtedly move on to other, more sophisticated networked devices to produce visual and textual content to be shared with others in building their networked self. Nevertheless, through such toys they presumably will have learned the value of self-development and expression, even when confined to the user-device relationship. These toys firmly anchor contemporary identity in the affordances of one's interactive electronic possessions. They set the stage for additional, sometimes more invasive, device features that can develop interactivity in more subtle and troubling ways. Among these are technologies that develop the device's awareness and surveillance of its user, often through similar optical sensing features. Some of these technologies, their affective power and the potential pitfalls they bring, will be described and explored in the next chapter.

CHAPTER 5

Sensing a Presence

As demonstrated in the previous chapter, recognizing ourselves and shaping our visual identity through the personal media device and its affordances is a major component of contemporary media interactivity. However, this process goes both ways. Just as we recognize ourselves through our devices, our devices have developed new ways of recognizing us. Just as we shape a sense of who we are through our device interactions, our devices create an image of us and our behaviour in return. We may play with the camera on our phone, for example, but in a sense our phone can play with us through its visualizing and sensing capabilities. These capabilities often impact our decisions. They encourage us to reshape our actions or behaviour, such as how we move our finger across the screen or how we frame a shot. Perhaps more important, this influence can extend well beyond the moments when we consciously interact with the object as sensor data is collected twenty-four hours a day and can be leveraged to individually shape the device's relationship with its user.[1]

Recognition Systems

The multiple modalities of visual recognition, representation, and affirmation unleashed in the user-device relationship through selfie production have been augmented – but also problematized – by the inclusion of facial detection and recognition systems. This stands as much for the Kidi Secrets Selfie Journal children's toy seen at the end of the last chapter as it does for the Samsung Galaxy, iPhone, and other contemporary smart devices. The popularity of making and sharing selfies made the face a fundamental component of interaction between users and their hardware. In this context, automated facial detection and recognition could be construed as an extension or deepening of the terms of this relationship. Face detection is integral to many photography apps, for example, locating and often enhancing a face within the image field (by adding lighting, smoothing skin, or reducing blemishes) to produce more satisfying selfies. Media critic Alexis Madrigal notes that these automated aesthetic functions are "ubiquitous and low temperature, but no less effective."[2]

In essence, detection and recognition systems represent an algorithmic and overt confirmation – on a regular basis – of the device's acknowledgment and seeming understanding of its user. Often set as a constantly running feature of the device's programming, facial detection and recognition can initiate or facilitate any interaction between the device and the user. This state of permanent, wakeful observation on the part of the device, however, also raises significant concerns around the potential and likelihood for enhanced tracking, surveillance, and profiling as the device can detect, analyze, and record the user's bodily traits and movements (rather than merely the *device*'s movements, as is the case with GPS tracking or cellular tower pinging and triangulation).

Automated facial detection and recognition systems employ algorithms to find, interpret, and match faces. Facial detection systems can scan for the presence of a face in front of the lens to facilitate portrait photography or to gauge a user's level of attention to the device. Facial recognition is most commonly used as a security feature, allowing an owner to unlock their device simply by looking at the screen from relatively close range. Through machine learning in neural networks supported by vast data collection and analysis, these technologies broaden the parameters and meanings of the face-based interactions with devices already established in selfie-making. They build on the existing intimacy and enjoyment – and societal participation – in making selfies and social media videos of the self to forge a relationship in which the device engages and acknowledges the user's face in diverse ways, producing a more nuanced user-device relationship across a variety of daily interactions. The widespread acceptance of such systems – despite potential privacy risks – may lie in the personal, affective qualities they embody and produce. Like selfie practices, they can imply a sense of intimacy and complicity between device and user. They also can intersect with or mimic practices of networked self-imagery, as in the affinities of facial recognition systems with face-scanning games such as those from FaceApp and FaceLab. Continuing advances in emotion recognition and affective computing will likely transform this emphasis on the face and its actions into a relationship more closely resembling that of human face-to-face interactions. However, one can say that existing affordances in portable, face-based visual technologies already have produced circumstances where the face becomes an active player in the interface at a potentially continuous level.

Device-based facial recognition systems represent perhaps the most overt and discussed face-oriented personal media technology today. Facial recognition locking systems have been included in smartphones produced by Apple, Samsung, Google, Huawei, LG, and Asus, among others. Facial recognition features function as a form of acknowledgment and affirmation based on the device's intimate knowledge of the owner as a unique, physical presence. Like many digital technologies addressed in this book, facial recognition capabilities for personal media were developed and marketed well before they became popular. And early on, they were more closely tied to the mobile photographic techniques that would fuel the selfie. In 2005, for example, Japanese electronics company OMRAN produced the OKAO Vision Face Recognition Sensor for portable devices. "Users register their own face image to their unit with the unit's camera. To use the unit, the user simply takes his or her own photo," states a press release from the product's launch.[3] At the time, OMRAN researchers described this technology as part of a larger project of "face understanding" systems, suggesting not only recognition but also comprehension on the part of the device when these visual technologies were employed.[4] In 2011, Google provided facial recognition device locks with its Android 4.0 operating system. Introduced in the Samsung Galaxy Nexus, the feature's frequent failures in recognizing owners' faces and its easy deception by two-dimensional images in the place of an actual face hampered its adoption as a convenient or effective security measure.[5] Facial recognition security systems gained in effectiveness and popularity after 2017, however, when Samsung and Apple introduced more accurate and sophisticated systems in the Galaxy series, the iPhone, and the iPad.

Facial recognition security systems in portable, personal devices have conformed to two basic modelling types: two-dimensional and three-dimensional. For both types, a device's optical technologies compare the visual information gathered by sensors at a particular moment against previously recorded and stored information to determine whether there is sufficient correspondence between the two to warrant unlocking the system. Two-dimensional systems typically rely only on the device's camera to make face images that are then compared to photographic samples created when the security feature was first activated. The OKAO system released in 2005 employed this method. As we would understand it today, it required the user to take a selfie with their device each time they wished to unlock it. This image would then be compared with the initial "registration" image for correspondences in form, proportion, and spatial relationships across features. Samsung Galaxy Nexus also relied on two-dimensional imaging, though its photographing process was automatic. As late as 2023, some personal media facial recognition systems continued to rely on comparisons between two-dimensional images.[6]

Three-dimensional systems produce 3-D scans of the face that are compared to previous 3-D mappings. These systems usually supplement the device's standard camera with an infrared camera and dot projector. For example, Apple's Face ID – available on most iPhone models since iPhone X, as well as on the iPad Pro – employs user proximity and ambient light sensors to determine proper illumination levels for the recognition process. Based on this data an infrared flood illuminator adds supplemental light (if necessary) as the dot projector blankets the face in a pattern of over thirty thousand dots. The infrared camera captures the reflected light from these steps and uses the data to produce a real-time 3-D model of the surface of the face. This is compared to a stored model of the user's face to determine whether a sufficient threshold of resemblance has been achieved to unlock the device. The use of infrared lighting – beyond the spectrum detectable by the human eye – coupled with a rapid processing time of about a second makes these photographic and verification processes virtually undetectable to the user.[7] "Nothing has ever been simpler, more natural or effortless," explained Apple executive Phil Schiller at Face ID's launch in 2017, using language typical to the unveiling of nearly every new personal media technology. However, Schiller went further, declaring that "Face ID learns your face. It learns who you are. And it adapts to you as your face changes over time."[8] His claims suggest a deeper knowledge on the part of the device. It's not just familiar with a facial terrain, Schiller implies, it is familiar with a specific subject – "who you are" – and it can adjust to accommodate this changing self.

Of course, the idea of recognizing – let alone "knowing" – the user has its limits. While personalizing the device relationship at the level of spatial and optical interaction, these features can pose access problems for some users. A significant and widespread example from the early 2020s was the increased use of face masks in public spaces as a response to the COVID-19 pandemic. With the nose and mouth obscured by a mask, users found it difficult or impossible to employ device-level facial recognition systems.[9] Resetting Apple's Face ID with a mask covering only one side of the mouth and nose during the initial scanning process, for example, could allow some users to unlock their devices while subsequently wearing a mask, but this was less effective than full-face recognition.[10] That example points to a greater underlying problem, however: facial recognition locks, which have become increasingly available and popular, cannot be used in those contexts where covering the nose and mouth has long been an ordinary and perhaps necessary aspect of daily life. Indeed, popularizing facial recognition systems has played into hegemonic, mainly Western ideologies that equate full visibility of the face with liberty, equality, truthfulness, and authenticity. This popularization subtends, for example, political debates in France, Italy, Canada, the US, and elsewhere that often revolve around non-Western immigrants and the visibility of the face as a presumed basic requirement of the public sphere and participatory democracy.[11] As such, facial recognition systems on personal devices can contribute to the marginalization of people in circumstances where the face must be covered, whether for health, climatic, cultural, religious, or personal reasons. Here the device may recognize the user in the privacy of their home, but not when their face is partially covered in public, thus technologically reinforcing marginalization and perceptions of face coverings in public spaces as diminishing identity, agency, and social participation. That someone with their face partially covered may be easily recognized by friends and colleagues, for example, but not by the facial recognition system of the device they carry at all times, can also undermine belief in the device "learn[ing] who you are" and "adapt[ing] to you."

Perhaps exacerbating these divisions, the development and accuracy of facial recognition has been greatly aided precisely by the public circulation of the photographed face in the rise of making and sharing images of identified individuals on searchable social media accounts. Uploading selfies, school portraits, headshots, and other photos where the face figures prominently has created a massive resource of facial imagery tied to verifiable identities through traceable account IDs and photo tagging on Facebook, Instagram, X, and other sites. Facebook began using its two-dimensional facial detection and recognition systems – ominously called DeepFace – in 2010 to identify and automatically tag account holders in posted photos. After extended pressure over privacy and tracking concerns, Facebook converted this to an opt-in feature in 2019, before removing the systems entirely from the platform in 2021 and claiming to have deleted all archived data. Google Photos continues to automatically tag faces in its app, having introduced a manual tag option in 2019.[12] By scraping openly available data from social media platforms, companies and institutions developing facial recognition software have been able to benefit from the social value placed on portrait image sharing to design, test, and refine their systems.[13] Hence, contemporary facial recognition systems and applications – particularly in their implementation in personal media – are not supplemental to selfie culture, but rather its outgrowth.

Face Games

This process of online facial imagery feeding the growth of facial analysis software comes full circle – creating a sort of affective feedback loop – in the popularity of face-based apps that turn facial imagery into a field of play for identity and social exchange. Emphasizing the face's value in social media interactivity through intense algorithmic analysis, apps such as FaceApp, FaceLab, and Reface have adapted aspects of facial detection and recognition technologies to produce image effects for users to share with their social media networks. Other apps, including Fantastic Face, Face Secret, and Beauty Scanner – Face Analyzer, have claimed to employ face scanning software to forecast one's social acceptance, economic success, and general well-being. Augmented-reality filters developed for Instagram and other platforms pretend to scan the live screen image of a user's face to match it with different characters from Disney or Pokémon.[14] Many of these apps and filters require the user to take front-facing, eye-level selfies, just as facial recognition locks might ask, as the base images for modification or analysis. FaceApp, for example, allows users to "improve your selfie or just have fun" with editing choices of hairstyles, tattoos, and backgrounds, as well as more radical physical changes, including aging and gender swapping effects. Beauty Scanner – Face Analyzer "looks into geometric proportions of facial features … and the distance between those" to generate a "face attractiveness score" and even provide physiognomic analysis of the user's "character."[15]

Apps of this genre capitalize on connotations of selfies as enjoyable self-explorations that allow – and even encourage – creators to play with visual codes in expressing their personality and character while relying on the technological processes and popular associations of face scanning and recognition. These apps extend interactions between user and device around self-imagery while diversifying the user's exploration of the visual codes and social constraints of identity. This is especially true with imaging features around aging, gender, and even, in some cases, race and ethnicity.[16] Through such bundles of features, these apps claim to "know you" and your potential, whether that involves showing you how you will look in thirty or forty years or scoring how you look now and how lucky you can expect to be today. Their appeal rests largely on projecting personalization through detailed evaluation, even as they often use biased datasets that can produce generalizations and perpetuate stereotypes.[17]

Often categorized as "entertainment" by the companies that make them and the platforms that distribute them, these products may be perceived as game apps by their users. Nevertheless, they trade on beliefs and practices with strong social and political consequences. As seen in the claims of Beauty Scanner – Face Analyzer, for example, they derive from historical pseudo-sciences such as physiognomy, phrenology, and eugenics that tie an individual's physical traits to their social value, intellectual aptitude, and moral qualities.[18] These systems were developed in the eighteenth and nineteenth centuries, overlapping to an extent with the rise of the social sciences, and their legacy remains strong today. In explaining that "the reason physiognomy shaped people's thinking so strongly was that it didn't always come in its most virulent, racist guise – a lot of it was well-intentioned, a little nostalgic, and ultimately pretty harmless," literary critic Adrian Daub indicates both why such face-based apps may be popular and why they receive little criticism, even when facial recognition technologies and their implementation have drawn strident rebuke for the instrumentalization of racism.[19]

In addition to these issues, face-based apps also may save and share the images and personal data of their users with third parties amassing biometric databases or refining the artificial intelligence behind facial recognition systems. This has been a concern with FaceApp, for example. Produced by Russian developer FaceApp, Inc., the app has uploaded user photos onto its servers for editing, rather than running editing tools on users' devices, raising questions about data storage and unauthorized use.[20] Daily horoscope and "luck" predictors can produce a particularly rich database on individuals through archives of day-to-day uploads that can be useful for tweaking facial recognition systems in development. Based in part on photographic mediation as a measure of an individual's value and merit, the increasing popularity of gamified manifestations of facial recognition – given the troubling genealogies of facial recognition-based gameplay – contributes to normalizing biometric visual recognition systems across diverse social and political contexts. This can foster not only tolerance of, but also belief in, increasingly invasive facial recognition systems as simple extensions of existing popular visual practices of making meaning through the classification and hierarchization of groups and populations. Perhaps not surprisingly, facial recognition companies have helped legitimate these games by openly promoting them as useful applications of automated facial recognition. For example, FaceFirst, a leading US facial recognition software developer, has touted Face Secret as one of the "best mobile facial recognition apps."[21]

Indeed, playing games based on the device's recognition of the face starts in electronics for young children. Returning to the Kidi Secrets Selfie Journal examined earlier, the device's pledge to keep a child's secrets materializes not only in its numeric password but also its facial recognition lock. When the toy's facial recognition system is activated, the device's speaker tells the child to centre their face in the onscreen circle. "Hey, you! I can't wait to hear about your day," it states once it recognizes the child. If it does not recognize the child it states, "Your face hasn't been detected," and allows the child to use their numeric password. If that fails, the device glibly asserts, "Sorry, this isn't your diary," and shuts off.[22]

Through these simple, clear steps, the toy makes strong value judgments about the user. If it recognizes the child, it appears eager to get more input from them; if it does not, it simply cuts all receptive capacity, "ghosting" the child if only for the interval that the device is turned off and on so a new attempt can be made. This frames the device as a safe haven for "secrets," as the toy's name makes clear. Like adult face-based apps, the Kidi Secrets Selfie Journal's suite of games includes diagnostic and forecasting tools predicated on presenting and scanning the child's face. Its Face Fun game offers a FaceApp-like blending experience where the child and a friend can take turns presenting their face for scanning to "see how similar you both are." The Magic Ball game resembles Fantastic Face or Face Secret as the child centres their face in a "crystal ball" to take a photo that generates their "daily fortune." Such games encourage and reward recording the face and submitting to digital facial analysis as a regular part of childhood.[23] They represent the extension of disciplinary power over the child's body. While this power historically has been housed in institutions like elementary schools, it now plays to the child's sense of private agency and engagement in the conditioning interaction with their toy's sensors and processors.

VTech's adoption of facial recognition systems toward the affective interactivity of the Kidi Secrets Selfie Journal may be chilling, but it reflects how facial recognition systems work within wider personal media use. Facial recognition as a means of establishing an affective relation with the device is as much a part of device use for adults as it is for children. In its effort to make Face ID feel less like machine facial scanning and more like a friendly interchange, for example, Apple based the app's icon on its happy Mac and Finder graphics (see figure 5.1). When setting up Face ID for personal use, the user sees an animated, blinking version of the app icon at the centre of the screen and adjusts the device until the icon is superimposed over their face onscreen. Through this manoeuvre the lively "face" of the gazing device and the face of the user gazing back symbolically merge in the frame of the screen. At Face ID's launch, at least one tech critic

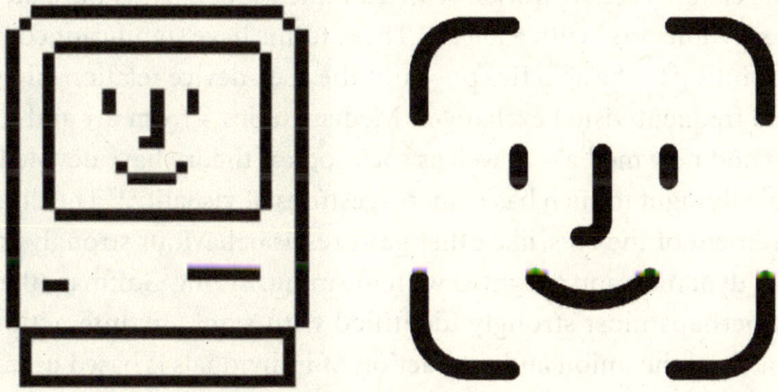

Figure 5.1
Apple Macintosh's Happy Mac start-up icon, left, as introduced in 1984, and iPhone's Face ID icon, as introduced in 2017.

interpreted the choice of the smiling, "transparent" Mac-like icon as an attempt by Apple to belie the app's intrusiveness: "So when you … point the new iPhone X at your face, instead of warming up to that old familiar anthropomorphic happy Mac grinning back at you, you'd do well to remember that this is the first step in a march toward a future in which your password is your body."[24] After set-up, Face ID's smiling icon would appear at the bottom of the screen during any subsequent facial recognition process (e.g., Apple Pay transactions or signing into some third-party apps), as though it is the eyes of the device's smiling face that determines if the user is familiar.

Facial recognition device locks may be popular in spite of their potential security risks because they conveniently merge with other features of the device, such as facial detection in camera apps. "Authenticating with your face seems like a natural choice when it comes to smartphones. Talk about convenient – you were going to look at the phone anyway, right?" states one tech reviewer.[25] Another explains, "I *love* Face ID. The beauty of it is that you get strong authentication that is almost invisible. I pick up my phone, and it's unlocked. I open my banking app, and a second or so later, I'm looking at my bank balance. They say the best user interfaces are invisible, and that to me is very nearly true of Face ID."[26]

Apple claims Face ID works "with a simple *glance*." Samsung states that its system "unlock[s] with a *look*."[27] These terms have significant connotations, pointing to the affective power of the user-device relationship based on these frequent visual exchanges. Media studies – from art and film to gaming and new media – as well as sociological theory have devoted considerable thought to such basic micro-gestures of visuality.[28] The direction or movement of the eyes, like other gestures, is behaviour strongly shaped by social dynamics and freighted with meaning. Erving Goffman, the sociologist perhaps most strongly identified with symbolic interactionism, explains that "the union and interaction of individuals is based upon mutual glances. This is perhaps the most direct and purest reciprocity which exists anywhere." Indeed, Goffman claims, "The totality of social relations of human beings, their self-assertion and self-abnegation, their intimacies and estrangements, would be changed in unpredictable ways if there occurred no glance of eye to eye."[29]

Glances can bear diverse connotations, particularly if they are prolonged or repeated, depending on environmental circumstances (street, school, office, restaurant, bus) and the physical and social markers of the participants (age, gender, race), let alone other cultural factors. Just as a glance in social encounters can be parsed to generate differing, and even competing, meanings, users and developers can envision facial recognition within a frame of interpersonal performativity. This is enhanced through interfaces such as the Face ID set-up. Indeed, as one reviewer protested, "Hold on, I need to make eye contact with my phone until it decides to acknowledge me[?]"[30] This complaint casts the technology as a social relationship between user and device hinging on conventions of eye contact and acknowledgment. Google has warned its Pixel customers that just looking in the direction of their phones can unlock them "even when you don't intend to," suggesting that the device can find meaning in a glance where there is none.[31] What this indicates, however, is a suggested awareness or consciousness on the side of the device. Piggybacking on facial recognition, attention awareness features that run constantly with the goal of detecting not only the user's attempts to interact with the device but also their intention to do so reflect this category of algorithmically determining identity *and* motive through presence and movement.

Attention and Awareness

Through the technological architecture and capacities of affordances such as facial recognition, devices can continually monitor users' behaviour with "attention aware" features that function with or without direct interaction. Even if an iPhone or iPad user chooses not to set up Face ID, for example, the device will nevertheless scan continually for a face whose eyes are oriented toward the screen. Apple explains: "The TrueDepth camera intelligently activates to support attention aware features, like dimming the display if you aren't looking at your device or lowering the volume of alerts if you're looking at your device." The Safari web browser (as well as some other apps) "checks to determine if you're looking at your device" and turns off the screen if it appears you are not.[32]

Attention awareness aims to further tailor the device as a knowing, reactive object that appears to make qualitative judgments (e.g., determining what constitutes attention or engagement) about user and interactivity alike. Whereas Face ID is oriented toward a specific user to suggest the device knows them as a unique individual, awareness features are meant to suggest a more general understanding of human behaviour and usage, regardless of identity. Thus, Motion Sense – Google's awareness system introduced with the Pixel 4 smartphone – relies on radar rather than optical sensors to "tell when you're nearby, but not who you are."[33] Oriented toward proximate behaviour, then, attention awareness adjusts the material terms of interaction based on the conditions, much as people do when interacting and communicating with each other in a shared, physical space.

In discussing these attention awareness features, users sometimes describe them as though interacting with others. "If you get a phone call, it will ring at normal volume, but only until it sees that you're looking at the screen. Then it lowers the volume since it already has your attention," explains one user in a MacRumors forum on attention awareness. "They're really subtle features that just seem so polite," adds another.[34] The continuous adjustments by the device based on its optical capture and algorithmic processing of the user's physical orientation to the device – even if the user is making no physical contact with it – mimic the adjustments in human interactions noted by Goffman and George Herbert Mead. For example, the volume adjustment component of attention awareness functions much like a person who will speak loudly to get another person's attention but then speak considerably more softly once they have it. With technologies such as TrueDepth and Face ID the face is constantly mediated by the device. Dot projection emitted from and received by the device translates the subtlest contours and movements of the face into a stream of data that is assessed and reassessed by the underlying software to determine a user's qualitative state (i.e., paying attention or not) and adjust the device's settings based on that presumed state.

Attention awareness as an interactive system joins two concepts, one assigned to the user and the other attributed to the device. Detecting attentiveness or attention in someone remains a qualitative judgment. As any teacher knows too well, a student may be looking directly at them during a classroom lecture but paying little attention to what is being shown or said. Similarly, daydreaming is a good example of a form of attention – in this case oriented to the workings of the imagination – that can be undetectable or misinterpreted through visual analysis of demeanour. A student could be intensely focused, but not on the lecture before them. The concept of "awareness" is also telling in Apple's framing of device-level processes. Describing the underlying technology of this affordance as "awareness," rather than, say, "detection," implies a deeper cognitive process on behalf of the device. *Merriam-Webster* defines "awareness" as "*knowledge* and *understanding* that something is happening or exists."[35] Being "aware" of one's surroundings means not only detecting the physical characteristics of the environment but also having the capacity to make judgments about it based on those characteristics.

These terms endow the technological process with a socio-cultural component moving beyond mere perception to an underlying understanding. Indeed, in visual theorist Jonathan Crary's work on the genealogy of attention, he identifies attention as a modern social and political construction centred on disciplining bodies for production and consumption. "What is important to institutional power … is simply that perception function in a way that insures a subject is productive, manageable, and predictable, and is able to be socially integrated and adaptive," Crary states.[36] In the development of what he terms "attentive practices" Crary explains that "discursive objects, material practices, and representational artifacts do not occupy qualitatively different strata but are equally involved in the production of effects of power and new types of subjectivities."[37]

A technological affordance such as attention awareness, tied intimately to the workings of an ever-present, accompanying (and interdependent) body, produces a tightening disciplinary loop between device and user. If the awareness of attention is meant to be attributed to the device in always monitoring the user's presence and movements, it also exists on the user's part. The device's reaction to the slightest movements or actions by the user can make the user more acutely aware of the device's presence and responsiveness. The device seems to awaken at the user's slightest movement. It can be awakened by a mere glance in its direction, which can be convenient, but also unnerving. The device's wakening may also, perhaps, awaken our desire or need for interaction. Filters available through Instagram, Snapchat, TikTok, and many other photo and video making and sharing apps have helped forge this bond or at least have made surveillance and tracking capacities appear to be harmless fun. This technology is behind the popular face and movement tracking lenses on numerous apps, for example, which allow various augmented-reality filters – from oversized eyes and tongues to fluttering fairy wings – to appear a part of the user's onscreen body as they move around the frame, even in real time. Such social media applications present the device's capacity for unwavering observation of the user and their movements as a central tool for creative interaction.

Scrutinizing mechanisms and effects of attention within contemporary social and technological frameworks, literary theorist Yves Citton has described the need for an "ecology" of attention extending from the current "economy" of attention. In the economy of attention, a superabundance of media materials and texts vie for everyone's temporally and psychologically constrained attention. An ecology of attention, Citton explains, addresses not only attention as an economic issue but also as an environmental one, and would particularly encompass our immersion in "biophysical" environments and the "affective and aesthetic meshwork" of media environments.[38] Citton's schema of this ecology has three levels: collective attention, joint attention, and individual attention. Examining relationships across these three levels can elucidate "attention aware" interface design and its potential social consequences for shaping personal relationships with technology. For Citton, collective attention is the macro level of unified social action, which he claims is required to intervene ("forcefully and/or virally") in media systems that condition attention.

Joint and individual attention are the micro relationships of attention. Joint attention is the "co-presence of human beings whose attentions directly influence each other," as when someone in your presence turns to look at something and you follow their gaze to do the same. "Joint attention plays a crucial role in conversations ... We learn to become intelligent and social human beings by tuning our attention in and out of other people's attention, whether at the level of collective or of joint attention," Citton explains. Indeed, from this description joint attention would be the basic condition for communication and interaction between beings and bodies. Individual attention is, simply, when "I as a subject face an object of attention" such as a screen.[39]

The performativity of personal media interfaces typically privileges joint attention. The user and device react and respond to each other. This takes place even as it could be said that the relationship is an example of individual attention, since the user is absorbed in their interaction with the screen. Attention awareness – as a design goal and material reality – works across concepts of joint and individual attention. In bridging these concepts it shapes the user-device relationship in ways that resemble "the co-presence of human beings" while remaining "a subject facing an object of attention" where no other human presence is necessary (i.e., beyond live videoconferencing, texting, phone calls, and the like). As Crary remarks of the relationship between attention and power, attention can be understood in two broad, and seemingly antithetical, ways: attention appears as "the means by which an individual observer can transcend those subjective limitations and make perception its own, and attention is at the same time a means by which a perceiver becomes open to control and annexation by external agencies."[40]

Computer scientists Lars-Erik Janlert and Erik Stolterman have described a profile of interaction based on the presence and quality of eight characteristics. Among these are "attention demand" and "awareness level," which they see as closely related and entwined.[41] Attention demand involves the extent to which an interaction requires a user's attention. This can be measured objectively, they assert, but it also involves a subjective component. When a user takes on a new system or activity – such as a new technological capacity or an updated interface with design changes and added components, their sense of attention will be high. Once they have sufficient knowledge and practice, however, their subjective sense of attention may diminish while their objective attention (e.g., tapping the right zones or selecting the right options in a menu) remains stable. Awareness level involves the extent to which the user is conscious that interaction is taking place between themselves and surrounding devices and systems. "High attention demand implies high user awareness of the interaction, but if the attention demand is low the user's awareness may vary from the minimum required to higher levels," they explain. "The actual awareness level can partly be under the user's own control in situations where other demands on the user's attention are not pressing."[42]

The balance and degree of attention demand and awareness level vary across the optically based interactive technologies that have been examined in this and previous chapters. These variations may help shape our understandings of – and attitudes toward – these technologies and their role in our everyday social behaviour. Negative perceptions of activities like selfie-making, for instance, can be related to the practice's attention and awareness requirements. The degree of attention to, and awareness of, the device in selfie-making is relatively high. As users become more familiar with the technical possibilities and limitations of their device for making such images, their subjective attention may decrease, yet their awareness will remain high. This intensity of awareness – even when demands of attention diminish with increased expertise with the device – is critical to the experience of producing selfies. Compare this, for example, to other activities one might undertake with the device, such as a phone conversation, listening to music, reading a blog, or scrolling a feed. All are activities where one can easily become less aware of the device as the focus remains on the content rather than the delivery system.

Drawing from Janlert and Stolterman, it could be said that this awareness is the conscious decision of the user and remains significantly under their control. First, this is the case because selfie-making is a voluntary activity. Second, it is also so because the user understands that selfie-making can entail a relatively complex physical interaction with the device. It is not merely the setting of a timer on the device's camera, though this can easily be done to produce an adequate portrait of the self. It is instead frequently a form of negotiation between device, user, and their surroundings. In this interaction the user is experiencing themselves through a device that makes them highly aware of both themselves as an object and agent, and the device as an object and agent. This can be particularly so when working with automatic camera settings, which will continuously adjust qualities such as exposure and focal area and distance as the sensors recognize changes in the incoming data from the space before the lens. Even with automatic settings, users must regularly adjust the orientation of the device, their own position, and, to the extent possible, their surroundings to produce a satisfying image.

This intense attention to, and awareness of, the user-device relationship in activities like selfie-making contrasts with mobile optical surveillance and tracking features that attempt to shift the "burden" of awareness away from the user to the device. Attention awareness is "polite" precisely because it seems to react quickly and efficiently to the user's movements, requiring a minimum of attention on the part of the user toward the device. Indeed, the perfect attention awareness system is one where the device is constantly monitoring the user, but the user may take notice of this process only when they wish to engage with the device. In selfie production, the attention appears to derive from the user's (self) absorption in their fixation on the device. With attention awareness, it is the device that appears ever attentive and constantly fixated on the user. (Facial recognition locks would appear to occupy some middle ground between these two extremes of selfie practices and device-based awareness features.)

Therein may lie the difference – especially when compounded with additional social factors and intersectional vectors such as gender, race, and age – in approaches and attitudes to these distinct aspects of personal media visuality. Self-image making on the part of the user and automatic imaging on the part of the device both involve the intersection of awareness and attention with ideas of entanglement and enchantment, as the user-device relationship is at the heart of both processes. However, in making selfies and related visual artifacts, the user leverages entanglement and enchantment as technological components in the exploration of self through the affective power of gestural performativity. Identity is generated and affirmed through the deliberate encounter with the device and surroundings. In the device's default behavioural monitoring systems and resulting interface adjustments, conversely, such conscious exploration is lost as the device's computations find ways to conform to behavioural cues (that is, to read movement as performance) without the user taking notice. The user is permanently immersed in the technological entanglement of the device's sensing capabilities, but that entanglement barely registers in cognitive perception. Despite these seemingly diametrically opposed differences, each of these processes ultimately may contribute to the same result – a tightening of the bond between users and their devices as a significant affective relationship functioning within a wider social field, and a deepening grip of institutional power structures in our smallest attempts at self-examination, affirmation, or agency.

In constantly observing, recording, and analyzing user behaviour even when the user is not directly interacting with the device, these awareness features may have long-term consequences for shaping the user-device relationship. Even before these capabilities emerged, however, the perception of device awareness independent of user interaction was already present through other means of constant recognition and solicitation of the user. Push notifications and alerts, a part of phone culture since the first years of the century, have framed networked communication as the responsibility of the device as a helpful intermediary requiring regular attention and input. These conditions, central to the experience of these devices, will be explored in the next chapter.

CHAPTER 6

Nurturing Dependence

We hold our portable, personal media devices out at different angles to look back at us for taking photos or livestreaming. We tap, rub, and caress their glass faces to do and make things. We ask them questions or make requests through their voice-activated virtual assistants. And when they beep, chime, vibrate, or illuminate, we reflexively pick them up and hold them close. All in all, they get abundant attention. Observed from the outside, all these interactions across the day suggest these devices hold an extraordinarily privileged place in our lives. As we have seen, even when it appears that we are not interacting with them, their various sensors can continue observing in a constant state of vigilance, awaiting the moments when we are close or when we make a sound. Under these conditions, if they have power in their battery, then they are interacting – or at least attempting to interact – with our bodies. In the case of wearable networked devices, this interactive relationship has become more intense. With a smartwatch or fitness tracker, the device may indeed always interact with the body, processing a constant flow of biometric data accessible through the device's fixed position against the user's skin.

This chapter follows the extension of self into the personal media object to its eventual conclusion by examining how networked interactions facilitated by smartphones and wearables have tended toward a pattern of constant recognition and solicitation of the user. The relationship between us and our devices has changed from one where we (or another person trying to contact us) initiate the process of interaction to one where the device, through advanced sensing technology and enhanced networked processing, more and more frequently initiates interactions and works to reshape our habits, our priorities, and our sense of who we are. As it generates a more detailed picture of us through an increasing number of interconnected technological features and data points, it can attune its behaviour in multiple, minor ways. This can be enhanced and intensified by artificial intelligence models that shift the device into an even broader "awareness" of the user, beyond merely monitoring movement and attention to gauging and manipulating mood and motives. These developments threaten to deepen power imbalances between users and the corporations behind these products and services. New modes of data extraction and assetization, coupled with increasingly sophisticated and adaptable interfaces, can produce granular modifications in the user-device relationship outside the user's control or understanding that, over time, can fundamentally impact networked sociality and user agency.

Creepiness and Relational Artifacts

Common parameters of personal media use contribute to what theorist Wendy Hui Kyong Chun has described as the "creepiness of new media" in their diverse demands upon, yet seeming attentiveness to, the user.[1] Through default settings such as push notifications and alerts that surface data to the screen when the user is not actively using associated apps, the device's regular interruptions of everyday activities position it as an engaged intermediary, ceaselessly fielding, finding, and filtering information for the user, while nevertheless requiring regular feedback in return.[2] A 2023 study of American teenagers found that they received a "barrage" of such notifications. Equipping their phones with activity monitoring software, the study registered a median of 237 notifications a day, with a quarter of these coming during school hours.[3] By turning off or otherwise reducing these notifications, the user may gain some peace, but they also may feel they risk ignorance about what's happening (a circumstance known as FOMO, short for "fear of missing out"). This system of notifications and alerts is – it is worth noting – supplemented by geolocative and network tracking data that can be leveraged to generate suggestions for products, social contacts, or further personalization.[4]

Chun has formulated the equation "Habit + Crisis = Update" to describe contemporary, networked personal media use. Driven by the development and expansion of social media, which now impacts nearly all networked electronic interactions, everyday usage often involves regularly reacting to material offered up by the device. Our reactions can be deliberate communicative responses to others in the network, such as sending an emoji in reply to a text. However, they also may be actions we would not perceive as responses, such as merely opening a notification and looking at it, which are nevertheless recognized and recorded as data by the device and underlying systems. Or they may seem to blur these two possibilities, as when we open a text and the sender gets a notification that we have done so, even if we do not respond to the text. All of these actions entail a change in condition in the device and a reaction to that change, which produces a new, different condition. Habit plus a "crisis" (that is, a development that requires a reaction), leads to a change in the system. And how the device interacts with its user is shaped, and reshaped, in part by the outcome of all these daily "crises" and updates.

Writing about the "era of social media," Chun states, "Automatically recognized changes of status have moved from surveillance to evidence of one's ongoing existence. A true sign of trouble is the lack of signs or updates."[5] Contemporary media multiply these automatic changes for each of us with automatic notifications, offers, software updates, security patches, and interface tweaks. Any of these could be called a crisis, according to Chun, noting that crises are "moments that demand real-time responses." All these changes pass through our device, all of them impact our relationship with it. "In crisis, new media has found its value, its punctuating device," Chun states. "Crises have been central to making the Internet a mass medium to end mass media: a ~~mass~~ *personalized* device."[6]

In considering the manifestations and consequences of the types of automated feedback systems described by Chun as entangling users and devices (and eventually networks), let's turn to two examples from different time periods, targeted at very different users: key chain virtual pets of the 1990s and wrist-mounted fitness and activity trackers of the 2010s and 2020s. Devised as portable, everyday items that interact with the user precisely around habit and crisis (though small-scale crises, for the most part), virtual pets were marketed primarily as toys for children, while wearable trackers are often marketed as adult tools to achieving and maintaining healthy lifestyles. While virtual pet devices exist today mostly as a niche market suffused in media nostalgia, trackers represent a growing market of networked wearables not only for consumers but also for businesses and institutions seeking to exercise greater control over workers, reduce sick time, and increase productivity.[7] Despite these significant differences, both digital pets and trackers offer useful insights into the development of symbiotic relationships between devices and users and the different affective implications built through these relationships, since the messages of both are not from other humans but are automatically generated by the device itself.

Digital pets and trackers can also be viewed within the lens of "relational artifacts" developed by sociologist Sherry Turkle. For Turkle, relational artifacts are computational objects that appeal to our emotions and sense of empathy by exhibiting qualities of companionship.[8] Digital pets encourage us to take care of them; fitness trackers encourage us to take care of ourselves. In developing the theory, Turkle and her team studied "robot creatures" like Furbys, yet the changing features and actions of the more static objects studied here bring them within scope.[9] The tracker is not only a data collection and display device but also the user's coach or trainer, setting goals and measuring progress. And, of course, features like voice assistance underpinned by machine learning and generative AI are making these relational artifacts in our lives more and more the main networked artifacts we use, whatever their outward form.

Wear-Care

Wearable fitness and activity trackers such as Fitbit and biometrics-tracking watches such as Apple Watch and Samsung Galaxy represent perhaps the most extensive application of crises and companionship to the material conditions of physical interaction between user and device as interdependent, animated beings. By constantly monitoring the user's physiology and physical activity and notifying them to modify behaviour (e.g., vibration alerts or screen notifications to warn of prolonged stasis), a tracker functions much like a caregiver. Media ethics researcher Btihaj

Ajana states that trackers "'prod' the user to take action rather than just collect data." Ajana explains, "By playing the role of a 'friend' who knows the user well or the role of an authority such as a nurse or a doctor, self-tracking devices and apps aim to enhance the persuasive effect on one's behaviour."[10] Indeed, it could be argued that the user ultimately is providing reciprocal care to the device by feeding it a constant stream of personal data and giving it regular attention. These devices have become a primary tool of the quantified self (QS) movement, which promotes collecting and analyzing multiple metrics of one's daily activity toward greater self-awareness, personal improvement, and good health.[11] They also represent a turn in personal media devices toward biopolitics and the "'neoliberal' ethos of (self) governance and health management whereby individuals are increasingly expected to be in charge of their own health and wellbeing."[12] Health, data extraction, and behavioural quantification and monetization are embedded in the user-device relationship as both user and device constantly adjust their actions to the behavioural changes of the other.

Fitbit has been a pioneer in health and fitness trackers. Founded in 2007, it was acquired by Google in 2021, giving the tech giant access to a wealth of individual health data that can be integrated with a user's data from other Google products and services (e.g., search engine activity, Google Nest surveillance, YouTube viewing, Waze route-finding, etc.). Fitbit's Sense smartwatch, to give one example, can gather a wide range of health data from its wearer (see figure 6.1). The Fitbit Sense includes an electrodermal activity (EDA) sensor to detect stress. Its ECG app will send notifications for irregular heart rhythms (AFib). Its Health Metrics dashboard measures breathing rate, skin temperature, and blood oxygen levels. The device's sleep app charts REM as well as duration and depth of sleep while using audio sensors for snoring and noise detection. These features allow twenty-four-hour monitoring and data harvesting of a user's bodily behaviour, activity intensity, and even their mental state. This comprehensiveness across a range of behavioural and vital signs implies that the device is best worn more or less constantly to provide the most accurate picture of personal health and signal any medical concerns as soon as they arise. Even devices that are not marketed primarily as health trackers may offer such monitoring. The Apple Watch, sold as much as a style accessory as a useful networked device, offers heart rate monitoring through an optical heart sensor that can measure the wrist's pulse wave and generate notifications for ab-

Figure 6.1
A Fitbit Sense displaying heart rate, "active zone" minutes, and sleep minutes, in addition to the day and time.

normally high or low rates, as well as for irregular beating. It also uses an optical detector to track oxygen levels in the bloodstream and measures sleep REM and depth. Its step tracking measures not only walking distance but also walking "quality" through step length and symmetry.[13] The Samsung Galaxy Watch offers equivalent features, as well as "body composition analysis" measuring "body fat, skeletal muscle, body water, Body Mass Index (BMI) and more."[14] Garmin markets its Venu smartwatch as a "GPS smartwatch," in keeping with the company's roots in satellite-guided navigational equipment for boats, cars, and the military. Nevertheless, it claims the Venu offers "more health stats than you've ever seen on a watch," including heart rate, sleep quality, and blood oxygen, respiration, stress, and energy levels.[15]

In the development of personal media at the end of the twentieth century, human biomedical interaction with portable, personal devices was envisioned primarily as cyborgian advances in implanted devices that would become one with the body. Certainly, such devices have been developed. However, these interventions directly into the body have been limited, for the most part, to treating specific medical conditions or needs. Examples include pacemakers to correct cardiac irregularities, deep brain stimulators for epilepsy or Parkinson's disease, and infusion pumps for administering medication directly into the bloodstream over long periods.[16] Far more biomedical monitoring is done through external consumer wearables, and the scope, depth, and accuracy of their data collection are continuously increasing.[17] Sociologist Deborah Lupton refers to it as "lively data" that is steadfastly "about the lives of humans: about their bodily functions, behaviours, social relationships, moods and emotions." This data is shared with the user through the interface to inform and modify behaviour, yet it also has a life of its own as it can be collected and shared by private corporations for other profitable purposes.[18]

In their book on self-tracking, researchers Gina Neff and Dawn Nafus point out that tracking data "can be useful, powerful, tedious, pleasurable, underwhelming, wrong, or just beside the point in a variety of everyday contexts."[19] Within the mechanisms of information and surveillance capitalism, much of this data is produced and collected through required or default settings. Our devices share much of this data with us, even if unwanted or seemingly beside the point. Through this glut of information collection and representation the device creates a data mirror that reflects us back at ourselves by, in fact, refracting our behaviour – caught by sensors – through the language and connotations of data management. Taking care of ourselves, in some ways, may mean taking care of our data. This is why, for example, people using trackers may feel as though their exercise or workouts do not "count" if the physical activity has not been sensed, quantified, and analyzed by their device or its apps.[20] And manufacturers of such devices encourage wearing the device for extended periods to collect as much biometric and behavioural data as possible. To this end, Fitbit recommends only taking a break and removing the Sense when the user takes a shower, "although you can shower while wearing your watch," it reassures device owners.[21]

Media theorist José van Dijck has argued that the basic meaning of sharing has changed in fundamental ways in recent years. Sharing with others or sharing with the platforms to reach others – called "connectedness" by van Dijck – is "transparent," while sharing with platforms that is subsequently shared by underlying companies with other platforms – termed "connectivity" – is opaque and rarely disclosed.[22] Through the material performativity of intimacy described in the foregoing chapters, sharing would also produce a third category – sharing with the device. What this would entail is the interaction between device and user across data that ostensibly seems to be contained between the device and the user. This would apply less to messages on social media platforms and similarly consciously networked data, and apply more to step counts, heart rate, and other data that is shared with the device and reflected back at the user without any sense, perhaps, that this data may enter larger networks and be stored, analyzed, or shared elsewhere. Under these conditions, sharing is an intimate practice between user and device that may build trust, even as that shared behavioural information is passed along to other, unknown entities, potentially for intentions beyond those expected by the user. Accordingly, Apple sought in 2023 to differentiate its devices as more private than its competitors' by emphasizing how the corporation does not share such health and behaviour data with other companies.[23]

Neff and Nafus explain that "self-tracking takes place in social situations. The numbers of self-tracking may focus on the individual, but they stem from fundamental beliefs about how societies function."[24] These fundamental beliefs themselves are evolving, however, as mores around privacy, sharing, and social participation have changed. Self-tracking is more and more a networked activity, no longer limited to a microchip on a non-networked watch or pedometer, let alone a notebook and a pen. In this constant and even excessive sharing through the device, these numbers begin to represent how society functions rather than the specific needs or desires of the individual. For example, health data collected through commercial devices and apps, ostensibly for personal use and benefit, may be used for other interactions with the individual. It can be leveraged for crafting targeted offers of health insurance or promoting specific drugs or health products to the user. It also could be used as part of large data sets amassed from many users to shape health policy more broadly for societies and populations or to design new products or interfaces.

In relating fitness trackers to surveillance and social inequalities, health culture scholars Katelyn Esmonde and Shannon Jette have described a "Fitbit subject assemblage."[25] The term is grounded in Michel Foucault's theories of self-discipline within socio-political power structures and Gilles Deleuze and Felix Guattari's concept of entanglements between humans, non-humans, and discourse that can generate desire and affect. Esmonde and Jette's research underscores how expectations and applications of personal media devices can reinforce or exacerbate deep-rooted inequalities around class, gender, and race. Fitness trackers can be used as tools of power not only by tech companies that collect medical and behavioural data but also by companies and institutions that require employees or clients to wear the devices to monitor health and productivity. Fitness trackers do not only promote self-evaluation; they also promote "positive" behavioural change based on device feedback and notifications. As Esmonde and Jette note, populations that have less leisure time or increased caregiving and domestic responsibilities (as has historically been the case for women – especially working-class women of colour) are less likely to adhere to the device's recommendations and goals. They are also more likely to feel guilty about their inability to meet the device's expectations. "These devices make legible the numbers that position a person as healthy or unhealthy. It is not only a person who interprets confessions and diagnoses ill health; in this case, it is a step counter and an app that do so," Esmonde and Jette explain.[26]

Feeding the Device

This interdependent relationship around health and well-being through alerts, notifications, and updates recalls the circumstances of portable digital pets in the 1990s. First introduced in Asia, toys such as Tamagotchi, released in 1996, and Giga Pets, released a year later, came in colourful, egg-shaped plastic cases. Tethered to key chains, these toys had three or four control buttons and a small screen about the size of a quarter (see figure 6.2).[27] Tamagotchi's manufacturer, Japanese toy company Bandai, sold four hundred million Tamagotchi worldwide within the toy's first year and a half.[28] (By comparison, it took Apple *five years* to sell as many iPhones.)[29] With this global success, these toys represent a pivotal moment in the evolution of the update-centric relationships that have become the norm between users and their personal media devices. However, in proportion to their popularity and significance, they remain under-represented in the socio-cultural history of computing and personal media, as the connection between digital toys and wider media is seldom made.[30]

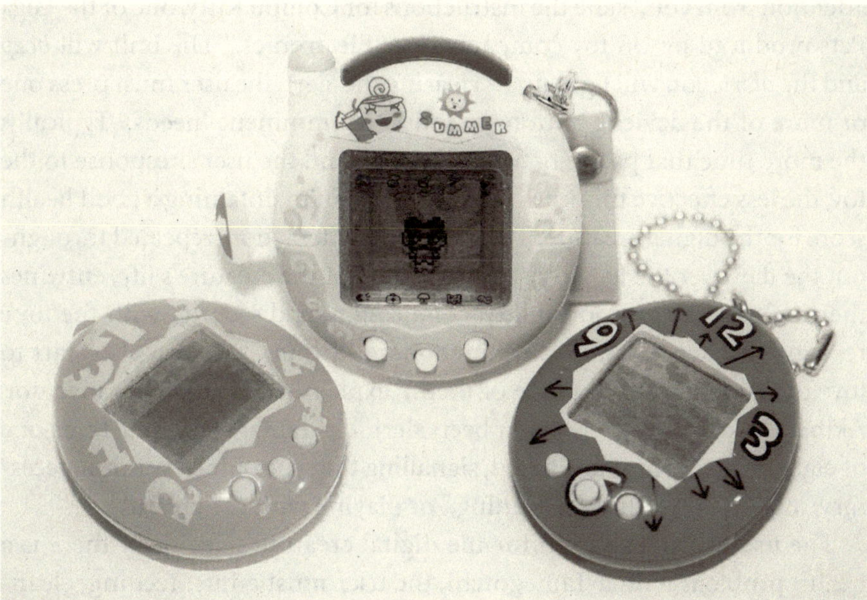

Figure 6.2
Several models of Tamagotchi by Bandai.

The role of habit and crisis identified by Chun in personal media is central to the functioning and affective impact of these toys, as the onscreen creature's development into a healthy digital being depends on an intersubjective, technological intimacy between user and device. Having researched Tamagotchi, Turkle claims, "Although primitive as relational artifacts, the Tamagotchis demonstrated a fundamental truth of a new human–machine psychology. When it comes to bonding with computers, *nurturance* is the 'killer app' (an application that can eliminate its competitors). When a digital creature entrains people to play parent, they become attached."[31] Bringing together object mobility with frequent interactions around caregiving, anthropologist Anne Allison claims "nomadic machines like the *tamagotchi* become a person's constant companion almost more than anything outside the body itself."[32]

Tamagotchi and Giga Pets require a user's frequent intervention, normally prompted by beeps coming at irregular intervals, to ensure the device's well-being. "At various times, your pet will require a certain kind of attention from you," state the instructions for Compu Kitty, one of the Giga Pets produced by US toy company Tiger Electronics. "The unit will *beep* and the *alert* icon will light up."[33] Hearing the alert, the user must press one or more of the device's buttons to satisfy its imminent "needs." Typically, the more time that passes between the alert and the user's response to the toy, the less effective this intervention will be in maintaining a good health score for the digital creature. This pattern of interaction, repeated throughout the day over the five to twenty-five days of the creature's life, entwines the user's sense of responsibility, compassion, and security with the toy's recognition, dependency, and functioning. "I think that you also start to love them when you take care of them," explained Tamagotchi's inventor, Akihiro Yokoi, in 1997.[34] After a beep alert, the Tamagotchi user finds one of eight or ten icons illuminated, signalling the type of intervention necessary, including "feeding," "cleaning," or playing with the creature.

The user must also monitor the digital creature's health. If there is a health problem with a Tamagotchi, the user must adjust feeding, cleaning, or playing interventions or administer "medicine." Additionally, Tamagotchi may beep for none of these reasons, which means it is simply misbehaving and must be disciplined through further button pressing. Indeed, as with all other cases, in disciplining the creature it is ultimately the user who is being disciplined by adjusting their behaviour and turning their attention to the device amidst irregular alerts while attending to their own daily needs and activities. As Compu Kitty's instructions explain, among the device's several icons and buttons "you cannot choose [the alert] icon. Instead, this icon will light up to let you know that your pet needs something."[35]

Even when a user responds promptly to a Tamagotchi or Giga Pet alert, it is rarely a matter of simply pressing a button to silence the device. Take, for example, administering medicine to Tamagotchi. According to the instructions accompanying the device, users must "press the A button until the medicine icon is highlighted, then press the B. Sometimes 2 or 3 injections are needed before Tamagotchi is well."[36] Feeding also requires pressing A, then B several times, while trying to avoid overfeeding (in which case the creature will refuse to eat). "There are a total of 4 hearts on the 'Happy' and 'Hunger' screens and they start out empty," the Tamagotchi instructions explain. "The more hearts that are filled, the better satisfied Tamagotchi is. You must feed or play with Tamagotchi to fill the empty hearts.

If you keep Tamagotchi full and happy it will grow into a cute, happy cyber creature." If a user ignores alerts, is late to respond to them, or provides an incomplete response by tapping the wrong buttons or not tapping the right button enough times, then the creature suffers in its development. "If you neglect Tamagotchi, it grows into an unattractive alien," the device's instructions warn users.[37]

Updating

"It seems that the shape, personality, and life of each Tamagotchi is based on how well you take care of it," the Tamagotchi instructions explain.[38] "Seems" is an intriguing term in qualifying these statements, signalling that the user may have an impact on the device's behaviour, but that the device also may produce results independent of a user's interventions. The description aptly sums up the contemporary relationship we have with our personal media devices. Our behaviour certainly contributes to how they perform for us, but we never have complete control over their behaviour, as we never fully know how algorithms produce outcomes for us, nor whether those outcomes are based on machine learning or also derive from – or factor in – the behaviour of other users, whose actions are entirely independent of our own.

Anne Allison argues that "The care taken by children in raising their digital pets encouraged a degree of personalization and emotional closeness with cybertechnology previously unseen with kids."[39] As mentioned earlier, the affordances and psychological conditioning these devices produced from the 1990s on are relevant, and even uncanny, when facing the trends of the 2020s and potentially beyond. Indeed, the Tamagotchi-clutching millennial children of the 1990s are now the smartphone-clutching millennials entering middle age. The increasing frequency of software update alerts by personal media devices today (and the apps they house) has transformed them into something like digital pets. Consider this description in a 2023 news piece on software update notifications: "Once the day begins, these notifications can pop up at inconvenient and distracted times." However, "that screen-blocking software update notification that keeps coming back may be annoying to a phone user, but ignoring it for too long is a mistake."[40] While the device typically functions smoothly before update alerts, if users ignore these alerts and do not execute the required updates, functionality may diminish, much as the Tamagotchi or Giga Pet may start misbehaving or get sick if alerts are ignored or interventions delayed. Although security updates are often critical in reducing or eliminating vulnerabilities in software, version updates may be only minor tweaks to the look or functioning of an app or operating system. Version updates may have little impact on performance in the short term, yet, if they are systematically neglected, they can compromise not only the functioning of the specific app or operating system but also its compatibility with other software components. Research shows that users are often reluctant to make even critical updates after having problems with less significant updates, and that update notifications generally can trigger annoyance and confusion.[41]

App and device manufacturers often recommend automatic updating to avoid such potential problems, but nearly any app or device's help centre will have conversation threads of frustrated users who find updates have changed or diminished the functionality of the product. Advice is readily available online for how to make or remove updates if your device is acting strange.[42] If a device behaves oddly after an update, it is perceived as the fault of the update, not the device. As such, updating can become a delicate balancing act of responding to some alerts but not others. Similarly, maintaining digital pets is a balancing act that sometimes includes unnecessary alerts, for which the user must refrain from indulging the pet with feedings, play, and so on. Performing these tasks blindly in response to these alerts will only make the pet more disagreeable. In these cases, the user must either ignore or discipline the pet.[43] This uncertainty surrounding update notifications – will the change enhance, protect, or diminish the device and the user's experience? – fuels ambivalence toward them.

Updating, of course, is not only a matter of accepting software changes for our devices. It also can refer to our level of participation on platforms, particularly social media apps. Status updates, location updates, activity updates… these actions on our part are an essential component of online connectedness. When we make changes to our profiles or accounts, when we post new content or react to existing content, we often produce a ripple across the surface of these platforms, triggering updates or notifications to any number of our followers, and even *potential* followers identified and targeted by the app. When we update, we create new alerts for others, and vice versa. And system updates and status updates only compound as we increase the number of devices and apps we use.

It is no coincidence that social media platforms capitalized on updating and intensified the practice through the development of platform-specific versions of the types of digital pets developed by Bandai, Tiger Electronics, and others. In 2007, Facebook created the Facebook Platform, a format that allowed third-party software developers to create products that would function within a user's Facebook experience. These products, such as games, could interact with Facebook affordances and features like notifications to friends and followers of status changes. One of the first third-party accessories to appear was SuperPoke! Pets by Slide, arriving on the social media site within a month of Platform's release.[44] SuperPoke! Pets gave users a choice of twelve pets. Once selected, the user would take care of the virtual pet through the platform and attend to any signalled needs, much like Tamagotchi or a Giga Pet. The requirements of taking care of this pet ensured that Superpoke! pet owners would access and use Facebook regularly. "You must check in daily to keep the care meters from running down to zero. Washing, feeding, tickling and giving your pet a play date once a day will keep him happy and earn extra income for your pet's household," explained one site offering SuperPoke! Pets tips.[45] The simple updating of the pet could blur into a user updating their own status and content on the site, as well as seeing updates of other users in their newsfeed. Organizing playdates, of course, required interacting with other Facebook users who had SuperPoke! pets. Additional Facebook games, such as Pet Society by Playfish (2008) and PetVille by Zynga (2010), offered similar opportunities for interaction with virtual pets and other users who owned them on the platform.[46]

This frequent, datafied caregiving – necessary for the survival of these virtual pets – builds an empathetic relationship between user and onscreen character that incorporates the device as the sole means of interaction. Caregiving is not just a matter of giving attention, but of taking the time to provide the *right* attention to meet the pet's specific and changing needs. Developmental psychologist Alison Gopnik has theorized that "one of the principal mechanisms for establishing … relationships of care is caring itself." As Gopnik explains, "We don't care for others because we love them, we love them because we care for them."[47] The intensity and variety of care required for virtual pets forges bonds between the user and the pet. Recall the claim of Tamagotchi's inventor: "You also start to love them when you take care of them."[48] These may not be long-lasting bonds, but within the relatively short lifetime of the pet, they can be strong, so that forgetting or losing the key chain device that ostensibly houses the pet could cause significant stress, panic, or pain. When we care for our other personal media devices in similar ways – regular interactions, responding to cues at irregular and frequent intervals, keeping them by our side – similar bonds may emerge, even if we do not consciously recognize our device as another being. This may explain, for example, the common experience of phantom vibration syndrome (described in chapter 3) not as sensitivity to the possibility of communication from others, but rather as the plea of the device itself as an animated object requiring care.

Laying out the development of "growing games" as a popular video game genre in Japan in the 1980s and 1990s, media scholar Machiko Kusahara notes that Tamagotchi represented a radical shift from PC-based games for taking care of virtual beings from fish to baby princesses. "Tamagotchi broke the boundary of growing games ... by removing visual and behavioural realism from the growing simulation and focusing on psychological impact," Kusahara states.[49] With its small, monochrome, pixelated screen, the Tamagotchi did not offer much in terms of an immersive screen world, even by the standards of the time. The realism of the toy, in terms of transforming the creature into a convincingly living being, was the production of its differing, unpredictable alerts, reinforcing the "habit + crisis" model described by Chun.

Designer Judith Donath has explored the qualities that will trigger affective connections with digital pets over other interactive objects or programs. For Donath, the metaphor of the animal is reinforced by "the design of interaction between owner and 'pet,' through a combination of autonomous behaviour, dependency, intensive interaction, and ongoing development, [which] engenders deep devotion to them."[50] This interaction is amplified by two design attributes, according to Donath: embodiment through the device and the device always being on. Even though the device is "physically... unremarkable," Donath notes that "the pet is the whole physical package, not just the image on the screen. Seeing the pet as an object, rather than a program, helped lend it credence as a creature." By remaining always on, the device supports an "illusion of aliveness."[51]

As seen in the examples and contexts studied throughout this book, personal media devices can be understood as expansions of the self. The user's care for the device and device's seeming care for the user intensify that expansion. For digital toys that gamify care, the user's attempts at meeting the device's survival needs are blatantly quantified. SuperPoke! Pets had care meters; Tamagotchi had health meters. Early instructions for Tamagotchi explained that "you determine the mood, health, and behavior of the Tamagotchi with the health meter."[52] Giga Pets had health and happiness scores. These varied scoring schemes, like rudimentary ranking and analytics mechanisms foreshadowing later score-based health apps and device features, were at the heart of maintaining the proper functioning of these virtual beings.[53] As Allison states, "This is the rubric of the *tamagotchi*: a pet that goes virtually anywhere but whose existence is rooted in, and mimetic of, corporeal upkeep."[54]

The consequences for neglecting alerts or administering improper care was an increasingly unhealthy pet and even premature death. Tamagotchi might live for weeks but, if neglected, could die in days. "Just forget to feed it for one day, or miss cleaning the toilet for a few hours – it would become seriously ill and even die if not given medicine," explains Kusahara.[55] While death was inevitable with Tamagotchi, it was the threat of poor development and early death due to misuse that raised the stakes of user-device interaction. Within the context of the mid-1990s, this intense user-device relationship was seen as unusual and harmful, especially for children. The *New York Times* noted that Tamagotchi is "a dictatorial little toy that threatens to die if the child stops playing with it."[56] A *Smithsonian Magazine* piece on the twenty-fifth anniversary of Tamagotchi includes testimony to the psychological effect of the toy's virtual death. "I remember, very clearly, standing in the kitchen when my sister found out that her Tamagotchi died, and just how traumatic that was for her," states one Tamagotchi user of their experience of the toy as a child.[57] Tamagotchi that died in "infancy" would simply end with a fading screen. Those that lasted to maturity would have a death sequence that depicted a ghost by a gravestone (in the Japanese model) or an angel among stars (in the English-language model).[58]

Amidst criticism for hooking kids on intensive cycles of care that, after a couple weeks, resulted in the loss of the virtual being they had worked so hard to keep alive, Bandai made changes to Tamagotchi functionality. A pause button was added, for example. While Tamagotchi and Giga Pets typically "slept" at night and made no beeps, they would beep once or twice an hour during the day. Like the Do Not Disturb settings available on most phones today, the pause button was particularly helpful for users in contexts where the devices were restricted or prohibited, such as schools. A *New York Times* editorial criticizing the toys mused that, in light of such changes, "with any luck, the kids will lose interest in a pet that no longer requires their constant attention."[59]

These and similar virtual pets would position portable, digital devices as personal companions for many young people at the turn of the millennium, preparing them for the type of frequent interactions we have with our devices today, especially in terms of updating and monitoring. Writing in 2007, Kusahara remarked, "Now looking back, the interaction a user could have with Tamagotchi was not a happy or entertaining one at all. It was in fact a game, because users tried it repeatedly (if not too shocked by the death) to obtain all possible forms of metamorphosis [of the creature] … The biggest lesson was that users should be able to *enjoy* virtual characters. There was little sense of humor in Tamagotchi, after all."[60]

Gopnik has described caring for others as a "kind of expansion of the self."[61] However, in writing about the self and computing's relational artifacts (such as robots and interactive toy creatures), Turkle warns:

> If our experience with relational artifacts is based on the fiction that they know and care about us, can the attachments that follow be good for us? Or might they be good for us in the "feel good" sense, but bad for us as moral beings? The answers to such questions do not depend on what robots can do today or in the future. These questions ask what *we* will be like, what kind of people *we* are becoming as we develop increasingly intimate relationships with machines.[62]

It is relatively clear that Tamagotchi and Giga Pets did not care for their users. They were the needy ones – their happiness meter was theirs, after all, not ours – and it was up to us to maintain them in good health. Part of that good health was simply interacting with them, however, to build an affective relationship between user and device. Today, the metrics go both ways, as device performance (especially it being "up to date") and our performance are constantly measured and analyzed, with data and notifications frequently shared for both. As this process intensifies, with more user data collected and more nuanced data packaging and analysis from the device, the expansion that Gopnik and Turkle describe will only continue.

Writing for *PCMag* in 2018, Benj Edwards commented that "these keychain buddies taught a generation of 1990s kids about responsibility and/or how difficult it can be to take care of a help[l]ess creature. They were a cultural touchstone for a generation."[63] What seemed like an extraordinary transgression in affective transference and intimacy a quarter-century ago now cleaves toward the norm for users and their devices as the relationship – and its multiple forms of material interaction and exchange – is increasingly perceived as mutually beneficial. Nearly every portable, networked media device today offers daily alerts, notifications, and updates. While device and app settings may allow us to silence or turn off these signals by the device on a case-by-case basis, it is rare that they are ever turned off entirely. This may be because of user resignation to the persistence of networked devices or this may be because of the user's fear of missing out. The sense of being connected through the device is enhanced by the way the device continually lets us know that changes are happening. Users may also be concerned about the well-being of the device and its apps. Sometimes these signals are inconsequential, but at other times they can alert the user to security patches and other updates that protect the device and its apps from attacks. It may be a combination of these reasons. And even if you turn off notifications, sometimes updating an app or system will automatically reactivate them. Whatever the individual circumstances, the result is habitual processes of interaction with the device that extend beyond simply communicating with others. In the case of fitness and activity trackers, these signals may be seen as notifications or alerts by and about the user's body. The device's chime or beep can be the equivalent of a burp, a howl, or a yawn, alerting the user to the body's needs and changes. The connection between device and body could not be any closer. And just as the device alerts the user to take care of their own body and well-being, the device can alert the user to take care of its body and well-being.

Conclusion

Before presenting some final observations, let's reacquaint ourselves with the object of our inquiry. Set this book down for a moment and grab your nearest personal media device. It could be your phone, your watch, or your tablet. Perhaps you may not need to set this book down at all, if you are reading these words on a device. In either case, after all that has been presented in the preceding chapters, take a moment to appreciate the object. Consider again how this small, rather plain-looking thing can produce such a rich variety of effects: sounds, vibrations, light and colour modulations, and so on. Recall the potential affective impact that can be produced from the combination of these effects, depending on device settings, place, time of day, and user needs and desires. Tapped into wireless networks and the device's own operating system, the material capabilities of this unobtrusive piece of glass, metal, and plastic transform it into an animated, adaptable, and personalized presence in our lives. Its many actions demand our attention in different ways, again hinging on circumstances and settings. These are not just signals, but invitations to interact, engage, and share. The device is not only a tool – like a land line phone, a reflex camera, or a TV remote – but also a companion that seems to need our attention as much as we might need it.

The conditions just described – converting a small, plain object into a marvel of interactive and affective power – did not materialize in a breakthrough moment of discovery, a fortuitous accident, or a serendipitous coincidence. They did not arrive bundled in an R&D demo, a sensational product drop, or a developers' conference keynote speech (despite any number of YouTube videos, puff pieces, or marketing visuals that might suggest otherwise). As this book has shown, the power of the personalized, interactive media device emerges out of a remarkable array of objects, gadgets, practices, desires, and needs spanning over a half century. Its seeds are in 1970s improvised kit computers, 1980s operating system cursors, 1990s key chain toy pets, 2000s MP3 player cases and appliqués, and 2010s rear- and front-facing cameras. And there are more seeds elsewhere. The examples and episodes explored in the preceding chapters are far from exhaustive in describing the development and consequences of these devices and their interaction with humans. Nevertheless, what you have read represents an ever-shrinking tip of the iceberg, as processes and features become increasingly embedded behind the screen and beyond our awareness.

Across these diverse historical objects and contexts emerge design features and patterns of interaction that engage the senses to make the device intimate and complicit. Admittedly, media and media devices have been intimate for centuries. From handwritten letters, paperback books, and portrait miniatures, to cameras, magic lanterns, and walkie-talkies, portable media objects and content have reshaped our relationship to the environment and society on an individual level for many, many years. The contemporary devices studied here, however, not only structure intimacy across object, content, and networks but also root it in the range and complexity of potential interactions between device and user. Design features such as the shape and texture of devices, as well as responsive elements like touch screens, facial recognition, and automatic volume modulation make familiarity and awareness a transactional certitude for both the device and its user across their interactions. Ironically, even increased networking capabilities (from the simple phone conversation or text of early cellphones to advanced graphics and live audiovisual streaming on devices today) may contribute to greater intimacy and complicity with the device than with the people we may communicate with through the device. While telecommunications networks should represent an opportunity for users to engage directly with other people, more often than not they have facilitated users' engagement with software and algorithms that sort, reframe, and even modify content made by others. For example, using a social media app is often more about engaging with the specifics of the system as they manifest themselves in the interface than about interacting with other people. The app will often personalize content to maximize engagement with the platform, prioritizing suggested sensational or provocative content over content or messages produced by a user's social contacts (e.g., TikTok's For You tab as a default over its Following tab). We may even experience direct communications from others – a text or a phone call – as disrupting our relationship with the device as we attempt to engage with it and its networked behaviour, rather than with live human beings.

These circumstances condition people, reshaping their behaviour and habits, as effects and features backed by networked computing build emotional dependency while multiplying paths and forms of device interactivity. Just as the 1990s handwriting recognition systems studied in chapter 3 trained users to adapt their pen strokes to communicate effectively with the device, or the digital pet alerts considered in chapter 6 necessitated timely reactions to keep a virtual pet healthy, the device is a disciplining tool subtly reshaping both body and mind to its needs. This process now stretches twenty-four hours a day as the device channels the collective power of some of the world's largest corporations into highly personalized doses of content and effects based on patterns of behaviour detected when the user is awake and asleep. For as long as the device remains near the user, as seen in chapter 5, it collects data on movement, engagement, and personal habits to determine and target cues for further engagement. Under these circumstances, we could say it is not only the user or device that is needy but also the seemingly limitless avarice of an all-sensing, ever-recording networked capitalism, where even a moment's "distraction" of the user away from the device represents corporate loss in data assets and revenue. That this corporate neediness is partially masked by the intervening object (i.e., I give the device my data so *it* knows me better and aligns with my lifestyle and personality) is perhaps the most striking example of how power can circulate and impact our lives even in moments when we feel most removed from such societal forces (as when lying on the sofa just "killing time" with our phone).

Having tied these devices to a half-century of communication technologies and consumer electronics that have augmented, realigned, and concentrated power in building intimacy and affect between users and their devices, we may turn now to the question of their future. Amid all the changes in technology, media practices, and the social fabric of society in recent years, studies as late as 2023 suggest that our relationship with, and dependence on, these devices is only becoming more complex.[1] Smartphones, smartwatches, and the like have accompanied us almost everywhere only for the last twenty years (if that), yet it has become difficult to imagine how life was before. Using maps, road signs, and the knowledge of locals to find our way seems so twentieth-century, even if GPS was not commonly used on phones until the 2010s. And now that our device speaks to us to show us the way, we rarely speak to anyone else for directions. As addressed earlier, especially regarding locative technologies in chapter 2 and identity recognition systems in chapter 4, these objects double for us in the networked world. Our phone or watch (linked to our phone) is our principle identifying object. In some jurisdictions during the COVID-19 pandemic, for example, proof of immunization for access to shared spaces (restaurants, theatres, meeting rooms, etc.) came from an app on the phone. A paper note from a doctor or clinic was not only useless but also suspect. Proving our identity through two-factor verification, to give another example, almost always involves our phone.

But why is so much faith put in these devices as irrefutable evidence of our being? Simply put, the personal media device has become our interface with nearly everything, much as our face had been the primary interface with others for thousands of years. It is hard to imagine some other product or object becoming such a widely accepted proof our identity, short of bodily implanted technology or totalizing sensing systems like universal facial recognition covering all spaces, public and private (which, ironically, would bring us back to the face as a primary interface!). It may happen that technology will be implanted in the body, so the network can pass through our flesh directly to our neural links. It is also possible that our environments will recognize us with such precision (through ubiquitous face, speech, and movement recognition, for example) that many of the transactions we now conduct through our devices will be accomplished without them. Perhaps neural decoders will navigate our thoughts and activate retina-level screens so we can network without speaking, moving, or even opening our eyes. For decades such scenarios have been theorized and predicted (consider the cyborgian imaginary of the 1990s), but using our hands – and sometimes our voice – to interact with independent objects still seems to be the way to get most things done. Part of the social resistance to these other options may also be the spectre of loss of individual control and privacy even while, as this book has argued throughout, the individual control and privacy of our hand-held devices is more phantasmagoria than fact.

In the current context, however, we might consider the relationship between these devices and two other global technological trends that have broad consequences for the future flow and concentration of power in societies: artificial intelligence (AI) and smart environments of networked infrastructures. Since the 2010s, AI increasingly has moved out of corporate and institutional research centres into widespread use across a variety of applications. It captured the attention of the general public in 2021–22 with the release of free, easy-to-use generative AI applications like ChatGPT and DALL-E. This shift has been fuelled by developments in neural networks, foundational large language models (LLMs), and generative adversarial networks (GANs) underpinned by the enormous data and computing power of big tech.

Generative AI of the ChatGPT, DALL-E, and Gemini sort creates data – text, images, sound – meant to resemble existing data. Trained on, and tested against, human creations (books, songs, speeches, photographs, etc.), generative AI can produce content that mimics the tastes, habits, and idiosyncrasies of humans. Generative AI contributes to more human-like interactions with devices and platforms. Chatbots and voice-based assistants like Siri or Google Assistant behave more like humans and less like clusters of prepackaged modular responses. Deep learning AI models, on the other hand, detect patterns in data and predict potential outcomes. In user-device relationships, deep learning can be effective for analyzing behaviour at both the micro and macro level (i.e., individual users and large groups). This has powerful implications for the future role personal media devices can play in our lives. Harvesting mass amounts of physiological, optical, and interactive data, deep learning AI models can guide and nuance user-device interactions based on fast, complex, and ever-changing algorithms at a level not yet experienced. As we build longer histories with these devices and the products we use on them, the enormous capacity and speed of these learning models may be able to predict behaviour in the moment based on years of our device use, tailoring interface and content accordingly second to second. In this regard, AI may be seamlessly integrated into existing user-device relationships, creating further advantages for platforms in an already imbalanced relationship.

Smart environments involve sensors and high-speed data networks to put objects, architectures, and spaces into constant communication in ways that can continually modify these environments and the experiences of those inhabiting them. A child of cybernetics and an extension of pervasive computing and the Internet of Things (IoT), smart environments underpin systems such as cashierless shopping, self-driving transportation, and automated medication delivery in hospitals. They also include systems beyond a user's knowledge, such as energy grids. In many cases (like hospitalization or shopping), accurate identification and tracking of individuals is paramount to adjusting spaces and experiences effectively at a personal level. At present, our personal networked media devices frequently serve as the determining link between us and these environments. If AI nuances our interactions with the personal media device, in such smart environments the device can convey a sense of control over our circumstances. We can adjust settings and preferences on the device, for example, to alter how it interacts with any given space, machine, or system. However, smart environments are another reason why misplacing, forgetting, or losing one's phone can be a harrowing experience. Without the device, surrounding smart entities, like the car, the retail shop, or the home, will "ghost" you.

In both AI and smart environments, we can see how a personal media device becomes a valued asset or partner for their technological processes. Reliance on the device suggests user autonomy even as these systems can undermine agency, choice, and equal access and opportunity across users. In our current dependency on the devices studied here, there remains one critical element of comfort that these other options may not offer, however (if "comfort" is even the right word, given that these devices are configured to give us a sense of comfort and reassurance in picking up and using them). Amid the invasive, affective, and addictive features our personal devices contain, there still is an "off" button that dangles the possibility of shutting down the device and escaping networked existence, if only for a couple of hours. Granted, we rarely – if ever – entirely shut off our devices. Even when we go to bed, we tend to put them in one mode or another, rather than shut them down. The imperatives of society – with more and more organizations and companies shedding humans and paper-based transactions – make this option less and less of an option in reality. Yet, it is still there, however impractical it is becoming. Were these operations or the infrastructure of these devices to move entirely to our bodies or our environments, however, even that rarely used option might disappear. In that moment, the personal media device and user would truly merge, becoming entirely one and the same. Where, then, would we place our attention, our affection?

Notes

Introduction

1 Sharif Mowlabocus, "The 'Mastery' of the Swipe: Smartphones, Transitional Objects and Interstitial Time," *First Monday* 21, no. 10 (3 October 2016), https://doi.org/10.5210/fm.v21i10.6950.

2 Sherry Turkle, *Alone Together: Why We Expect More from Technology and Less from Each Other* (New York: Basic Books, 2011), 1.

3 Thomas Beauvisage and Kevin Mellet, "Datassets: Assetizing and Marketizing Personal Data," in *Assetization: Turning Things into Assets in Technoscientific Capitalism*, ed. Kean Birch and Fabian Muniesa (Cambridge, MA: MIT Press, 2020), 75–95.

4 J.C.R. Licklider, "Man-Computer Symbiosis," *IRE Transactions on Human Factors in Electronics* HFE-1, no. 1 (March 1960): 4–11.

5 Armin Beverungen, Timon Beyes, and Lisa Conrad, "The Organizational Powers of (Digital) Media," *Organization* 26, no. 5 (September 2019): 621–35, 624.

6 See Steve Jones's idea on the "digitization of memory" as a key component of contemporary culture. Steve Jones, "People, Things, Memory and Human-Machine Communication," *International Journal of Media & Cultural Politics* 10, no. 3 (September 2014): 245–58. This is also addressed in Nicholas Agar, *How to Be Human in the Digital Economy* (Cambridge, MA: MIT Press, 2019); and Ben Jacobsen and David Beer, *Social Media and the Automatic Production of Memory: Classification, Ranking, and the Sorting of the Past* (Bristol: Bristol University Press, 2021).

7 Nick Srnicek, "Auxiliary Organs: An Ethics of the Extended Mind," in *The Imaginary App*, ed. Paul D. Miller and Svitlana Matviyenko (Cambridge, MA: MIT Press, 2014), 72–3.

8 There were about seven billion mobile phone subscriptions worldwide in 2024, for a world population of just over eight billion people. See Petroc Taylor, "Smartphone Mobile Network Subscriptions Worldwide 2016–2028," Statista, 22 May 2024, https://www.statista.com/statistics/330695/number-of-smartphone-users-worldwide/.

9 Edward W. Constant II, "The Social Locus of Technological Practice: Community, System, or Organization?," in *The Social Construction of Technological Systems*, ed. Wiebe E. Bijker, Thomas P. Hughes, and Trevor Pinch (Cambridge, MA: MIT Press, 1987), 231.

10 For occasions where these theories have been employed in such contexts, see Rogers Brubaker, *Hyperconnectivity and Its Discontents* (Cambridge, UK: Polity Press, 2022); Nathan Jurgenson, *The Social Photo: On Photography and Social Media* (London: Verso, 2019); Richard Ling, *New Tech, New Ties: How Mobile Communication Is Reshaping Social Cohesion* (Cambridge, MA: MIT Press, 2008); and Terje Rasmussen, *Personal Media and Everyday Life: A Networked Lifeworld* (Basingstoke: Palgrave Macmillan, 2014).

11 Wendy Hui Kyong Chun, *Updating to Remain the Same: Habitual New Media* (Cambridge, MA: MIT Press, 2016); Sherry Turkle, *Life on the Screen: Identity in the Age of the Internet* (New York: Simon & Schuster, 1995); Turkle, *Alone Together*; Christina Dunbar-Hester, *Hacking Diversity: The Politics of Inclusion in Open Technology Cultures* (Princeton, NJ: Princeton University Press, 2020); Sharon Y. Tettegah and Safiya Umoja Noble, eds., *Emotions, Technology, and Design* (London: Academic Press, 2016); and Mikael Wiberg, *The Materiality of Interaction: Notes on the Materials of Interaction Design* (Cambridge, MA: MIT Press, 2017).

12 Erkki Huhtamo and Jussi Parikka, eds., *Media Archaeology Approaches, Applications, and Implications* (Berkeley, CA: University of California Press, 2011), 3.

13 Huhtamo and Parikka, *Media Archaeology*; Erkki Huhtamo and Doron Galili, "The Pasts and Prospects of Media Archaeology," *Early Popular Visual Culture* 18, no. 4 (2020): 333–9.

14 Clemens Apprich and Götz Bachmann, "Media Genealogy: Back to the Present of Digital Cultures," in *Digitisation: Theories and Concepts for Empirical Cultural Research*, ed. Gertraud Koch (London: Routledge, 2017): 293–306, 296.

15 Barry Smart, *Michel Foucault*, rev. ed. (London: Routledge, 2002), 33–8.

16 These cities are the headquarters of Alphabet (Google's parent company),

Meta, Apple, and Microsoft, four global corporations collectively worth over $10 trillion in market capitalization in 2024 and that directly affect practically every smartphone and internet user on Earth through their electronics, apps, services, and data centres.

17 Jenny L. Davis, *How Artifacts Afford: The Power and Politics of Everyday Things* (Cambridge, MA: MIT Press, 2020), 11. Emphasis in original.

18 Anita Say Chan, *Predatory Data: Eugenics in Big Tech and Our Fight for an Independent Future* (Berkeley, CA: University of California Press, 2025); Brandeis Hill Marshall, *Data Conscience: Algorithmic Siege on our Humanity* (Hoboken, NJ: Wiley, 2022); Cathy O'Neil, *Weapons of Math Destruction: How Big Data Increases Inequality and Threatens Democracy* (New York: Crown, 2016); Lisa Nakamura, *Digitizing Race: Visual Cultures of the Internet* (Minneapolis: University of Minnesota Press, 2007).

19 Patrick Grother, Mei Ngan, and Kayee Hanaoka, *Face Recognition Vendor Test (FRVT), Part 3: Demographic Effects* (Washington, DC: National Institute of Standards and Technology, 2019), https://doi.org/10.6028/NIST.IR.8280; Joy Buolamwini, *Unmasking AI: My Mission to Protect What Is Human in a World of Machines* (New York: Random House, 2023); Sarah McIntyre, Saad S. Nagi, Francis McGlone, and Håkan Olausson, "The Effects of Ageing on Tactile Function in Humans," *Neuroscience* 464 (1 June 2021): 53–8, https://doi.org/10.1016/j.neuroscience.2021.02.015.

20 Joachim Israel, "Social Responsivity as Elementary Human Action," *Acta Sociologica* 31, no. 3 (1988): 231–40. See also George Herbert Mead, *Mind, Self, and Society*, ed. Charles W. Morris (1934; repr., Chicago: University of Chicago Press, 2015); Lars-Erik Janlert and Erik Stolterman, *Things That Keep Us Busy: The Elements of Interaction* (Cambridge, MA: MIT Press, 2017), 105–6.

21 For an example of such a focus in researching issues of networked identity and intimacy, consider Howard Gardner and Katie Davis, *The App Generation: How Today's Youth Navigate Identity, Intimacy, and Imagination in a Digital World* (New Haven: Yale University Press, 2013).

22 Janlert and Stolterman, *Things That Keep Us Busy*, 20.

23 Michelle Drouin, *Out of Touch: How to Survive an Intimacy Famine* (Cambridge, MA: MIT Press, 2022), 118.

24 Wiberg, *Materiality of Interaction*, 34.

25 Mowlabocus, "'Mastery' of the Swipe"; Marina Everri, "'Space Invaders': Are Smartphones Really Transforming Parents and Adolescents' Ways of

Communicating?," *Parenting for a Digital Future* (blog), 1 March 2017, https://blogs.lse.ac.uk/parenting4digitalfuture/2017/03/01/space-invaders-are-smartphones-really-transforming-parents-and-adolescents-ways-of-communicating/; and Trevor Haynes, "Dopamine, Smartphones & You: A Battle for Your Time," Science in the News, Harvard University Graduate School of Arts and Sciences, 1 May 2018, https://sitn.hms.harvard.edu/flash/2018/dopamine-smartphones-battle-time/.

26 Daniel Miller, *Stuff* (Cambridge: Polity, 2010), 6. Regarding this concept, see also Ainissa Ramirez, *The Alchemy of Us: How Humans and Matter Transformed One Another* (Cambridge, MA: MIT Press, 2020).

27 Alan Kay, "User Interface: A Personal View," in *Multimedia: From Wagner to Virtual Reality*, ed. Randall Packer and Ken Jordan (New York: W.W. Norton, 2002), 124.

28 Shoshana Zuboff, *The Age of Surveillance Capitalism: The Fight for a Human Future at the New Frontier of Power* (New York: PublicAffairs, 2019).

29 Ganaele Langlois, Joanna Redden, and Greg Elmer, *Compromised Data: From Social Media to Big Data* (New York: Bloomsbury Academic, 2015); Sung-Yueh Perng, Rob Kitchin, and Leighton Evans, "Locative Media and Data-driven Computing Experiments," *Big Data & Society* 3, no. 1 (January–June 2016), https://doi.org/10.1177/2053951716652161; Sachin Banker and Salil Khetani, "Algorithm Overdependence: How the Use of Algorithmic Recommendation Systems Can Increase Risks to Consumer Well-Being," *Journal of Public Policy & Marketing* 38, no. 4 (October 2019): 500–15.

30 Zizi Papacharissi, ed., *The Networked Self: Identity, Community, and Culture on Social Network Sites* (New York: Routledge, 2011); Brian Massumi, *Parables for the Virtual: Movement, Affect, Sensation* (Durham, NC: Duke University Press, 2002), 128; Lee Rainie and Barry Wellman, *Networked: The New Social Operating System* (Cambridge, MA: MIT Press, 2012), 3.

31 Rainie and Wellman, *Networked*, 6.

32 Margaret E. Morris, *Left to Our Own Devices: Outsmarting Smart Technology to Reclaim Our Relationships, Health, and Focus* (Cambridge, MA: MIT Press, 2018), xxi.

33 *Merriam-Webster*, s.v. "neediness," accessed 3 February 2025, https://www.merriam-webster.com/dictionary/neediness.

34 *Oxford English Dictionary*, s.v. "neediness," accessed 3 February 2025, https://www.oed.com/search/dictionary/?scope=Entries&q=neediness.

35 Carli Ochs and Andreas Sonderegger, "What Students Do While You Are

Teaching – Computer and Smartphone Use in Class and Its Implication on Learning," in *Human-Computer Interaction* – *INTERACT 2021*, ed. Carli Ardito et al., Lecture Notes in Computer Science 12933 (Cham: Springer, 2021): 501–20, https://doi.org/10.1007/978-3-030-85616-8_29.

36 Terje Rasmussen refers to this as the personalization of information, versus the personalization of media. The former involves mass media techniques for making generalized content appear "'closer' to the audience," while the latter adapts technology to specific uses and needs at the individual level. See Rasmussen, *Personal Media and Everyday Life*, 6.

37 In this regard, actor-network theory may be useful in exploring the user-device relationship, though its focus on networks places it outside the goals of this study, which centres on material and spatial interactions between individual bodies and devices. See Bruno Latour, *Reassembling the Social: An Introduction to Actor-Network Theory* (Oxford: Oxford University Press, 2005); Wiebe E. Bijker, Thomas P. Hughes, and Trevor Pinch, eds., *The Social Construction of Technological Systems: New Directions in the Sociology and History of Technology* (Cambridge, MA: MIT Press, 1987).

38 Laine Nooney, *The Apple II Age: How the Computer Became Personal* (Chicago: University of Chicago Press, 2023), 9.

39 *Oxford English Dictionary*, s.v. "personal," accessed 3 February 2025, https://www.oed.com/search/dictionary/?scope=Entries&q=personal.

40 *Oxford English Dictionary*, s.v. "medium," accessed 3 February 2025, https://www.oed.com/search/dictionary/?scope=Entries&q=medium.

41 Unsigned review of *A Revived Ministry, Our Only Hope for a Revived Church*, in *The Eclectic Review* 20 (July–December 1846): 23–40, 33. Emphasis in original.

42 "The Church, Its Authority," *Newchurchman* 2, no. 2 (April 1843): 65–127, 101.

43 Samuel Harris, *The Self-Revelation of God* (New York: Charles Scribner's Sons, 1887), 454–5.

44 *The Patent, Trade-Mark, and Copyright Journal of Research and Education* 1, no. 1 (June 1957), 163. Emphasis in original.

45 Erwin H. Ephron, "Are the People You Want Watching?," *Media/Scope* 11 (October 1967): 46–9, 120–4, 120.

46 Marshall McLuhan, *Understanding Media: The Extensions of Man* (New York: McGraw-Hill, 1964).

47 William H. Gilbert, ed., *Public Relations in Local Government* (Washington, DC: Institute for Training in Municipal Administration, 1975).

48 Wilbur Schramm, *Men, Messages, and Media: A Look at Human Communication* (New York: Harper & Row, 1973), 113–14.

49 See, for example, advertisements for the Pocket Kozy camera, *McClure's Magazine*, advertising supplement, November 1897, 69.

50 RCA Victor ad, *Popular Mechanics*, July 1951, 1.

51 Dyna-mite Pocket Radio ad, *Popular Mechanics*, September 1952, 64.

52 Tinytone Pocket Personal Radio ad, *Popular Mechanics*, January 1957, 88.

53 Viscount Electronics ad, *New York Times Magazine*, 16 October 1966, 124.

54 See, for example, Eric Freedman, *Transient Images: Personal Media in Public Frameworks* (Philadelphia: Temple University Press, 2010); Katie Day Good, "From Scrapbook to Facebook: A History of Personal Media Assemblage and Archives," *New Media & Society* 15, no. 4 (June 2013): 557–73.

55 *The International Encyclopedia of Media Effects*, s.v. "Personal Media," by Nancy Thumim, ed. Patrick Rössler, Cynthia A. Hoffner, and Liesbet van Zoonen, last modified 8 July 2016, https://onlinelibrary.wiley.com/doi/full/10.1002/9781118783764.wbieme0180.

56 Marika Lüders, "Conceptualizing Personal Media," *New Media & Society* 10, no. 5 (October 2008): 683–702, 684.

57 Ibid., 685.

58 Rasmussen, *Personal Media and Everyday Life*, 5.

59 Ibid., 8.

60 For examples beyond those provided here, see Joel C. Kuipers and Joshua A. Bell, introduction to *Linguistic and Material Intimacies of Cell Phones*, ed. Joshua A. Bell and Joel C. Kuipers (Abingdon: Routledge, 2018), 6.

61 The vast amount of personal material stored on these devices – potentially dating back years – convinced the United States Supreme Court that devices seized as evidence during arrests could only be searched by law enforcement for evidence pertaining to the immediate cause of detainment. Despite being generally sympathetic to law enforcement and relatively lenient in terms of search and seizure, the court ruled that there was simply too much information about people on their phones, potentially allowing authorities to search all corners of one's life from a simple disorderly conduct or drug arrest. See *Riley v. California*, 573 US 373 (2014), no. 13–132.

62 Norman J. Medoff and Barbara K. Kaye, *Electronic Media: Then, Now, and Later*, 3rd ed., electronic ed. (New York: Routledge, 2017).

63 Cynthia A. Hoffner, Sangmi Lee, and Se Jung Park, "'I Miss My Mobile

Phone!': Self-Expansion via Mobile Phone and Responses to Phone Loss," *New Media & Society* 18, no. 11 (December 2016): 2452–68.

64 Stefan Tams, Renaud Legoux, and Pierre-Majorique Léger, "Smartphone Withdrawal Creates Stress: A Moderated Mediation Model of Nomophobia, Social Threat, and Phone Withdrawal Context," *Computers in Human Behavior* 81 (April 2018): 1–9; A.L.S. King, A.M. Valença, A.C.O. Silva, T. Baczynski, M.R. Carvalho, and A.E. Nardi, "Nomophobia: Dependency on Virtual Environments or Social Phobia?," *Computers in Human Behavior* 29, no. 1 (2013): 140–4; B.W. Park and K.C. Lee, "The Effect of Users' Characteristics and Experiential Factors on the Compulsive Usage of the Smartphone," *Ubiquitous Computing and Multimedia Applications* 151 (2011): 438–46.

65 Jason M.Cuéllar and Todd H. Lanman, "'Text Neck': An Epidemic of the Modern Era of Cell Phones?," *Spine Journal* 17, no. 6 (June 2017): 901–2; Xiaofei Guan et al., "Gender Difference in Mobile Phone Use and the Impact of Digital Device Exposure on Neck Posture," *Ergonomics* 59, no. 11 (November 2016): 1453–61; Michael Gradisar et al., "The Sleep and Technology Use of Americans: Findings from the National Sleep Foundation's 2011 Sleep in America Poll," *Journal of Clinical Sleep Medicine* 9, no. 12 (December 2015): 1291–9; Liese Exelmans and JanVan den Bulck, "Bedtime Mobile Phone Use and Sleep in Adults," *Social Science & Medicine* 148 (January 2016): 93–101; Jan Van den Bulck, "Text Messaging as a Cause of Sleep Interruption in Adolescents, Evidence from a Cross Sectional Study," *Journal of Sleep Research* 12, no. 3 (September 2003): 263.

Chapter One

1 Laine Nooney, *The Apple II Age: How the Computer Became Personal* (Chicago: University of Chicago Press, 2023), 7.

2 *Time*, cover, 3 January 1983.

3 Sherry Turkle, "Always-On/Always-On-You: The Tethered Self," in *Handbook of Mobile Communication Studies*, ed. James E. Katz (Cambridge, MA: MIT Press, 2008), https://doi.org/10.7551/mitpress/7445.003.0013.

4 Oliver Garfield, GENIACS: *Simple Electric Brain Machines and How to Make Them; Also: Manual for Geniac Electric Brain Construction Kit No. 1* (New York: Berkeley Enterprises, 1955), 2.

5 Mark Frauenfelder, *The Computer: An Illustrated History from Its Origins to the Present*, 2nd ed. (London: Carlton Books, 2013), 114.

6 Lionel de Bournonville, Arthur L. Samuel, and M.V. Wilkes, "Computers in 1984," *New Scientist* 21, no. 380 (27 February 1964): 528–31, 530.

8 Alan Kay, "User Interface: A Personal View," in *Multimedia: From Wagner to Virtual Reality*, ed. Randall Packer and Ken Jordan (New York: W.W. Norton, 2002), 124. Emphasis in original.

8 One of the first uses of the term "personal computer" in general settings was Hewlett-Packard's marketing of its HP-65 programmable pocket calculator in 1974 as "the 'personal computer,'" though, as Paul Ceruzzi notes, "the trade press was hesitant to call them computers." Paul E. Ceruzzi, *A History of Modern Computing*, 2nd ed. (Cambridge, MA: MIT Press, 2003), 214. See also Chung C. Tung, "The 'Personal Computer': A Fully Programmable Pocket Calculator," *Hewlett-Packard Journal* (May 1974): 2–7.

9 "Small" and "home" are used in Carl Helms, "The State of the Art," *Byte* 1, no. 3 (November 1975): 6–7, 88, 6; "hobby" is used in Wayne Green, *Hobby Computers Are Here!* (Peterborough, NH: 73 Magazine, 1976) and Harold L. Singer, "The Hobby Computer Explosion: What's Happening and Where Is It Heading in the Future?," in *Computers the Next 5 Years: Evolution or Revolution: Compcon Spring 76: Twelfth IEEE Computer Society International Conference* (Long Beach, CA: IEEE, 1976): 216–17.

10 Edmund C. Berkeley, "Simple Simon," *Scientific American*, November 1950, 40–3, 40.

11 Lisa Gitelman and Geoffrey B. Pingree, "Introduction: What's New About New Media," in *New Media, 1740-1915*, ed. Lisa Gitelman and Geoffrey B. Pingree (Cambridge, MA: MIT Press, 2003), xii.

12 Stewart Brand, "SPACEWAR: Fanatic Life and Symbolic Death among the Computer Bums," *Rolling Stone*, 7 December 1972, 50–8.

13 Tung-Hui Hu, *A Prehistory of the Cloud* (Cambridge, MA: MIT Press, 2016), 46–7.

14 Among the personal computer pioneers who took LSD are Stewart Brand, Douglas Engelbert, and Steve Jobs. Jobs called it "one of the two or three most important things he had done in his life." John Markoff, *What the Dormouse Said: How the Sixties Counterculture Shaped the Personal Computer Industry* (New York: Viking, 2005), xix and 58–68.

15 See, for example, Fred Turner, *From Counterculture to Cyberculture: Stewart Brand, the Whole Earth Network and the Rise of Digital Utopianism* (Chi-

cago: University of Chicago Press, 2008). Even when this imbalance is recognized, it is not necessarily rectified. In Martin Campbell-Kelly and William Asprey's history of the computer, for example, they note the role of hobbyists and kit building yet devote greater attention to the work of individuals such as Steve Jobs and Bill Gates than computer kit culture. Martin Campbell-Kelly et al., *Computer: A History of the Informaton Machine*, 3rd ed. (Boulder, CO: Westview Press, 2014), 229–41. See also Stan Augarten, *Bit by Bit: An Illustrated History of Computers* (New York: Ticknor & Fields, 1984), 253–81; Mark Frauenfelder, *The Computer: An Illustrated History from Its Origins to the Present*, 2nd ed. (London: Carlton Books, 2013), 114–55.

16 Markoff, *What the Dormouse Said*, xv.

17 See, for example, Ceruzzi, *A History of Modern Computing*, 224–6; Campbell-Kelly et al., *Computer*, 232–5.

18 Markoff, *What the Dormouse Said*, 251–2.

19 Mikael Wiberg, *The Materiality of Interaction: Notes on the Materials of Interaction Design* (Cambridge, MA: MIT Press, 2017), 8.

20 Campbell-Kelly et al., *Computer*, 236.

21 Untitled and unattributed article, *The Computer Hobbyist* 1, no. 4 (February 1975): 1.

22 Campbell-Kelly et al., *Computer*, 232–3.

23 William H. Whyte, *The Organization Man* (New York: Simon & Schuster, 1956).

24 There were some exceptions. Though most advertisements for Altair microcomputers simply described their design strengths, computing potential, and competitive pricing, a few promoted the devices as a means of popular liberation. "Imagine a land where computers are in the hands of the people. Creative people from farmers to merchants to students to engineers to housewives to dentists to poets," reads an advertisement entitled "The Land of Altair." Altair advertisement, *Byte* 2 (October 1975), 48–9.

25 Stephen B. Gray, "Building a Computer of Your Own," in *The Best of Creative Computing*, vol. 1, ed. David H. Ahl (Morris Plains, NJ: Creative Computing Press, 1976), 107–8, 108.

26 Campbell-Kelly et al., *Computer*, 233.

27 GENIAC ad, *Popular Science* 173, no. 4 (October 1958): 261.

28 Garfield, *GENIACS*, 2.

29 Steven M. Gelber, *Hobbies: Leisure and the Culture of Work in America* (New York: Columbia University Press, 1999), 262.

30 Ibid., 269 and 294.

31 Ibid., 288. Gelber's insights are reinforced by Paul Atkinson, whose work on DIY similarly identifies two types of DIY: proactive and reactive. Proactive DIY is largely creative and open as participants develop their own projects, goals, and styles, according to Atkinson, while reactive is more structured and scripted, based on kits and templates "involving the assembly of predetermined components." See Paul Atkinson, "Amateur Design," in *A Companion to Contemporary Design since 1945*, ed. Anne Massey (Hoboken, NJ: John Wiley & Sons, 2019), 373–92.

32 "The 8080 Is Here," *Computer Hobbyist* 1, no. 2 (December 1974): 3.

33 Steve Gray, "Building a MITS Altair 8800: First Impressions," in *Best of Creative Computing*, vol. 2, ed. David H. Ahl (Morristown, NJ: Creative Computing Press, 1984), 272–4, 272. Elsewhere, Paul Freiberger and Michael Swaine explain that the front-panel board became detached and had to be attached "by dozens of wires – a task requiring hours of tedious work by the owner." Paul Freiberger and Michael Swaine, *Fire in the Valley: The Making of the Personal Computer* (Berkeley, CA: Osborne/McGraw-Hill, 1984), 41.

34 Jim C. Warren, "Editor's Preface," *Dr. Dobb's Journal of Computer Calisthenics and Orthodontia* 1 (September 1976), i.

35 Jef Raskin, "Personal Computers: A Bit of Wheat Amongst the Chaff," *Dr. Dobb's Journal of Computer Calisthenics and Orthodontia* 1, no. 8 (September 1976): 242–45, 242.

36 Louis E. Frenzel, "What's Involved in Kit Building?," *Byte* 2, no. 3 (March 1977): 50–60, 50.

37 Rachel P. Maines, *Hedonizing Technologies: Paths to Pleasure in Hobbies and Leisure* (Baltimore: Johns Hopkins University Press, 2009), 3.

38 Ceruzzi, *A History of Modern Computing*, 230–1. For an account of "becoming very tired of toggling in data" and devising a solution, see Herman DeMonstoy, "An Octal Front Panel," *Byte* 1, no. 9 (May 1976): 38–40, 38.

39 Freiberger and Swaine, *Fire in the Valley*, 42.

40 Even when peripherals were added for ease of use and interaction, the process was a personalized one. As a contributor to *Byte* wrote in 1976, "A friend has recently completed assembly of an ALTAIR 8800 and is interfacing a TV typewriter and an audio cassette recorder for bulk storage … Another popular approach is to use a tele-typewriter … A traditionalist, looking back a couple generations, might opt for a key punch of maybe 036

vintage." Thomas C. McIntire, "How to Save the BYTES," *Byte* 1, no. 6 (February 1976): 46–7, 46.

41 Carl Helmers, "Assembling Programs by Hand," *Byte* 1, no. 7 (March 1976): 52–61, 52.

42 Michael L. Smith, "Building Your Own Interface … Tips from a Professional," *Kilobaud*, no. 6 (June 1977): 22–8, 22.

43 Dennis E. Hamilton, "It's Your Hobby! The Critics Be Hanged," *Kilobaud*, no. 13 (January 1978): 108.

44 Lars-Erik Janlert and Erik Stolterman, *Things That Keep Us Busy: The Elements of Interaction* (Cambridge, MA: MIT Press, 2017), 21.

45 Nooney, *Apple II Age*, 33.

46 These calculations are based on the names of ninety-nine individual subscribers (i.e., not companies or institutions) that appeared in *Computer Hobbyist* between December 1974 and February 1975. *Computer Hobbyist* 1, nos. 2–4 (December 1974–February 1975).

47 Christina Dunbar-Hester, *Hacking Diversity: The Politics of Inclusion in Open Technology Cultures* (Princeton, NJ: Princeton University Press, 2020), 36.

48 Nathan Ensmenger, "'Beards, Sandals, and Other Signs of Rugged Individualism': Masculine Culture within the Computing Professions," *OSIRIS* 30 (2015): 38–65, 43.

49 Wayne Green, "Computers Are Here – Are You Ready?," *73 Magazine* (October 1975): 40–6, 40.

50 Marie Hicks, *Programmed Inequality: How Britain Discarded Women Technologists and Lost Its Edge in Computing* (Cambridge, MA: MIT Press, 2017); Janet Abbate, *Recoding Gender: Women's Changing Participation in Computing* (Cambridge, MA: MIT Press, 2012); Jennifer S. Light, "When Computers Were Women," *Technology and Culture* 40, no. 3 (1999): 455–83; Allison Marsh, "The Hidden Figures Behind Bletchley Park's Code-Breaking Colossus," IEEE Spectrum, 31 December 2019, https://spectrum.ieee.org/the-hidden-figures-behind-bletchley-parks-codebreaking-colossus; Nathan L. Ensmenger, *The Computer Boys Take Over: Computers, Programmers, and the Politics of Technical Expertise* (Cambridge, MA: MIT Press, 2010).

51 Theodor H. Nelson, *Computer Lib/Dream Machines* (n.p.: Theodor H. Nelson, 1974), 2.

52 Glenna Matthews, *Silicon Valley, Women, and the California Dream* (Palo Alto, CA: Stanford University Press, 2003); David N. Pellow and Lisa

Sun-Hee Park, *The Silicon Valley of Dreams: Environmental Injustice, Immigrant Workers, and the High-Tech Global Economy* (New York: New York University Press, 2002); Rachel Grossman, "Women's Place in the Integrated Circuit," *Radical America* 14, no. 1 (1980): 29–50; Les Levidow, "Women Who Make the Chips," in *Women, Work, and Gender Relations in Developing Countries: A Global Perspective*, ed. Parvin Ghorayshi and Claire Belanger (Westport, CT: Greenwood Press, 1996).

53 Susan B. Dixon, "MITS Production Department Emphasizes Quality Construction Not Mass Production," *Computer Notes* 3, no. 3 (August 1977): 4–5.

54 *Creative Computing* 1, no. 2 (January–February 1975), 21.

55 Heather Lynne McWilliams, "Daddy and His Computer," *Creative Computing* 1, no. 1 (November–December 1974): 20. The piece had previously appeared in *Datamation* (May 1973).

56 John Molnar, "Chasing Those Naughty Bits," *Kilobaud*, no. 2 (February 1977): 22–4.

57 Steve Pollini, "My Computer Just Stares at Me…," *Computer Notes* 2, no. 2 (July 1976): 13, 22–3, 13.

58 Pete Cornell, "IMSAI Owners – Beware of the Memory Clobbering Phantom!," *Dr. Dobb's Journal of Computer Calisthenics and Orthodontia* 1, no. 8 (September 1976): 17.

59 Steve Ciarcia, "Having a 'Private Affair' with Your Computer," *Byte* 2, no. 4 (April 1977): 18–31.

60 This resonates with other male-dominated hobbies of the post-war era. For example, in his book on masculinity and amateur pilot culture after World War II, Alan Meyer points out that one pilot's wife wrote an article for a plane hobbyist magazine describing herself as an "airport widow." Alan Meyer, *Weekend Pilots: Technology, Masculinity, and Private Aviation in Postwar America* (Baltimore: Johns Hopkins University Press, 2015), 2.

61 Sherry Turkle, *Life on the Screen: Identity in the Age of the Internet* (New York: Simon & Schuster, 1995), 32.

62 John Zarrella, "Assembling an Altair 8800," *Byte* 1, no. 4 (December 1975): 78–80.

63 Ibid., 79.

64 Robert D. Grappel and Jack Hemenway, "Jack and the Machine Talk (or, The Making of an Assembler)," *Byte* 1, no. 12 (August 1976): 52–63.

65 Richard S. Simpson, "A Date with KIM," *Byte* 1, no. 9 (May 1976): 8–12.

Incidentally, when Steve Jobs developed Macintosh in the 1980s, he stated that "computers and society are out on a first date in this decade." See Steven Levy, *Insanely Great: The Life and Times of Macintosh, the Computer that Changed Everything* (New York: Viking, 1994), 26.

66 Yogesh M. Gupta, "True Confessions: How I Relate to KIM," *Byte* 1, no. 12 (August 1976): 44–8.

67 "Top Names of the 1960s," Social Security, accessed 3 February 2025, https://www.ssa.gov/oact/babynames/decades/names1960s.html.

68 Robert Grater, "Giving KIM Some Fancy Jewels," *Byte* 2, no. 7 (July 1977): 126–7.

69 R. Travis Atkins, "A New Dress for KIM (A Brief Case History)," *Byte* 2, no. 9 (September 1977): 26–7, 26.

70 Sheila Clarke, "My Friend is a Computer Junkie," *Kilobaud*, no. 6 (June 1977): 136–7, 136.

71 Ibid., 136–7.

72 Barbara Henderson, "Computer Widow," *Kilobaud*, no. 1 (January 1977), 99.

73 Ibid.

74 UNESCO and EQUALS Skills Coalition, *I'd Blush If I Could: Closing Gender Divides in Digital Skills through Education* (n.p.: UNESCO, 2019), 101.

75 As quoted in Emily Lever, "I was a Human Siri," Intelligencer, *New York*, 26 April 2018, http://nymag.com/intelligencer/smarthome/i-was-a-human-siri-french-virtual-assistant.html.

76 Heather Suzanne Woods, "Asking More of Siri and Alexa: Feminine Persona in Service of Surveillance Capitalism," *Critical Studies in Media Communication* 35, no. 4 (2018): 334–49; Marie Louise Juul Søndergaard and Lone Koefoed Hansen, "Intimate Futures: Staying with the Trouble of Digital Personal Assistants through Design Fiction," in *Proceedings of the 2018 Designing Interactive Systems Conference* (DIS '18) (New York: ACM, 2018), 869–80; Florian Habler, Valentin Schwind, and Niels Henze, "Effects of Smart Virtual Assistants' Gender and Language," in *Proceedings of Mensch und Computer 2019* (MuC '19), ed. Florian Alt, Andreas Bulling, and Tanja Döring (New York: ACM, 2019), 469–73; Ian Bogost, "Sorry, Alexa Is Not a Feminist," *Atlantic*, 24 January 2018, https://www.theatlantic.com/technology/archive/2018/01/sorry-alexa-is-not-a-feminist/551291/.

77 A product review for the Apple II in the March 1978 issue of *Byte* describes it as "one of the best examples of the concept of the complete 'appliance' computer. This variety of computer is sold as a finished product off the

shelves of the retailer's shop or by mail from the manufacturer's warehouse." Carl Helmers, "An Apple to Byte," *Byte* 3, no. 3 (March 1978): 18–24, 30–2, 35, 40–6.

78 Campbell-Kelly et al., *Computer*, 238 and 242.

79 Mitchell Waite and Michael Pardee, *Microcomputer Primer*, 2nd ed. (Indianapolis: Howard W. Sams and Co., 1980), 13.

80 Dennis E. Hamilton, "It's Your Hobby! The Critics Be Hanged," *Kilobaud*, no. 13 (January 1978): 108.

81 Louis E. Frenzel, Jr, "What Ever Happened to Computer Hobbyists?," *Interface Age* 7, no. 5 (May 1982): 108–10.

82 Ibid., 109.

83 Lawrence R. Zeitlin, "The Ultimate Personal Computer," *Kilobaud*, no. 9 (September 1977): 30–2. Reprinted from *Datamation* (May 1977): 131–7.

84 Ibid., 30.

85 Indeed, the article preceding Zeitlin's in that issue is a guide to building an ASCII keyboard. Robert Brehm, "Build Your Own ASCII Keyboard … With Serial and Parallel Output," *Kilobaud*, no. 9 (Sept. 1977): 22–7.

86 Luigia Camaioni et al., "The Role of Declarative Pointing in Developing a Theory of Mind," *Infancy* 5, no. 3 (2004): 291–308; Jeremy I.M. Carpendale and Ailidh B. Carpendale, "The Development of Pointing: From Personal Directedness to Interpersonal Direction," *Human Development* 53, no. 3 (2010): 110–26.

87 Wiberg, *Materiality of Interaction*, 20.

Chapter Two

1 "Hewlett-Packard's Personal Computer," *Personal Computer World* 3, no. 11 (November 1980): 11.

2 R.P. Dolan, "In This Issue," *Hewlett-Packard Journal* 31, no. 7 (July 1980): 2.

3 Wireless remote controls for networked media devices, such as the Philco Mystery Control, already existed with radio in the 1930s and 1940s. However, these controls did not require users to point the control at the device. Because the visual component of television requires viewers to be physically oriented toward the device, however, TV remote control manufacturers often opted for directional signal systems that required pointing the hand-held device at the television. See Caetlin Benson-Allott, *Remote Control* (New York: Bloomsbury Academic, 2015).

4 "Space Command TV by Zenith," Zenith Radio Corporation, *The Saturday Evening Post*, 9 November 1957, 123. These conditions could create or exacerbate unequal access to a device otherwise available to everyone in the environment. For example, research in the 1990s suggested that in normative family contexts the father typically had most control over the remote, followed by the mother and children. See David Morley, *Televisions, Audiences, and Cultural Studies* (London: Routledge, 1992).

5 Ivan Edward Sutherland, "Sketchpad, a Man-Machine Graphical Communication System" (PhD diss., Massachusetts Institute of Technology, 1963), 54.

6 Noah Wardrip-Fruin and Nick Montfort, eds., *The New Media Reader* (Cambridge, MA: MIT Press, 2003), 109.

7 See Thierry Bardini, *Bootstrapping: Douglas Engelbart, Coevolution, and the Origins of Personal Computing* (Palo Alto, CA: Stanford University Press, 2000); Scott Mace, "Light Pen Technology Looks to the Micro," *InfoWorld* 5, no. 52 and 6, no.1 (December 1983–January 1984), 61–2.

8 "The mouse introduced with the first Macintosh, the M0100, bears more than a modest resemblance to the Macintosh itself – same material, color, texture, and relative geometry. Edges bear a thick chamfer to improve hand fit and match the distinctive chamfer of Macintosh case. The result is continuity and coherence with the whole." William Lidwell and Gerry Manacsa, *Deconstructing Production Design* (Beverly, MA: Rockport Publishers, 2009), 124.

9 Douglas Engelbart, *Augmenting Human Intellect: A Conceptual Framework* (Menlo Park, CA: Stanford Research Institute, 1962), 70–1.

10 George A. Michael, "Survey of Graphic Data Processing Equipment for Computers," in *Use of Computers in Analysis of Experimental Data and Control of Nuclear Facilities*, ed. Bernard I. Spinrad (Oak Ridge, TN: US Atomic Energy Commission, 1967), 133–76, 163.

11 Aliyah Morgenstern, "Early Pointing Gestures," in *Gesture in Language: Development Across the Lifespan*, ed. Aliyah Morgenstern and Susan Goldin-Meadow (De Gruyter Mouton; American Psychological Association, 2022): 47–89, 47.

12 *Merriam-Webster*, s.v. "index," accessed 3 February 2025, https://www.merriam-webster.com/dictionary/index.

13 Charles S. Peirce, *Philosophical Writings of Peirce*, ed. Justus Buchler (New York: Dover Publications, 1956), 107.

14 Mary Ann Doane, "Indexicality: Trace and Sign," *differences* (2007), 2–3.

15 Ibid., 2.

16 Paul E. Ceruzzi, *A History of Modern Computing*, 2nd ed. (Cambridge, MA: MIT Press, 2003), 261.

17 Lucilla Cardinali et al., "Tool-Use Induces Morphological Updating of the Body Schema," *Current Biology* 19, no. 13 (14 July 2009): 1157; Mareike Pazen et al., "Predictive Perception of Self-generated Movements: Commonalities and Differences in the Neural Processing of Tool and Hand Actions," *NeuroImage* 206 (2020): 116309, https://doi.org/10.1016/j.neuroimage.2019.116309.

18 Jessica K. Witt and Dennis R. Proffitt, "Action-Specific Influences on Distance Perception: A Role for Motor Simulation," *Journal of Experimental Psychology* 34, no. 6 (2008): 1479–92.

19 Morgenstern, "Early Pointing Gestures," 49.

20 Doug Engelbart Institute, "1968 Demo – Douglas C. Engelbart, PhD et.al.," accessed 3 February 2025, https://dougengelbart.org/pubs/video/fjcc68/Englebart's-1968-Transcription.html. My emphasis.

21 Melvin Merkin, "In Love with Lisa," *Creative Computing* (October 1983): 12–20, 14. My emphasis.

22 "Macintosh!," *St. Mac*, February 1984, 12.

23 Sherry Turkle, *Life on the Screen: Identity in the Age of the Internet* (New York: Simon & Schuster, 1995), 35.

24 Luigia Camaioni et al., "The Role of Declarative Pointing in Developing a Theory of Mind," *Infancy* 5, no. 3 (2004): 305, 307.

25 Turkle, *Life on the Screen*, 23.

26 John Markoff, "For PC's the Mouse Will Reign," *New York Times*, 12 October 1988, D1.

27 Steven Levy, *Insanely Great: The Life and Times of Macintosh, the Computer that Changed Everything* (New York: Viking, 1994), 99. My emphasis.

28 To compete with the Macintosh and other mouse-based computers, Hewlett-Packard marketed the HP-150 desktop computer. Users could input commands by touching buttons on the HP-150 screen, in essence communicating by touching the "face" of the computer. However, HP's system consisted of a grid of infrared emitters and sensors embedded in the screen's bezel, so the system sensed proximity to the screen – rather than contact – as the finger broke the path of the infrared light passing just

above the screen's surface. The HP-150 screen surface was no more sensitive than that of the Lisa, Mac, or any other computer on the market.

29 Cathal O'Madagain, Gregor Kachel, and Brent Strickland, "The Origin of Pointing: Evidence for the Touch Hypothesis," *Science Advances* 5, no. 7 (10 July 2019): 1–8, 1. See also Jeremy I.M. Carpendale and Ailidh B. Carpendale, "The Development of Pointing: From Personal Directedness to Interpersonal Direction," *Human Development* 53 (2010): 110–26; Noburo Masataka, "From Index-Finger Extension to Index-Finger Pointing: Ontogenesis of Pointing in Preverbal Infants," in *Pointing: Where Language, Culture and Cognition Meet*, ed. Sotaro Kita (Mahwah, NJ: Lawrence Erlbaum, 2003), 69–84.

30 O'Madagain, Kachel, and Strickland, "The Origin of Pointing," 7.

31 Paul DeGroot, "Boom in Palm Computers not Likely to Subside," *Globe and Mail*, 26 February 1999, R5.

32 Michael McCandless, "Palm and the Handheld Revolution," *IEEE Expert* 12, no 6 (November-December 1997): 6.

33 Katie Hafner, "Web Phone: The Next Big Thing?," *New York Times*, 15 April 1999, G1.

34 Myles White, "A Notebook for Every Need," *Toronto Star*, 27 May 1997, D6.

35 David Pogue, *PalmPilot: The Ultimate Guide* (Sebastopol, CA: O'Reilly, 1999).

36 Ibid.

37 *Merriam-Webster*, s.v. "stylus," accessed 3 February 2025, https://www.merriam-webster.com/dictionary/stylus.

38 *Oxford English Dictionary*, s.v. "stylus," accessed 3 February 2025, https://www.oed.com/dictionary/stylus_n?tab=factsheet#20353375; *The Oxford Dictionary, Thesaurus, and Wordpower Guide* (Oxford: Oxford University Press, 2001), 1287.

39 *PalmPilot Handbook* (n.p.: 3Com, 1997), 6.

40 Apple, "What Is Newton?," YouTube video, 25 July 2011, 3:46, https://www.youtube.com/watch?v=lkg4EAK0Y30.

41 Sonja Neef, José van Dijck, and Eric Ketelaar, *Sign Here! Handwriting in the Age of New Media* (Amsterdam: Amsterdam University Press, 2006), 10.

42 Carrie Noland, *Agency and Embodiment* (Cambridge, MA: Harvard University Press, 2009), 2. Emphasis in original.

43 Apple, "Welcome to Newton," YouTube video, 6 May 2006, 8:10, https://www.youtube.com/watch?v=64QuJdJmCbA.

44 Cary Lu, "A Small Revelation: Newton has Arrived – at Long Last," *MacWorld*, September 1993, 102–6, 102.

45 Lesley Gourlay, *Posthumanism and the Digital University: Texts, Bodies, and Materialities* (London: Bloomsbury Academic, 2020), 127.

46 Ibid.

47 Jeff Rice, *The Rhetoric of Cool: Composition Studies and New Media* (Carbondale, IL: Southern Illinois University Press, 2007), 137.

48 Sutherland, "Sketchpad," 8.

49 Pogue, *PalmPilot*; *PalmPilot Handbook*, 6.

50 Kevin Fogarty, "Portable Devices Must Be Practical," *Computerworld* 32, no. 4 (26 January 1998): 69–70, 70.

51 Cary Lu, "A Small Revelation: Newton Has Arrived," 106.

52 Vilém Flusser, *Gestures* (Minneapolis: University of Minnesota Press, 2014), 20.

53 The *Wall Street Journal* referred to it as a "pocket-phone-cum-computer." Dennis Kneale, "IBM, BellSouth Team Up to Sell 'Simon,'" *Wall Street Journal*, 29 October 1993, B1.

54 IBM, *Simon Says "Here's How": Users Manual* (n.p.: IBM Corporation, 1994), 1, 9, 15, and 20.

55 Bloomberg Business News, "I.B.M. Device to Be Shown," *New York Times*, 1 November 1993, D3. The *Toronto Star* coverage is an exception: "At the touch of a finger, the screen can change to reveal a personal phonebook, appointment schedule or notepad." See Richard Morochove, "Pentium Computer Processor Appears to Offer Best '94 Value," *Toronto Star*, 3 January 1994, B6.

56 Steve Jobs, "iPhone 2007 Presentation," YouTube video, 13 May 2013, 7:30, https://www.youtube.com/watch?v=vN4U5FqrOdQ.

57 It is worth noting that styluses sold for touch screen devices today typically have a soft tip to replicate the contact of the finger but are also working ink pens or markers.

58 Doug Engelbart Institute, "1968 Demo – Douglas C. Engelbart, PhD et.al." My emphasis.

59 For example, see Jason Farman, *Mobile Interface Theory: Embodied Space and Locative Media*, 2nd ed. (New York: Routledge, 2021); Nanna Verhoeff, *Mobile Screens: The Visual Regime of Navigation* (Amsterdam: Amsterdam University Press, 2012); and Rowan Wilken, ed., Special Issue on Locative Media, *Convergence* 18, no. 3 (August 2012).

60 Lawrence Letham and Alex Letham, GPS *Made Easy: Using Global Positioning Systems in the Outdoors*, 5th ed. (Seattle: Mountaineers Books, 2008).

61 Frank van Diggelen, "The Smartphone Revolution," GPS *World*, 1 December 2009, https://www.gpsworld.com/wirelesssmartphone-revolution-9183/.

62 Emporia Telecom, *Emporia Elegance Plus* GPS (Linz: Emporia Telecom Produktions und Vertriebs, 2012), 28.

63 Stephen Shankland, "Google Latitude Keeps Tabs on Friends' Locations," CNET, 4 February 2009, https://www.cnet.com/tech/mobile/google-latitude-keeps-tabs-on-friends-locations/; Scott Gilbertson, "Google Latitude Broadcasts Your Location," *Wired*, 4 February 2009, https://www.wired.com/2009/02/google-latitude/.

64 Charlie Sorrel, "Third-Party GPS for iPhone," *Wired*, 20 September 2007, https://www.wired.com/2007/09/third-party-gps/.

65 Apple, "Find My," accessed 3 February 2025, https://www.apple.com/icloud/find-my/.

66 David Meyer, "Why You Should Care about GPS in Mobiles," ZDNET, 17 January 2007, https://www.zdnet.com/article/why-you-should-care-about-gps-in-mobiles/.

67 "Cellphone Software Could Pose Privacy Risk," *New Scientist* 196, no. 2630 (17 November 2007): 27.

68 See, for example, "Stream of Consciousness," a 1997 episode of the science fiction series *The Outer Limits*. *The Outer Limits*, season 3, episode 5, "Stream of Consciousness," directed by Joe Zimniki, written by David Shore and Leslie Stevens, featuring George Newbern, Suki Kaiser, and Shane Meier, aired 7 February 1997.

Chapter Three

1 Matthew Fulkerson, *The First Sense: A Philosophical Study of Human Touch* (Cambridge, MA: MIT Press, 2013), 5–6.

2 John D. Miller, *Beads and Prayers: The Rosary in History and Devotion* (London: Burns & Oates, 2001); Shauna Huffaker, "Prayer Beads," in *Encyclopedia of Islam*, ed. Juan E. Campo (New York: Facts on File, 2009), 558–9.

3 Michel Foucault, *Discipline and Punish: The Birth of the Prison*, trans. by Alan Sheridan (New York: Vintage Books, 1977), 138.

4 Sophia Berolo, Richard P. Wells, and Benjamin C. Amick III,

"Musculoskeletal Symptoms Among Mobile Hand-held Device Users and Their Relationship to Device Use: A Preliminary Study in a Canadian University Population," *Applied Ergonomics* 42 (2011): 371–8, http://dx.doi.org/10.1016/j.apergo.2010.08.010.

5 The packaging for USRobotics' Pilot 5000 device included illustrations of a user single-handedly interacting with the device in a shirt pocket and on a table. The largest illustration, however, showed the device held up in one hand with the fingers easily keeping the device upright.

6 David Pogue, *PalmPilot: The Ultimate Guide* (Sebastopol, CA: O'Reilly, 1999), preface.

7 Dylan Jones, *iPod, Therefore I am: Thinking Inside the White Box* (London: Bloomsbury, 2005), 14.

8 Heidi Rae Cooley, "It's All about the Fit: The Hand, the Mobile Screenic Device and Tactile Vision," *Journal of Visual Culture* 3, no. 2 (August 2004): 133–55, 137.

9 Ibid.

10 D.W. Winnicott, *Playing and Reality* (London: Tavistock Publications, 1971), 88.

11 Jones, *iPod*, 3–4.

12 Sharif Mowlabocus, "The 'Mastery' of the Swipe: Smartphones, Transitional Objects and Interstitial Time," *First Monday* 21, no. 10 (October 2016), https://doi.org/10.5210/fm.v21i10.6950; Peter Gleiberman, "The Use of Mobile Social Technology as Transitional Objects Impact on Personality Functioning" (PhD diss., Antioch University, 2020), https://aura.antioch.edu/cgi/viewcontent.cgi?article=1591&context=etds.

13 Penny Spikins, *Hidden Depths: The Origins of Human Connection* (York: White Rose University Press, 2022), 268–71.

14 Steve Hoober, "Design for Fingers, Touch, and People, Part 1," UXMatters, 6 March 2017, https://www.uxmatters.com/mt/archives/2017/03/design-for-fingers-touch-and-people-part-1.php.

15 Apple, "Reach the Top of the iPhone Screen with One Hand," iPhone User Guide, accessed 3 February 2025, https://support.apple.com/en-ca/guide/iphone/iph145eba8e9/ios.

16 Whitson Gordon, "All the Ways to Use Your Phone with One Hand," *Popular Science*, 21 October 2021, https://www.popsci.com/use-your-phone-with-one-hand/.

17 Jeramy Johnson, "How to Enable One-Handed Mode in Android 12," An-

droid Central, 26 May 2021, https://www.androidcentral.com/how-enable-one-handed-mode-android-12.

18 "Galaxy Z Fold6," Samsung, accessed 3 February 2025, https://www.samsung.com/ca/smartphones/galaxy-z-fold6/.

19 Jeffrey S. Young and William L. Simon, *iCon Steve Jobs: The Greatest Second Act in the History of Business* (Hoboken, NJ: Wiley, 2005), 284.

20 Connie Guglielmo, "What It Was Like to Watch Steve Jobs Introduce the iPod 20 Years Ago," CNET, 23 October 2021, https://www.cnet.com/tech/mobile/what-it-was-like-to-watch-steve-jobs-introduce-the-ipod-20-years-ago/.

21 Christopher Phin, "To All the iPods I've Scratched Before …," *Macworld*, 30 March 2015, https://www.macworld.com/article/225222/to-all-the-ipods-ive-scratched-before.html.

22 Steven Levy, *The Perfect Thing: How the iPod Shuffles Commerce, Culture, and Coolness* (New York: Simon & Schuster, 2007), 71–2.

23 Peter Buckley and Duncan Clark, *The Rough Guide to iPods and iTunes* (New York: Rough Guides, 2004), 29.

24 Lorraine Ross, "Tech Tattoos Can Turn a Hefty Profit," *Engravers Journal* 34, no. 8 (February 2009), https://www.engraversjournal.com/legacyarticles/2672/ (link defunct).

25 Dan Moren, "Analysis: Inside Apple's iPod Sales Figures," *Macworld*, 31 January 2008, https://www.macworld.com/article/189142/ipodsales-3.html.

26 Levy, *Perfect Thing*, 72.

27 Michael J. Miller, "HP Eyes Entertainment," *PC Magazine*, 19 October 2004, 26.

28 Steve Stoute, *The Tanning of America: How Hip-Hop Created a Culture That Rewrote the Rules of the New Economy* (New York: Gotham Books, 2011), 188.

29 "Other Peripherals," *GearAxis Unwired*, August 2005, 58; tech blogger Jillian Myers bemoaned, "I put one of those new iPod stickers on my iPod, after the promise of easy removal. Easy removal my ass!!" See Jillian Myers, "HP's iPod Tattoo Stickers," *Wired*, 28 September 2004, https://www.wired.com/2004/09/hps-ipod-tattoo/.

30 Michael Atkinson, *Tattooed: The Sociogenesis of a Body Art* (Toronto: University of Toronto Press, 2003), 27.

31 Dan Frakes, *Your iPod Life* (Berkeley, CA: Mac Publishing, 2006), 11.

32 "New users may initially wonder why there is nowhere to 'open it up' or

put the iPod in. Instead, you simply stretch the screen opening a bit wider and push the iPod into the case until you 'squeeze' it into the correct position." See Lisa Gade, "iSkin," MobileTechReview, 18 November 2005, https://www.mobiletechreview.com/iPod/iSkin-iPod.htm.

33 "Touchy Subjects," *Mac Life*, August 2008, 72.

34 Quoted in Guy Julier, *The Culture of Design* (London: Sage, 2013), 131.

35 J. D. Biersdorfer, *iPod & iTunes: The Missing Manual*, 3rd ed. (Cambridge: Pogue Press, 2005), 289.

36 Michael F. Roizen and Mehmet Oz, *YOU: The Owner's Manual for Teens* (New York: Scribners, 2011), 3.

37 Gade, "iSkin."

38 Guglielmo, "What It Was Like."

39 Julier, *Culture of Design*, 131.

40 John H. Day, "Inside iPod," Electronic Design, 19 January 2005, https://www.electronicdesign.com/technologies/displays/article/21760166/inside-ipod.

41 Julier, *Culture of Design*, 131.

42 Sergio M. Rezende, *Introduction to Electronic Materials and Devices* (Cham: Springer, 2022), 463.

43 See Karolina M. Lempert and Elizabeth A. Phelps, "Neuroeconomics of Emotion and Decision Making," in *Neuroeconomics: Decision Making and the Brain*, 2nd ed, ed. Paul W. Glimcher and Ernst Fehr (Boston: Elsevier/AP, 2014), 219–36; C. Edwards, "The Electrical Properties of Skin," in *The Physical Nature of the Skin*, ed. R.M. Marks, S.P. Barton, and C. Edwards (Lancaster: MTP Press, 1988), 209–14; and Jaime Vila, "Psychophysiological Assessment," in *Encyclopedia of Applied Psychology*, ed. Charles Donald Spielberger (Oxford: Academic Press, 2004), 197–204.

44 Vila, "Psychophysiological Assessment," 202.

45 Jones, *iPod*, 4.

46 Daniel Eran Dilger, "Apple Wins Rubberbanding Patent Case Against Motorola in Germany," *Apple Insider*, 13 September 2012, https://appleinsider.com/articles/12/09/13/apple_wins_rubberbanding_patent_case_against_motorola_in_germany.

47 Ibid.; Nick Wingfield, "Jury Awards $1 Billion to Apple in Samsung Patent Case," *New York Times*, 24 August 2012, https://www.nytimes.com/2012/08/25/technology/jury-reaches-decision-in-apple-samsung-patent-trial.html.

48 "Behavioral Changes: All Apps," Android for Developers, accessed 3 Feb-

ruary 2025, https://developer.android.com/about/versions/12/behavior-changes-all.

49 Alexandra Schneider, "The iPhone as an Object of Knowledge," in *Moving Data: The iPhone and the Future of Media*, ed. Pelle Snickars and Patrick Vonderau (New York: Columbia University Press, 2012), 55.

50 Dan-Mikael Ellingsen, et al., "The Neurobiology Shaping Affective Touch: Expectation, Motivation, and Meaning in the Multisensory Context," *Frontiers in Psychology* 6 (2015), https://doi.org/10.3389/fpsyg.2015.01986.

50 Francis McGlone, Johan Wessberg, and Håkan Olausson, "Discriminative and Affective Touch: Sensing and Feeling," *Neuron* 82, no. 4 (May 2014): 737–55, https://doi.org/10.1016/j.neuron.2014.05.001.

52 "Index," Galvactivator, accessed 3 February 2025, https://www.media.mit.edu/galvactivator/index2.html.

53 "Galvactivator," MIT Media Lab, accessed 3 February 2025, https://www.media.mit.edu/projects/galvactivator/overview/.

54 Sam Byford, "Demand Good Vibrations from Your Next Android Phone," *Verge*, 29 March 2018, https://www.theverge.com/circuitbreaker/2018/3/29/17175466/android-haptic-feedback-is-bad-why.

55 See David Parisi, *Archaeologies of Touch: Interfacing with Haptics from Electricity to Computing* (Minneapolis: University of Minnesota Press, 2018).

56 John Free, "Pocket Pagers: Beep into a Boom," *Popular Science* 211, no. 1 (July 1977), 78–9, 135.

57 "Sounds, Vibrations, and Notification on your Galaxy phone or Tablet," Samsung, accessed 3 February 2025, https://www.samsung.com/us/support/answer/ANS00089085/.

58 *Merriam-Webster*, s.v. "neediness," accessed 3 February 2025, https://www.merriam-webster.com/dictionary/neediness.

59 Sherry Turkle, *Alone Together: Why We Expect More from Technology and Less from Each Other* (New York: Basic Books, 2011), 16–17.

60 Michelle Drouin, Daren H. Kaiser, and Daniel A. Miller, "Phantom Vibrations among Undergraduates: Prevalence and Associated Psychological Characteristics," *Computers in Human Behavior* 28 (2012): 1491; see also M.B. Rothberg et al., "Phantom Vibration Syndrome among Medical Staff: A Cross Sectional Survey," *BMJ* 341, no. 7786 (2010): 6914, http://dx.doi.org/10.1136/bmj.c6914; Robert Rosenberger, "An Experiential Account of Phantom Vibration Syndrome," *Computers in Human Behavior* 52 (2015): 124–31.

61 Drouin, Kaiser, and Miller, "Phantom Vibrations," 1493.

62 Maurice Merleau-Ponty, *Phenomenology of Perception*, trans. Colin Smith (London: Routledge & Kegan Paul, 1962); Don Ihde, *Technology and the Lifeworld: From Garden to Earth* (Bloomington: Indiana University Press, 1990).

63 Rosenberger, "Experiential Account," 127–8.

64 Ibid., 128.

Chapter Four

1 Mark Andrejevic and Neil Selwyn, "Facial Recognition Technology in Schools: Critical Questions and Concerns," *Learning, Media and Technology* 45, no. 2 (2020): 115–28; Yaroslav Kuflinski, "How Facial Recognition Software Is Revolutionizing Hospital Security, Care, Human Resources," *Healthcare Today*, 29 August 2019, https://www.healthcareittoday.com/2019/08/29/how-facial-recognition-software-is-revolutionizing-hospital-security-care-human-resources/; Kashmir Hill, "Which Stores Are Scanning Your Face? No One Knows," *New York Times*, 10 March 2023, https://www.nytimes.com/2023/03/10/technology/facial-recognition-stores.html.

2 Rene Chun, "China's New Frontiers in Dystopian Tech," *Atlantic*, 15 April 2018, https://www.theatlantic.com/magazine/archive/2018/04/big-in-china-machines-that-scan-your-face/554075/; Yi Shu Ng, "Facial Recognition Is Now Being Used to ID and Publicly Shame Jaywalkers, Like You," *Mashable*, 21 June 2017, https://mashable.com/2017/06/21/china-facial-recognition-jaywalkers-shaming/; Paul Mozur, "One Month, 500,000 Face Scans: How China Is Using A.I. to Profile a Minority," *New York Times*, 14 April 2019, https://www.nytimes.com/2019/04/14/technology/china-surveillance-artificial-intelligence-racial-profiling.html.

3 Malkia Devich-Cyril, "Defund Facial Recognition," *Atlantic*, 5 July 2020, https://www.theatlantic.com/technology/archive/2020/07/defund-facial-recognition/613771/. For work on bias in automated facial recognition systems, see Patrick Grother, Mei Ngan, and Kayee Hanaoka, *Face Recognition Vendor Test (FRVT), Part 3: Demographic Effects* (Washington, DC: National Institute of Standards and Technology, 2019); Joy Buolamwini and Timnit Gebru, "Gender Shades: Intersectional Accuracy Disparities in Commercial Gender Classification," *Proceedings of Machine Learning Research* 81 (2018): 1–15.

4 Steven Levy, *Insanely Great: The Life and Times of Macintosh, the Computer that Changed Everything* (New York: Viking, 1994), 4.

5 "Cromemco Low Cost Optical Data Digitizer," *Cromemco: Specialists in Computer Peripherals, Catalog 76S* (Mountain View, CA: Cromemco, 1976), 7.

6 Terry Walker, Harry Garland, and Roger Melen, "Build Çyclops: First All Solid-State TV Camera," *Popular Electronics* 7, no. 2 (February 1975): 29.

7 Ibid.

8 For consideration of online photographic representations of the self beyond body images, see Katrin Tiidenberg and Andrew Whelan, "Sick Bunnies and Pocket Dumps: 'Not-Selfies' and the Genre of Self-Representation," *Popular Communication* 15, no. 2 (April-June 2017): 141–53.

9 Selfies became such a common topic of cultural discussion in 2013 that the *Oxford English Dictionary* chose "selfie" as its "word of the year." Silvia Killingsworth, "And the Word of the Year Is …" *New Yorker*, 19 November 2013, https://www.newyorker.com/culture/culture-desk/and-the-word-of-the-year-is.

10 Taylor Lorenz, "The Instagram Aesthetic Is Over," *Atlantic*, 23 April 2019, https://www.theatlantic.com/technology/archive/2019/04/influencers-are-abandoning-instagram-look/587803/; Joel Wright, "Influencers: Manage Your Selfies," *Adweek*, 31 October 2017, https://www.adweek.com/digital/joel-wright-hashoff-guest-post-influencers-manage-your-selfies/.

11 Michele Zappavigna, "Social Media Photography: Construing Subjectivity in Instagram Images," *Visual Communication* 15, no. 3 (2016): 271–92.

12 Apryl A. Williams and Beatriz Aldana Marquez, "The Lonely Selfie King: Selfies and the Conspicuous Prosumption of Gender and Race," *International Journal of Communication* 9 (2015): 1775–87; Valerie Barker and Nathian S. Rodriguez, "This Is Who I Am: The Selfie as a Personal and Social Identity Marker," *International Journal of Communication* 13 (2019): 1143–66.; Son Vivienne, "'I Will Not Hate Myself Because You Cannot Accept Me': Problematizing Empowerment and Gender-Diverse Selfies," *Popular Communication* 15, no. 2 (April–June 2017):126–40.

13 Theresa M. Senft and Nancy K. Baym, "What Does the Selfie Say? Investigating a Global Phenomenon," *International Journal of Communication* 9 (2015): 1588–606, 1592. See, for example, Marijke Naezer, "Sexy Selves: Girls, Selfies and the Performance of Intersectional Identities," *European Journal of Women's Studies* 27, no. 1 (February 2020): 41–56.

14 Hannah Betts, "Selfie-Obsessed: How Narcissism Became the New Normal," *Telegraph* (London), 2 November 2019, https://www.telegraph.co.uk/women/life/selfie-obsessed-narcissism-became-new-normal/; Nasim Mansurov, "The Generation of the Self-Obsessed," *Photography Life*, 16 April 2020, https://photographylife.com/the-generation-of-the-self-obsessed; Marc Beaulieu, "Experts Say Chronic Selfie Snapping Is Now a Real Condition Called 'Selfitis,'" CBC, 20 December 2017, https://www.cbc.ca/life/wellness/experts-say-chronic-selfie-snapping-is-now-a-real-condition-called-selfitis-1.4458635. For analysis of such media coverage and its consequences, see Jessica Leigh Maddox, "Fear and Selfie Loathing in America: Identifying the Interstices of Othering, Iconoclasm, and the Selfie," *Journal of Popular Culture* 51, no. 1 (February 2018): 26–49; Amy Adele Hasinoff, "The Media Panic about Teen Sexting," in *The Routledge Companion to Media, Sex and Sexuality*, ed. Clarissa Smith, Feona Attwood, and Brian McNair (New York: Routledge, 2018), 193–201.

15 Katie Warfield, "Im(matter)ial Bodies: A Material and Affective Rethinking of Selfies for Digital Literacy Resources," *Language and Literacy* 20, no. 3 (2018): 74.

16 Maddox, "Fear and Selfie Loathing in America," 31.

17 See, for example, Elisabetta Costa, "Affordances-in-Practice: An Ethnographic Critique of Social Media Logic and Context Collapse," *New Media & Society* 20, no. 10 (October 2018): 3641–56.

18 Katie Warfield, "Making the Cut: An Agential Realist Examination of Selfies and Touch," *Social Media + Society* 2, no. 2 (April 2016): 1, https://journals.sagepub.com/doi/full/10.1177/2056305116641706. It is worth pointing out that Warfield's theoretical work in this essay emerges from the intersection of digital materialism and agential realism.

19 Sumin Zhao and Michele Zappavigna, "Beyond the Self: Intersubjectivity and the Social Semiotic Interpretation of the Selfie," *New Media & Society* 20, no. 5 (May 2018): 1735.

20 Ibid., 1737.

21 Anirban Baishya, "#NaMo: The Political Work of the Selfie in the 2014 Indian General Elections," *International Journal of Communication* 9 (2015): 1688.

22 Nathan Jurgenson, *The Social Photo: On Photography and Social Media* (London: Verso, 2019), 56. See also Linh Nguyen and Kim Barbour, "Selfies

as Expressively Authentic Identity Performance," *First Monday* 22, no. 11 (2017), https://firstmonday.org/ojs/index.php/fm/article/view/7745/6561.

23 Charles Horton Cooley, *Human Nature and the Social Order* (1902; repr., New Brunswick, NJ: Transaction Publishers, 1983), 184.

24 Ibid.

25 Ibid.

26 Mirror-based self-portraits exist among the work of many twentieth-century photographers, including Diane Arbus, Cecil Beaton, Ilse Bing, Manuel Álvarez Bravo, Claude Cahun, Imogen Cunningham, Gisèle Freund, Lee Friedlander, Alfredo Molina La Hitte, Vivian Maier, Gordon Parks, Man Ray, Edward Steichen, Andy Warhol, and Weegee.

27 See Henri Lefebvre, *The Production of Space*, trans. Donald Nicholson-Smith (1974; repr., Oxford: Blackwell, 1991).

28 Mikael Wiberg, *The Materiality of Interaction: Notes on the Materials of Interaction Design* (Cambridge, MA: MIT Press, 2017), 135.

29 Ibid., 136.

30 See also Heekyoung Jung and Erik Stolterman: "Materiality is more about the relationship between people (user) and the material artifact in terms of how it is used out in the world." Heekyung Jung and Erik Stolterman, "Form and Materiality in Interaction Design: A New Approach to HCI," in *Proceedings of the Extended Abstracts on Human Factors in Computing Systems (CHI'11)* (New York: ACM Press, 2011), 399–408 (quoted in Wiberg, *The Materiality of Interaction*, 55).

31 Sabine Melchoir-Bonnet, *The Mirror: A History*, trans. Katharine H. Jewett (New York: Routledge, 2001), 23.

32 Ibid., 143.

33 Chris Broodryk, "The Selfie as Articulation of, and Response to, Indifference(s)," in *Voices from the South: Digital Arts and Humanities*, ed. Amanda Du Preez (Cape Town: AOSIS, 2018), 73.

34 Mark Pendergrast, *Mirror, Mirror* (New York: Basic Books, 2003), 249–50.

35 Nancy Martha West, *Kodak and the Lens of Nostalgia* (Charlottesville, VA: University Press of Virginia, 2000), 109–12. The Vanity was followed by the Kodak Coquette, released in 1930, which was reduced to the camera and a matching mirrored compact and lipstick holder.

36 Madeleine Marsh, *Compacts and Cosmetics: Beauty from Victorian Times to the Present Day* (Barnsley: Pen & Sword History, 2014), 91.

37 West, *Kodak and the Lens of Nostalgia*, 110.

38 David Pogue, *iPhone: The Missing Manual* (Sebastopol, CA: O'Reilly Media, 2007), 10.

39 Joe Hutsko and Barbara Boyd, *iPhone 5 All-in-One for Dummies* (Hoboken, NJ: John Wiley & Sons, 2013), 424.

40 Jon Stapley and Rod Lawton, "The Best Selfie Camera in 2020: Cameras and Camera Phones that Put You First!," *Digitialcameraworld*, 3 December 2019, https://www.digitalcameraworld.com/buying-guides/best-selfie-camera; Charles Arthur, "The Selfie Was Created Pretty Much by Accident… and That's How the Next Big Thing Could Appear," *Guardian*, 12 October 2015, https://www.theguardian.com/technology/2015/oct/12/selfies-front-facing-cameras-the-next-big-thing.

41 "Motorola A920 Original Press Release," Mobile Collectors, accessed 3 February 2025, http://www.mobilecollectors.net/phone/2900/Motorola-A920.

42 During his presentation, Steve Jobs used Face Time to call Apple designer Jony Ive in front of a live audience. Brian X. Chen, "Apple Unveils High-Resolution, Videoconferencing iPhone 4," *Wired*, 7 June 2010, https://www.wired.com/2010/06/live-blog-apples-iphone-centric-wwdc-2010/; John D. Sutter, "Will iPhone 4 Usher in Era of Video Calls?," *CNN*, 7 June 2010, http://www.cnn.com/2010/TECH/mobile/06/07/apple.iphone.video/index.html.

43 "How Do I Get Rid of 'Selfies' in Photos of iOS9?" Apple Communities, 19 September 2015, https://discussions.apple.com/thread/7225882.

44 Lisa Eadicicco, "How to Find All of the Selfies on Your iPhone," *Time*, 9 December 2016, https://time.com/4437819/how-to-find-selfies-iphone/. The beta of this feature apparently stored all front-facing camera shots in the selfies folder, even if there was no human present in the image. See Mikey Campbell, "Latest iOS 9 Beta Includes Separate Photos Folders for Selfies, Screenshots," *AppleInsider*, 8 July 2015, https://appleinsider.com/articles/15/07/08/latest-ios-9-beta-includes-separate-folders-for-selfies.

45 Anna Munster, "'Text and Walk without Fear': Apps and the Experience of Transparency," in *The Imaginary App*, ed. Paul D. Miller and Svitlana Matviyenko (Cambridge, MA: MIT Press, 2014): 111–24.

46 Ibid., 114.

47 Ibid., 113.

48 Jurgenson, *Social Photo*, 55–6.

49 Grace Y. Choi and Elizabeth Behm-Morawitz, "Teach Me About Yourself(ie):

Exploring Selfie-Takers' Technology Usage and Digital Literacy Skills," *Psychology of Popular Media Culture* 7, no. 3 (2018): 352–3.

50 For participant observation of such practices, see Warfield, "Making the Cut," 3–6.

51 Munster, "'Text and Walk without Fear,'" 113.

52 Alfred Gell, "The Technology of Enchantment and the Enchantment of Technology," in *Anthropology, Art and Aesthetics*, ed. Jeremy Coote and Anthony Shelton (Oxford: Clarendon Press, 1992), 44.

53 Ibid., 47.

54 Kenji Kawakami, Dan Papia, and Hugh Fearnley-Whittingstall, *The Big Bento Box of Unuseless Japanese Inventions: The Art of Chindogu* (New York: W.W. Norton, 2005).

55 Chris Plante, "In Defense of the Selfie Stick," *Verge*, 31 December 2014; Haley Goldberg, "Why the Selfie Stick Is 2014's Most Controversial Gift," *New York Post*, 17 December 2014, https://nypost.com/2014/12/17/why-the-selfie-stick-is-the-most-controversial-gift-of-2014/. For an extended critique of selfie sticks, see Chris Matyszczyk, "Want the Perfect Smiley Selfie? Carry a Big Silver Stick," *CNET*, 21 September 2014, https://www.cnet.com/news/want-the-perfect-smiley-selfie-carry-a-big-white-stick/.

56 Eli Epstein, "12 Gadgets Every 20-Something Should Own," *Mashable*, 23 January 2015, https://mashable.com/2015/01/23/essential-gadgets-millennials/. Another article states, "Never again stop to ask a stranger to take your photo. For one thing, people hate being asked." Lindsey Weber, "You Will Mock, Then Purchase a Selfie Stick," *Medium*, 29 December 2014, https://medium.com/why-2015-wont-suck/26-you-will-mock-then-purchase-a-selfie-stick-ea57f41dfda.

57 Tomas Chamorro-Premuzic, "Selfie Sticks Should Be Banned for Massaging Our Self-Obsession," *Guardian*, 27 August 2015, https://www.theguardian.com/media-network/2015/aug/27/selfie-stick-self-obsession-narcissism-technology; Emad Ahmed, "Selfie Sticks Mask a Bigger Problem We Have with Each Other – Interaction," *New Statesman*, 1 December 2015, https://www.newstatesman.com/science-tech/internet/2015/12/selfie-sticks-mask-bigger-problem-we-have-each-other-interaction; Nellie Bowles, "I Hate Selfie Sticks. Was the Human Arm Such a Problem?," *Vox*, 10 January 2015, https://www.vox.com/2015/1/10/11557602/i-hate-selfie-sticks-was-the-human-arm-such-a-problem.

58 Meagan Drillinger, "All about Me! The Era of the Selfie Stick," *Travel*

Weekly, 23 September 2015, https://www.travelweekly.com/Travel-News/Travel-Technology/The-era-of-the-selfie-stick.

59 Samsung Levant, "Galaxy A Series: Awesome is for Everyone," YouTube video, 30 December 2019, 0:48, https://www.youtube.com/watch?v=oLTrNq2MnBM.

60 Tech Ear, "Every Google Pixel Phone Ad (2016–2020)," YouTube video, 8 February 2020, 11:30, https://www.youtube.com/watch?v=xdTQuicWdO8.

61 Samsung Thailand, "สวยครบเครื่อง เพอร์เฟคทุกมุมมอง" [Fully equipped, perfect for every angle], YouTube video, 13 March 2019, video, 1:00, https://www.youtube.com/watch?v=6dNGyy4Fa_Y.

62 Gionee India, "Welcome to Alia's Selfiestan with Gionee," YouTube video, 21 March 2017, 1:43, https://www.youtube.com/watch?v=kZk-UsDUiFE.

63 Apple, "iPhone 11 Slofies – Introducing Slowmo Selfies," YouTube video, 11 September 2019, 0:27, https://www.youtube.com/watch?v=FVa467aRXtk.

64 George Herbert Mead, *Mind, Self and Society from the Standpoint of a Social Behaviorist*, ed. Charles W. Morris (Chicago: University of Chicago Press, 1934), 138.

65 Ibid., 141–2.

66 Touchless gesture has been developed by several phone companies but has been seen to have limited use except in the era of selfie taking. See Lauren Goode, "Touchless Gesture Controls on Phones? Think Bigger," *Wired*, 12 August 2019, https://www.wired.com/story/gesture-controls-phones-samsung-lg-google/.

67 LG Electronics Eastern Africa, "LG G3 Gesture Shot," YouTube video, 17 September 2014, 0:30, https://m.youtube.com/watch?v=wtoqKXdku60; "Gesture Shot," LG, accessed 3 February 2025, https://www.lg.com/us/mobile-phones/VS985/Userguide/279.html.

68 LG India, "Wave a 'Hi,' Count Till 3 and Pose!," Facebook post, 15 September 2014, https://www.facebook.com/lgindiapage/photos/wave-a-hi-count-till-3-and-pose-get-the-best-selfies-with-lgg3s-gesture-selfie-h/933372030024111/.

69 Samsung Australia, "Take a Selfie by Showing a Palm," accessed 14 July 2020, video, 1:00, https://www.samsung.com/au/getstarted/camera/take-a-selfie-by-showing-a-palm/.

70 Abhijeet Mishra, "All the Ways You Can Take Pictures on the Samsung Galaxy Note 9," *SamMobile*, 5 September 2018, https://www.sammobile.com/2018/09/05/galaxy-note-9-camera-pictures-tip.

71 Kaarina Nikunen, "Once a Refugee: Selfie Activism, Visualized Citizenship and the Space of Appearance," *Popular Communication* 17, no. 2 (April–June 2019): 154–70; Caterina Presi, Natalia Maehle, and Ingeborg Astrid Kleppe, "Brand Selfies: Consumer Experiences and Marketplace Conversations," *European Journal of Marketing* 50, nos. 9/10 (2016): 1814–34; Mark A. Rademacher, "'The Most Inspiring Bikini Photos You'll See This Summer': A Thematic Analysis of Mass Audiences' Interpretations of Ostomy Selfies," *New Media* 20, no. 10 (October 2018): 3858–78. Recent examples of research on women and girls and selfies include Mary McGill, "'Do I Really Look Like That?': Unpacking Discourses of Control and Discursive and Visual Dissonances in Young Women's Selfie-Practices," *Feminist Media Studies* (30 November 2022), https://doi.org/10.1080/14680777.2022.2150671; Alana Papageorgiou, Colleen Fisher, and Donna Crossa, "'It Just Sends the Message That You're Nothing But Your Body': A Qualitative Exploration of Adolescent Girls' Perceptions of Sexualized Images on Social Media," *Sexuality & Culture* 27 (2023): 462–81; Marijke Naezer, "Sexy Selves: Girls, Selfies and the Performance of Intersectional Identities," *European Journal of Women's Studies* 27, no. 1 (February 2020): 41–56; Wendi S. Williams and Anissa L. Moody, "Analyzed Selfie: Stereotype Enactment, Projection, and Identification among Digitally Native Black Girls," *Women and Therapy* 42, nos. 3–4 (October 2019): 366–84; Jolanda Veldhuis et al., "Me, My Selfie, and I: The Relations between Selfie Behaviors, Body Image, Self-Objectification, and Self-Esteem in Young Women," *Psychology of Popular Media* 9, no. 1 (January 2020): 3–13. For a consideration of masculinity and selfies, see Begonya Enguix and Erick Gómez-Narváez, "Masculine Bodies, Selfies, and the (Re)configurations of Intimacy," *Men* 21, no. 1 (April 2018): 112–30.

72 Chelsea P. Butkowski et al., "Quantifying the Feminine Self(ie): Gender Display and Social Media Feedback in Young Women's Instagram Selfies," *New Media & Society* 22, no. 5 (May 2020): 817–37. See also Antonio García-Gómez, "From Selfies to Sexting," *Girlhood Studies* 11, no. 1 (Spring 2018): 43–58, https://doi.org/10.3167/ghs.2018.110105; Giovanna Mascheroni, Jane Vincent, and Estefanía Jimenez, "'Girls Are Addicted to Likes So They Post Semi-Naked Selfies': Peer Mediation, Normativity and the Construction of Identity Online," *Cyberpsychology: Journal of Psychosocial Research on Cyberspace* 9, no. 1 (2015): https://doi.org/10.5817/CP2015-1-5.

73 Jurgenson, *Social Photo*, 59.

74 Butkowski et al., "Quantifying the Feminine Self(ie)," 818.

75 Anne Burns, "Selfie-Correction," *New Inquiry*, 4 August 2014, https://thenewinquiry.com/selfie-correction/.

76 Anne Burns, "Self(ie)-Discipline: Social Regulation as Enacted Through the Discussion of Photographic Practice," *International Journal of Communication* 9 (2015): 1716.

77 Ibid., 1717.

78 "Explore & More Selfie Phone," Skip Hop, accessed 3 February 2025, https://www.skiphop.com/skiphop-playtime-musical-crawling-toys/V_185650.html.

79 "JaRu's Color Me Cutie Cellfie Time Gloss," S&D Kids, accessed 3 February 2025, https://www.sndkids.com/products/ja-ru-girls-cellfie-time-phone-lip-gloss-with-mirror-258214.

80 What Kids Want, My Pretend Selfie Set, Amazon, accessed 3 February 2025, https://www.amazon.com.au/Pretend-Selfie-Phone-Stick-Photo/dp/B074V9MNFV.

81 VTech Toys UK, "VTech Toys UK – VTech Kidizoom Flix Selfie Camera – Toys for Kids – VTech Toys UK Advertisement," YouTube video, 18 October 2017, 4:07, https://www.youtube.com/watch?v=SjlIZDS8IEs.

82 "Kidi Secrets Selfie Journal," VTech Kids, accessed 3 February 2025, https://www.vtechkids.ca/en/product/detail/18803/Kidi_Secrets_Selfie_Journal.

Chapter Five

1 Marcin Straczkiewicz, Peter James, and Jukka-Pekka Onnela, "A Systematic Review of Smartphone-Based Human Activity Recognition Methods for Health Research," *NPJ Digital Medicine* 4 (2021): 148, https://doi.org/10.1038/s41746-021-00514-4; Jun-Ki Min et al., "Toss 'n' Turn: Smartphone as Sleep and Sleep Quality Detector," in *CHI '14: Proceedings of the SIGCHI Conference on Human Factors in Computing Systems* (New York: Association for Computing Machinery, April 2014): 477–86, https://doi.org/10.1145/2556288.2557220.

2 Alexis C. Madrigal, "No, You Don't Really Look Like That," *Atlantic*, 18 December 2018, https://www.theatlantic.com/technology/archive/2018/12/your-iphone-selfies-dont-look-like-your-face/578353/.

3 "OMRON Announces 'OKAO Vision Face Recognition Sensor,' World's First Face Recognition Technology for Mobile Phones," OMRON, 28 February 2005, https://www.omron.com/media/press/2005/02/n_280205.html.

4 Shihong Lao and Masato Kawade, "Vision-Based Face Understanding Technologies and Their Applications," in *Advances in Biometric Person Authentication, 5th Chinese Conference on Biometric Recognition, SINOBIOMETRICS 2004, Guangzhou, China, December 13–14, 2004*, ed. Stan Z. Li et al. (Berlin: Springer, 2005), 339–48.

5 Danyll Wills, "New Google Smart Phone Recognizes Your Face," *MIT Technology Review*, 19 October 2011, https://www.technologyreview.com/s/425805/new-google-smart-phone-recognizes-your-face/; Matt Hamblen, "Face Unlock Feature in Galaxy Nexus Seen as Novelty, Not Security," *ComputerWorld*, 22 November 2011, https://www.computerworld.com/article/1475166/face-unlock-feature-in-galaxy-nexus-seen-as-novelty-not-security.html; Greg Kumparak, "Yes, Android's New Face Unlock Feature Can Be Fooled with a Photo," *TechCrunch*, 11 November 2011, https://techcrunch.com/2011/11/11/android-facial-unlock-photo/.

6 In 2023 this was still the case with several phones from Motorola, Nokia, and Xiaomi. Even as late as 2020 most Android phones still relied only on the front-facing camera to produce 2D facial recognition, although there were some notable exceptions among high-end devices, such as the Samsung Galaxy S10 and the Huawei Mate 20 Pro. See Charles Hymas, "Smartphone Facial Recognition Technology Can be 'Unlocked with a Photo,'" *Telegraph* (London), 19 May 2023, https://www.telegraph.co.uk/news/2023/05/19/smartphones-facial-recognition-which-unlocked-photo/.

7 Jessica Dolcourt, "Is Pixel 4 Face Unlock Faster than iPhone's Face ID? We Found Out," *CNET*, 23 October 2019, https://www.cnet.com/news/pixel-4-face-unlock-faster-than-iphone-11-face-id-we-found-out/; John Koetsier, "Apple Finally Gets Face Unlock Right," *Forbes*, 23 September 2019, https://www.forbes.com/sites/johnkoetsier/2019/09/23/apple-finally-gets-face-unlock-right-iphone-11-and-ios-13/#324700eb5605.

8 Global News, "Apple Unveils iPhone X," YouTube video, 12 September 2017, 0:15, https://www.youtube.com/watch?v=aEoVcYQ8caM.

9 Alfred Ng, "Your Face Mask Selfies Could Be Training the Next Facial Recognition Tool," *CNET*, 15 May 2020, https://www.cnet.com/news/your-face-mask-selfies-could-be-training-the-next-facial-recognition-tool/.

10 Even iPhone's "alternate appearance" setting requires the nose and mouth to be visible. Lisa Eadicicco, "Unlocking Your iPhone While Wearing a Face Mask Is Difficult, but Here's the 1 Trick That Made Apple's Face ID Work for Me," *Business Insider*, 12 April 2020,

https://www.businessinsider.com/iphone-face-id-not-working-with-mask-try-workaround-trick-2020-4; Michael Potuck, "iPhone: How to Improve Face ID with a Mask," *9to5Mac*, 8 April 2020, https://9to5mac.com/2020/04/08/iphone-how-to-use-face-id-with-mask/.

11 Adriana Piatti-Crocker and Laman Tasch, "Veil Bans in Western Europe: Interpreting Policy Diffusion," *Journal of International Women's Studies* 16, no. 2 (January 2015): 15–29; Alessandro Ferrari and Sabrina Pastorelli, eds., *The Burqa Affair across Europe: Between Public and Private Space* (Farnham: Ashgate, 2013); Sherene H. Razack, "A Site/Sight We Cannot Bear: The Racial/Spatial Politics of Banning the Muslim Woman's Niqab," *Canadian Journal of Women* 30, no. 1 (2018): 169–89; Carla M. Zoethout, "Secularism Stated, Rejected, and Reaffirmed," *Journal of Religion* 17 (2015), https://cdr.creighton.edu/server/api/core/bitstreams/2a522608-ac8d-41c7-b075-c6896e053568/content; Emily Laxer, "We Are All Republicans: Political Articulation and the Production of Nationhood in France's Face Veil Debate," *Comparative Studies in Society and History* 60, no. 4 (October 2018): 938–67.

12 Sigal Samuel, "Facebook Will Finally Ask Permission before Using Facial Recognition on You," *Vox*, 4 September 2019, https://www.vox.com/future-perfect/2019/9/4/20849307/facebook-facial-recognition-privacy-zuckerberg; Elizabeth Dwoskin and Drew Harwell, "Facebook Is Ending Use of Facial Recognition Software, Deleting Data on More than a Billion People," *Washington Post*, 2 November 2021, https://www.washingtonpost.com/technology/2021/11/02/facebook-ends-facial-recognition/; Jacob Kastrenakes, "Google Photos Finally Lets You Manually Tag People in Pictures," *Verge*, 27 November 2019, https://www.theverge.com/2019/11/27/20985721/google-photos-tagging-manual-people-face-pictures. For an example of Facebook's research in this area, see Yaniv Taigman et al., "DeepFace: Closing the Gap to Human-Level Performance in Face Verification," in *CVPR '14: Proceedings of the 2014 IEEE Conference on Computer Vision and Pattern Recognition* (Washington: IEEE Computer Society, June 2014): 1701–8.

13 Joss Fong, "What Facial Recognition Steals from Us," *Vox*, 10 December 2019, https://www.vox.com/recode/2019/12/10/21003466/facial-recognition-anonymity-explained-video.

14 Tyler Coates, "'Which Character Are You?': Instagram Filters Are Radically Dumb," *Wired*, 14 January 2020, https://www.wired.com/story/movie-character-instagram-filter/.

15 "Beauty Scanner – Face Analyzer: About This App," Google Play, accessed 3 February 2025, https://play.google.com/store/apps/details?id=com.golden.ratio.face.

16 FaceApp briefly offered an "ethnicity filter" in 2017, but the company removed the filter after widespread negative media coverage. Two similar apps, FaceTruth and Future Seer, both offer "exotic" filters for selected Asian, Middle Eastern, and South American ethnicities. See James Vincent, "Popular Face-Aging App Now Offers 'Black,' 'Indian,' and 'Asian' filters," *Verge*, 9 August 2017, https://www.theverge.com/2017/8/9/16119296/selfie-editor-faceapp-racial-filters; Lucas Matney, "Update: FaceApp Pulls Ill-Advised 'Ethnicity Filters,'" *Techcrunch*, 9 August 2017, https://techcrunch.com/2017/08/09/faceapps-ill-advised-new-update-adds-ethnicity-filters/.

17 Stephen Monteiro, "Gaming Faces: Diagnostic Scanning in Social Media and the Legacy of Racist Face Analysis," *Information, Communication & Society* 26, no. 8 (2022), 1601–17, https://doi.org/10.1080/1369118X.2021.2020867; Niharika Jainet al., "Imperfect ImaGANation: Implications of GANs Exacerbating Biases on Facial Data Augmentation and Snapchat Selfie Lenses," Computer Science Statistics working paper, 2020, https://arxiv.org/pdf/2001.09528.pdf.

18 Averyl Dietering, "Facial Recognition, Physiognomy, and Racism," *Sundial*, 12 December 2019, https://medium.com/the-sundial-acmrs/facial-recognition-physiognomy-and-racism-ffc3d232a352; Adrian Daub, "The Return of the Face," *Longreads*, October 2018, https://longreads.com/2018/10/03/the-return-of-the-face/.

19 Daub, "The Return of the Face."

20 Chris Brownlee, "How Worried Should You Be About FaceApp?," *Slate*, 18 July 2019, https://slate.com/technology/2019/07/faceapp-old-photos-privacy-concerns-facial-recognition.html.

21 The FaceFirst website states that Face Secret is "a mobile app that analyzes a picture of your face to make predictions about you as a person, including your personality, age, ethnicity, and much more!" Jesse Davis West, "19 Best Mobile Face Recognition Apps for 2019," FaceFirst, accessed 14 July 2020, https://www.facefirst.com/blog/19-incredible-face-recognition-apps/.

22 *Parent's Guide: Kidi Secrets Selfie Journal* (n.p.: VTech Holdings Limited, 2018), 14.

23 Ibid., 23–4.

24 Adario Strange, "How Apple's iPhone X Is Using the Old 'Happy Mac' Icon to Make Face ID Less Creepy," *Mashable*, 13 September 2017, https://mashable.com/2017/09/13/apple-face-id-happy-mac-icon/.

25 Alex Perekalin, "Why Face Unlock Is a Bad Idea," *Kaspersky Daily*, 21 March 2018, https://www.kaspersky.com/blog/face-unlock-insecurity/21618/.

26 Ben Lovejoy, "Comment: In-Screen Touch ID Potentially Signals a Backward Step Ahead," *9to5Mac*, 5 September 2019, https://9to5mac.com/2019/09/05/in-screen-touch-id/.

27 "About Face ID Advanced Technology," Apple Support, accessed 3 February 2025, https://support.apple.com/en-ca/HT208108; Samsung for Business, "Which Biometric Authentication Method Is the Most Secure?," *Insights*, 12 February 2020, https://insights.samsung.com/2020/02/12/which-biometric-authentication-method-is-the-most-secure-2/. My emphasis.

28 Norman Bryson, *Vision and Painting: The Logic of the Gaze* (New Haven: Yale University Press, 1983); Mieke Bal, "Dispersing the Gaze: Focalization," in *Looking In: The Art of Viewing* (London: Routledge, 2004); John Ellis, *Visible Fictions: Cinema, Television, Video* (London: Routledge, 1982); Nicholas Mirzoeff, "The Subject of Visual Culture," in *The Visual Culture Reader*, ed. Nicholas Mirzoeff, 2nd ed. (London: Routledge, 2002); Chris Chesher, "Neither Gaze, nor Glance, but Glaze: Relating to Console Game Screens," *SCAN: Journal of Media Arts Culture* 1, no. 1 (January 2004), http://scan.net.au/scan/journal/display.php?journal_id=19.

29 Erving Goffman, *Behavior in Public Places: Notes on the Social Organization of Gatherings* (New York: Free Press, 1963), 93.

30 Laura Vitto, "The Internet Feels Appropriately Weird about Apple's Face ID," *Mashable*, 12 September 2017, https://mashable.com/2017/09/12/apple-face-id-memes/.

31 "Unlock Your Pixel with Your Face," Pixel Phone Help, accessed 3 February 2025, https://support.google.com/pixelphone/answer/9517039?hl=en.

32 "About Attention Aware features on your iPhone X or iPad Pro," Apple, accessed 3 February 2025, https://support.apple.com/en-ca/HT208245.

33 "Control Your Pixel without Touching It," Pixel Phone Help, accessed 3 February 2025, https://support.google.com/pixelphone/answer/9517454?hl=en.

34 "iPhone XR Attention Awareness Features," MacRumors, 11 January 2019, https://forums.macrumors.com/threads/attention-awareness-features.2164796/.

35 *Merriam-Webster*, s.v. "awareness," accessed 3 February 2025, https://www.merriam-webster.com/dictionary/awareness.

36 Jonathan Crary, *Suspensions of Perception: Attention, Spectacle, and Modern Culture* (Cambridge, MA: MIT Press, 1999), 4.

37 Ibid., 7.

38 Yves Citton, *The Ecology of Attention*, trans. Barnaby Norman (Cambridge: Polity, 2017), 1–24.

39 Yves Citton, "Multitude: Luigi Vitali in conversation with Yves Citton," *Dust* 6 (June 2014): 38–43, http://www.yvescitton.net/wp-content/uploads/2013/09/Citton-DustInterview-May21-2014.pdf.

40 Crary, *Suspensions of Perception*, 5.

41 Lars-Erik Janlert and Erik Stolterman, *Things That Keep Us Busy: The Elements of Interaction* (Cambridge, MA: MIT Press, 2017), 56–9.

42 Ibid., 56.

Chapter Six

1 Wendy Hui Kyong Chun, *Updating to Remain the Same: Habitual New Media* (Cambridge, MA: MIT Press, 2016), ix.

2 Lars-Erik Janlert and Erik Stolterman, *Things That Keep Us Busy: The Elements of Interaction* (Cambridge, MA: MIT Press, 2017).

3 Jenny S. Radesky et al., *Constant Companion: A Week in the Life of a Young Person's Smartphone Use* (San Francisco: Common Sense Media, 2023), 6.

4 Jason Farman, *Mobile Interface Theory: Embodied Space and Locative Media*, 2nd ed. (New York: Routledge, 2021); Nanna Verhoeff, *Mobile Screens: The Visual Regime of Navigation* (Amsterdam: Amsterdam University Press, 2012).

5 Chun, *Updating to Remain the Same*, 73.

6 Ibid., 74. Emphasis added.

7 Inbar Raber, Cian P. McCarthy, and Robert W. Yeh, "Health Insurance and Mobile Health Devices: Opportunities and Concerns," *JAMA* 321, no. 18 (2019): 1767–8, doi:10.1001/jama.2019.3353.

8 Sherry Turkle, "Authenticity in the Age of Digital Companions," *Interaction Studies* 8, no. 3 (2007): 501–17.

9 Sherry Turkle et al., "Relational Artifacts with Children and Elders: The Complexities of Cybercompanionship," *Connection Science* 18, no. 4 (2006), 347–61, https://doi.org/10.1080/09540090600868912.

10 Btihaj Ajana, "Digital Health and the Biopolitics of the Quantified Self," *Digital Health* 3 (2017): 1–18, 3.

11 Deborah Lupton, *The Quantified Self* (Cambridge: Polity, 2016).

12 Ajana, "Digital Health," 3.

13 Apple, "Healthcare: Apple Watch," Apple.com, accessed 3 February 2025, https://www.apple.com/ca/healthcare/apple-watch/.

14 Samsung, "Start Your Wellness Journey," accessed 3 February 2025, https://www.samsung.com/us/watches/.

15 Garmin, "Venu," accessed 3 February 2025, https://www.garmin.com/en-US/p/643260.

16 IEEE Transmitter, "From Pacemakers to Infusion Pumps – Medical Implants Require New Cybersecurity Solutions," 13 July 2022, https://transmitter.ieee.org/from-pacemakers-to-infusion-pumps-medical-implants-require-new-cybersecurity-solutions/.

17 For example, before the Fitbit Sense was released in 2020, the Fitbit Flex 2 in 2018 offered sleep and exercise tracking that assessed time and quality of activity, but did not include granulated data such as heart rhythm monitoring, blood oxygen levels, skin temperature readings, snore and noise detection, and the like. See Fitbit, Inc., Fitbit Flex 2, User Manual, version 1.2, 2018, https://staticcs.fitbit.com/content/assets/help/manuals/manual_flex_2_en_US.pdf.

18 Lupton, *Quantified Self*, 5.

19 Gina Neff and Dawn Nafus, *Self-Tracking* (Cambridge, MA: MIT Press, 2016), https://doi.org/10.7551/mitpress/10421.001.0001, 2.

20 Adriana Barton, "Tracking Down the Root of Our Self-Tracking Obsession," *Globe and Mail*, 23 February 2017, https://www.theglobeandmail.com/life/health-and-fitness/fitness/happier-and-healthier-getting-at-the-root-of-our-self-trackingobsession/article34120896/.

21 Fitbit, LLC, Fitbit Sense, User Manual, version 1.13, 2022, 12.

22 José van Dijck, *The Culture of Connectivity: A Critical History of Social Media* (Oxford: Oxford University Press, 2013), chapter 2.

23 Apple, *Health Privacy Overview* (May 2023), https://www.apple.com/ios/health/pdf/Health_Privacy_White_Paper_May_2023.pdf.

24 Neff and Nafus, *Self-Tracking*, 3.

25 Katelyn Esmonde and Shannon Jette, "Assembling the 'Fitbit Subject': A Foucauldian-Sociomaterialist Examination of Social Class, Gender and

Self-Surveillance on Fitbit Community Message Boards," *Health* 24, no. 3 (2020): 299–314.

26 Ibid., 309.

27 The Tamagotchi Mini had a 16 × 16 pixel screen. Like a fitness tracker, the Tamagotchi was originally conceived to be a watch-like device strapped to the user's wrist, but this was replaced by a key chain design. See Anne Allison, *Millennial Monsters: Japanese Toys and the Global Imagination* (Berkeley, CA: University of California Press, 2006), 164.

28 Machiko Kusahara, "Japanese Electronic Game Culture," in *Contemporary Youth Culture: An International Encyclopedia*, ed. Shirley Steinberg, Priya Parmar, and Brigit Richard (Westport, CT: Greenwood Press, 2006): 175.

29 "Unit Sales of the Apple iPhone Worldwide from 2007 to 2023," Statista, accessed 3 February 2025, https://www.statista.com/statistics/276306/global-apple-iphone-sales-since-fiscal-year-2007/.

30 Work on digital pets and their social significance includes Allison, *Millennial Monsters*; Turkle, "Authenticity in the Age of Digital Companions," and Machiko Kusahara, "The Art of Creating Subjective Reality: An Analysis of Japanese Digital Pets," *Leonardo* 34, no. 4 (2001): 299–302. Despite the ample possibilities of relating these devices to contemporary personal media, only a work like Laura Lawton's "Taken by the Tamagotchi: How a Toy Changed the Perspective on Mobile Technology," published in a University of Toronto student periodical, makes the connection. See Laura Lawton, "Taken by the Tamagotchi: How a Toy Changed the Perspective on Mobile Technology," *IJournal: Student Journal of the University of Toronto's Faculty of Information* 2, no. 2 (2017), https://theijournal.ca/index.php/ijournal/article/view/28127.

31 Turkle, "Authenticity in the Age of Digital Companions," 506. Emphasis in original.

32 Allison, *Millennial Monsters*, 186.

33 Tiger Electronics, Inc., *GigaPets Compu Kitty Instructions*, n.p., 1997.

34 Sheryl WuDunn, "Hatchling of Pet Lover Is Rage of Toylands," *New York Times*, 7 September 1997, 17.

35 Tiger Electronics, Inc., *GigaPets Compu Kitty Instructions*.

36 Bandai, *Tamagotchi Instructions*, n.p., 1997.

37 Ibid.

38 Ibid.

39 Allison, *Millennial Monsters*, 175.

40 Kaitlin Balasaygun, "The Biggest Risks in Procrastinating on iPhone, Android Software Updates," CNBC Tech Drivers, 5 February 2023, https://www.cnbc.com/2023/02/05/the-biggest-risks-in-putting-off-iphone-and-android-software-updates.html.

41 Kami Vaniea, Emilee Rader, and Rick Wash, "Betrayed by Updates: How Negative Experiences Affect Future Security," in *CHI '14: Proceedings of the SIGCHI Conference on Human Factors in Computing Systems* (New York: Association for Computing Machinery, April 2014), 2671–4, https://doi.org/10.1145/2556288.2557275. Michael Fagan et al., "A Study of Users' Experiences and Beliefs about Software Update Messages," *Computers in Human Behavior* 51 (2015): 504–19, http://dx.doi.org/10.1016/j.chb.2015.04.075.

42 Whitson Gordon and Jason Cohen, "Computer Acting Up? How to Uninstall a Windows Update," *PCMag*, 4 June 2022, https://www.pcmag.com/how-to/computer-acting-up-how-to-uninstall-a-windows-10-update.

43 Bandai, *Tamagotchi Instructions*.

44 Slide developed similar virtual pets for MySpace, Facebook's main competition among young users at that time.

45 Kellie Cardwell-Winters, "SuperPoke! Pets Walkthrough," Gamezebo, 2010, https://www.gamezebo.com/walkthroughs/superpoke-pets-walkthrough/.

46 Ines Di Loreto and Abdelkader Gouaich, "Facebook Games: The Point Where Tribes and Casual Games Meet," in *Proceedings of the IADIS International Conference on Game and Entertainment Technologies* (Freiburg: IADIS, 2010), 77–84. Zynga's FarmVille (2009) is perhaps the most popular third-party Facebook product that entails caring for virtual animals. Unlike the other products mentioned here, however, FarmVille's animals are generally not virtual pets, but virtual livestock, entailing very different user affective responses in terms of providing care and maintaining good health.

47 Alison Gopnik, "Alison Gopnik on a Revolution to Properly Value Caregivers," *Economist*, 18 June 2021, https://www.economist.com/by-invitation/2021/06/18/alison-gopnik-on-a-revolution-to-properly-value-caregivers. This is a variation of Gopnik's oft-quoted statement: "*We* don't *care* for children *because we* love *them*; *we* love *them because we care* for *them*." See Alison Gopnik, *The Carpenter and the Gardener* (New York: Farrar, Straus and Giroux, 2016), 87.

48 WuDunn, "Hatchling of Pet Lover."

49 Kusahara, "Japanese Electronic Game Culture," 175.

50 Judith Donath, *The Social Machine: Designs for Living Online* (Cambridge, MA: MIT Press, 2014), 70.

51 Judith Donath, "Artificial Pets," in *Encyclopedia of Animal Behavior: R–Z*, ed. Michael D. Breed and Janice Moore (Oxford: Academic Press, 2010), 955–6.

52 Bandai, *Tamagotchi Instructions.*

53 And the fitness tracking of Fitbit or Apple Watch similarly quantifies and evaluates. These do not simply measure sleep, for example, but sleep "quality." They establish targets, or allow users to establish targets, and measure their progress toward those benchmarks.

54 Allison, *Millennial Monsters*, 180.

55 Kusahara, "Japanese Electronic Game Culture," 177.

56 "Coddling the Virtual Pet," *New York Times*, 29 May 1997, A20.

57 Michelle Delgado, "Keeping Tamagotchi Alive," *Smithsonian Magazine*, 22 December 2021, https://www.smithsonianmag.com/innovation/keeping-tamagotchi-alive-180979264/.

58 Tamagotchi Wiki, "Death," Fandom, accessed 3 February 2025, https://tamagotchi.fandom.com/wiki/Tamagotchi_(1996_Pet)#Death.

59 "Coddling the Virtual Pet," *New York Times.*

60 Kusahara, "Japanese Electronic Game Culture," 178.

61 Gopnik, "Alison Gopnik on a Revolution."

62 Turkle, "Authenticity in the Age of Digital Companions," 513. Emphasis in original.

63 Benj Edwards, "The Golden Age of Virtual Pets," *PCMag*, 10 April 2018, https://www.pcmag.com/news/the-golden-age-of-virtual-pets.

Conclusion

1 Jay A. Olson et al., "Sex, Age, and Smartphone Addiction Across 41 Countries," *International Journal of Mental Health and Addiction* (2023), https://doi.org/10.1007/s11469-023-01146-3.

40 [illegible]

43 [illegible]

44 [illegible]

45 [illegible]

48 [illegible]

49 [illegible]

53 [illegible]

Epilogue

Index